Justice, Intervention, and Force in International Relations

This book analyzes the problems of current just war theory, and offers a more stable justificatory framework for non-intervention in international relations.

The primary purpose of just war theory is to provide a language and a framework by which decision-makers and citizens can organize and articulate arguments about the justice of particular wars. Given that the majority of conflicts that threaten human security are now intra-state conflicts, just war theory is often called on to make judgments about wars of intervention. This book aims to critically examine the tenets of just war theory in light of these changes, and formulate a new theory of intervention and just cause.

For Michael Walzer, the leading scholar of just war theory, armed humanitarian intervention is permissible only in cases of genocide, ethnic cleansing, widespread massacres, or enslavement. This book shows why this threshold is too restrictive in light of the progressive shift away from inter-state conflict as well as the emerging norms of "sovereignty as responsibility" and the "responsibility to protect." *Justice, Intervention, and Force in International Relations* aims to establish a new, stable foundation for non-intervention and a revised threshold for "just cause." In addition, this book demonstrates that over-reliance on the just cause category distorts understanding, analysis, and public discussion of the justice or injustice of resorting to war.

This new book will be of much interest to students of ethics, security studies, international relations and international law.

Kimberly A. Hudson is Deputy Director of the USAF Negotiation Center of Excellence and Assistant Professor of Social and Behavioral Science at the Air Force Culture and Language Center and the Air War College at Maxwell Air Force Base in Montgomery, Alabama. She has a PhD in Political Science from Brown University.

Contemporary security studies
Series Editors: James Gow and Rachel Kerr
King's College London

This series focuses on new research across the spectrum of international peace and security, in an era where each year throws up multiple examples of conflicts that present new security challenges in the world around them.

NATO's Secret Armies
Operation Gladio and terrorism in Western Europe
Daniele Ganser

The US, NATO and Military Burden-Sharing
Peter Kent Forster and Stephen J. Cimbala

Russian Governance in the Twenty-First Century
Geo-strategy, geopolitics and new governance
Irina Isakova

The Foreign Office and Finland 1938–1940
Diplomatic sideshow
Craig Gerrard

Rethinking the Nature of War
Edited by Isabelle Duyvesteyn and Jan Angstrom

Perception and Reality in the Modern Yugoslav Conflict
Myth, falsehood and deceit, 1991–1995
Brendan O'Shea

The Political Economy of Peacebuilding in Post-Dayton Bosnia
Tim Donais

The Distracted Eagle
The rift between America and old Europe
Peter H. Merkl

The Iraq War
European perspectives on politics, strategy, and operations
Edited by Jan Hallenberg and Håkan Karlsson

Strategic Contest
Weapons proliferation and war in the greater Middle East
Richard L. Russell

Propaganda, the Press and Conflict
The Gulf War and Kosovo
David R. Willcox

Missile Defence
International, regional and national implications
Edited by Bertel Heurlin and Sten Rynning

Globalising Justice for Mass Atrocities
A revolution in accountability
Chandra Lekha Sriram

Ethnic Conflict and Terrorism
The origins and dynamics of civil wars
Joseph L. Soeters

Globalisation and the Future of Terrorism: Patterns and Predictions
Brynjar Lia

Nuclear Weapons and Strategy
The evolution of American nuclear policy
Stephen J. Cimbala

Nasser and the Missile Age in the Middle East
Owen L. Sirrs

War as Risk Management
Strategy and conflict in an age of globalised risks
Yee-Kuang Heng

Military Nanotechnology
Potential applications and preventive arms control
Jurgen Altmann

NATO and Weapons of Mass Destruction
Regional alliance, global threats
Eric R. Terzuolo

Europeanisation of National Security Identity
The EU and the changing security identities of the Nordic states
Pernille Rieker

International Conflict Prevention and Peace-building
Sustaining the peace in post conflict societies
Edited by T. David Mason and James D. Meernik

Controlling the Weapons of War
Politics, persuasion, and the prohibition of inhumanity
Brian Rappert

Changing Transatlantic Security Relations
Do the US, the EU and Russia form a new strategic triangle?
Edited by Jan Hallenberg and Håkan Karlsson

Theoretical Roots of US Foreign Policy
Machiavelli and American unilateralism
Thomas M. Kane

Corporate Soldiers and International Security
The rise of private military companies
Christopher Kinsey

Transforming European Militaries
Coalition operations and the technology gap
Gordon Adams and Guy Ben-Ari

Globalization and Conflict
National security in a 'new' strategic era
Edited by Robert G. Patman

Military Forces in 21st Century Peace Operations
No job for a soldier?
James V. Arbuckle

The Political Road to War with Iraq
Bush, 9/11 and the drive to overthrow Saddam
Nick Ritchie and Paul Rogers

Bosnian Security after Dayton
New perspectives
Edited by Michael A. Innes

Kennedy, Johnson and NATO
Britain, America and the Dynamics of Alliance, 1962–68
Andrew Priest

Small Arms and Security
New emerging international norms
Denise Garcia

The United States and Europe
Beyond the neo-conservative divide?
Edited by John Baylis and Jon Roper

Russia, NATO and Cooperative Security
Bridging the gap
Lionel Ponsard

International Law and International Relations
Bridging theory and practice
Edited by Tom Bierstecker, Peter Spiro, Chandra Lekha Sriram and Veronica Raffo

Deterring International Terrorism and Rogue States
US national security policy after 9/11
James H. Lebovic

Vietnam in Iraq
Tactics, lessons, legacies and ghosts
Edited by John Dumbrell and David Ryan

Understanding Victory and Defeat in Contemporary War
Edited by Jan Angstrom and Isabelle Duyvesteyn

Propaganda and Information Warfare in the Twenty-first Century
Altered images and deception operations
Scot Macdonald

Governance in Post-Conflict Societies
Rebuilding fragile states
Edited by Derick W. Brinkerhoff

European Security in the Twenty-First Century
The challenge of multipolarity
Adrian Hyde-Price

Ethics, Technology and the American Way of War
Cruise missiles and US security policy
Reuben E. Brigety II

International Law and the Use of Armed Force
The UN charter and the major powers
Joel H. Westra

Disease and Security
Natural plagues and biological weapons in East Asia
Christian Enermark

Explaining War and Peace
Case studies and necessary condition counterfactuals
Jack Levy and Gary Goertz

War, Image and Legitimacy
Viewing contemporary conflict
James Gow and Milena Michalski

Information Strategy and Warfare
A guide to theory and practice
John Arquilla and Douglas A. Borer

Countering the Proliferation of Weapons of Mass Destruction
NATO and EU options in the Mediterranean and the Middle East
Thanos P. Dokos

Security and the War on Terror
Edited by Alex J. Bellamy, Roland Bleiker, Sara E. Davies and Richard Devetak

The European Union and Strategy
An emerging actor
Edited by Jan Hallenberg and Kjell Engelbrekt

Causes and Consequences of International Conflict
Data, methods and theory
Edited by Glenn Palmer

Russian Energy Policy and Military Power
Putin's quest for greatness
Pavel Baev

The Baltic Question During the Cold War
Edited by John Hiden, Vahur Made, and David J. Smith

America, the EU and Strategic Culture
Renegotiating the transatlantic bargain
Asle Toje

Afghanistan, Arms and Conflict
Post-9/11 security and insurgency
Michael Bhatia and Mark Sedra

Punishment, Justice and International Relations
Ethics and order after the Cold War
Anthony F. Lang, Jr.

Intra-State Conflict, Governments and Security
Dilemmas of deterrence and assurance
Edited by Stephen M. Saideman and Marie-Jo lle J. Zahar

Democracy and Security
Preferences, norms and policy-making
Edited by Matthew Evangelista, Harald Müller and Niklas Schörnig

The Homeland Security Dilemma
Fear, failure and the future of American security
Frank P. Harvey

Military Transformation and Strategy
Revolutions in military affairs and small states
Edited by Bernard Loo

Peace Operations and International Criminal Justice
Building peace after mass atrocities
Majbritt Lyck

NATO, Security and Risk Management
From Kosovo to Khandahar
M.J. Williams

Cyber-Conflict and Global Politics
Edited by Athina Karatzogianni

Globalisation and Defence in the Asia-Pacific
Arms across Asia
Edited by Geoffrey Till, Emrys Chew and Joshua Ho

Security Strategies and American World Order
Lost power
Birthe Hansen, Peter Toft and Anders Wivel

War, Torture and Terrorism
Rethinking the rules of international security
Edited by Anthony F. Lang, Jr. and Amanda Russell Beattie

America and Iraq
Policy making, intervention and regional politics
Edited by David Ryan and Patrick Kiely

European Security in a Global Context
Internal and external dynamics
Edited by Thierry Tardy

Women and Political Violence
Female combatants in ethno-national conflict
Miranda H. Alison

Justice, Intervention, and Force in International Relations
Reassessing just war theory in the 21st century
Kimberly A. Hudson

Justice, Intervention, and Force in International Relations

Reassessing just war theory in the 21st century

Kimberly A. Hudson

LONDON AND NEW YORK

First published 2009
by Routledge
2 Park Square, Milton Park, Abingdon, Oxon OX14 4RN

Simultaneously published in the USA and Canada
by Routledge
711 Third Avenue, New York, NY 10017

Routledge is an imprint of the Taylor & Francis Group, an informa business

First issued in paperback 2010

© 2009 Kimberly A. Hudson

Typeset in Times by Wearset Ltd, Boldon, Tyne and Wear

All rights reserved. No part of this book may be reprinted or reproduced or utilized in any form or by any electronic, mechanical, or other means, now known or hereafter invented, including photocopying and recording, or in any information storage or retrieval system, without permission in writing from the publishers.

British Library Cataloguing in Publication Data
A catalogue record for this book is available from the British Library

Library of Congress Cataloging in Publication Data
A catalog record for this book has been requested

ISBN13: 978-0-415-49025-2 (hbk)
ISBN13: 978-0-415-69158-1 (pbk)
ISBN13: 978-0-203-87935-1 (ebk)

For my family

Contents

	Acknowledgments	xii
	Introduction	1
1	Walzer's formulation of just cause	8
2	Walzer's innovations	19
3	Stable grounds for the non-intervention norm	43
4	Just cause	53
5	Other *jus ad bellum* categories	89
6	Intervention in Kosovo	126
	Conclusions	158
	Notes	166
	Index	186

Acknowledgments

This book could not have been written without lots of help of different varieties from many generous and wise souls. It is a joy to acknowledge some of them.

This book is based on research done for my Ph.D. dissertation, written at Brown University in Providence, Rhode Island. I owe a great deal of gratitude to my Ph.D. advisor, P. Terrence Hopmann. He provided round after round of challenging comments and suggestions for additions and revisions, generously taking along heavy drafts on his many journeys to faraway lands and sharing his encyclopedic knowledge of international relations and history. I am very grateful to him for his intellectual generosity, his guidance, and his kindness over the years. He is the best sort of scholar, teacher, and mentor. I count myself especially blessed to have been one of his students.

John Tomasi provided many focused, clear questions that improved and clarified my theoretical framework, especially about the non-intervention norm. He helped to shape the questions addressed in this book and to sharpen my arguments. Through the Political Theory Project, he provided many opportunities for the exchange of ideas (as well as financial support). I thank him for the inspiration and for the model he continues to provide.

John P. Reeder's generosity with his time, experience, and his intellectual gifts is awe-inspiring. Jock commented carefully on every chapter, and he provided many difficult and important objections. Some of these form the basis of the "objections" section in Chapter 4. Without his support and good-natured criticism and skepticism, this would have been a much different book.

I would also like to thank David Little and Fernando Teson for discussions about the threshold for just cause, and Thomas Biersteker and James Der Derian for comments on an early version of the project. Tom Maulucci, Robin Varnum, and Julie Walsh also provided comments on a later version. I also benefited from comments and questions following a talk at Air University in Summer 2008.

I presented many of the ideas that became chapters or parts of chapters in this book at conventions of the International Studies Association. Although I benefitted from many wonderful conversations at ISA, I would like to especially thank Mervyn Frost and Tony Lang for their comments and questions.

While I have only met Michael Walzer once, I am deeply indebted to him and his work (as are all students of just war).

Brown University was generous with institutional support from the Graduate School. I also benefited from support via the Watson Institute for International Studies, and the Political Theory Project at Brown University. Thanks to Patti Gardner, Suzanne Brough, and Dina Egge.

Lots of thanks also to Melissa Labonte, Erin Roberts, Angela Bruno, and Sarah Standing.

Finally, many thanks to Kate, Mimi, Spencer, Diane, Eddie, Uncle Dave, Ray, Cy, Elaine, Mike, Dani, Melissa, and John. My cats, Kitty and Delphis, sat next to me, or on my books, lap, and keyboard throughout most of the writing and kept the solitary process from being a lonely one. My family and my sweetheart, Donnie, have been very patient with my saying "no" to almost all family and social engagements (and household chores) during much of the writing of this book. They have been supportive in all the best ways.

Introduction

This book was inspired by Michael Walzer's monumental and extremely influential book, *Just and Unjust Wars: A Moral Argument with Historical Illustrations*. Although I am explicitly critical of several of Walzer's arguments, this project is written in the spirit of engaging and supplementing Walzer's work, not in the spirit of demolition. This book aims to address the central questions of *jus ad bellum* in light of changing attitudes toward sovereignty that have become ascendant since Walzer wrote *Just and Unjust Wars* and also in light of the increasing number of intra-state conflicts relative to inter-state wars.

Changing attitudes toward sovereignty are evident in the emerging norms of "sovereignty as responsibility," the "responsibility to protect," and the "responsibility to prevent," as well as in the work of international relations theorists in the liberal and constructivist schools. Unlike the realists, to whom Walzer sees his work as responding, who tend to view international relations as the a-moral, rational pursuit of narrow self-interest by rational unitary sovereign states, liberals emphasize interdependence and the possibility of cooperation, while constructivists stress the centrality of ideas as important for explaining and understanding international relations. Walzer's just war theory works well for a world where sovereign states are the only important actors and where inter-state conflict is the primary worry. However, as Thomas G. Weiss notes, there has been a "dramatic shift away from state-centric perspectives."[1] Presently, wars are most often internal wars between non-state actors and weak or repressive state authorities. Weiss quotes Kalevi Holsti, who puts the matter succinctly:

> The major problem of the contemporary society of states is no longer aggression, conquest, and the obliteration of states. It is, rather, the collapse of states, humanitarian emergencies, state terror against segments of local populations, civil wars of various types, and international terrorist organizations.[2]

Walzer's framework works very well for World War II, but international relations theorists are called upon with increasing frequency to analyze and make judgments about conflicts that do not lend themselves to a clear-cut aggressor-defender framework: "In the 1990's, for instance, 94% of wars resulting in 1000 or more battle deaths (the generally agreed, social-scientific definition to qualify as a *bona fide* war) were [civil wars]."[3] Walzer's framework is not ideal for addressing such wars, because in these conflicts it is difficult for outsiders to identify an unjust aggressor and just defender. Internally repressive states that are not aggressive against other states but threaten the security of their own people also pose a challenge to Walzer's non-intervention doctrine in light of the emerging norm of sovereignty as responsibility.

Walzer notes the increasing frequency of intra-state war and the more increasing frequency of appropriate occasions for armed humanitarian intervention (AHI) in the preface to the fourth edition of *Just and Unjust Wars*. Walzer asks: "How much human suffering are we prepared to watch before we intervene?"[4] and "How bad do things have to be on the other side of the border to justify a forceful crossing, to justify a war?"[5] Walzer has, up to the time of this writing, stood by his original answer as articulated in 1977; I explain Walzer's view at length in Chapter 1. By way of introduction here, I will summarize and say that for Walzer, foreigners may cross the border to rescue victims of genocide, enslavement, widespread massacres, or ethnic cleansing, or they may permissibly mount a counter-intervention if another external power has intervened first in a civil war, or they may assist secessionist groups under certain conditions. Any other offensive use of military force constitutes the crime of aggression and is unjust in Walzer's formulation. AHI is not permitted in Walzer's framework in cases where human suffering has not reached the level of genocide, ethnic cleansing, widespread massacres, or enslavement.

The first objective of this book is to show that Walzer's formulation of just cause is too restrictive and to work out a new formulation that is more stable. In light of the "progressive problem shift" away from inter-state conflict as well as the emerging norms of "sovereignty as responsibility" and the "responsibility to protect,"[6] there is a need for rethinking the foundations of both the non-intervention norm and the threshold for just cause.

The second aim of this book is to show that Walzer's focus on the just cause category of *jus ad bellum* cannot provide a sufficient framework for understanding, analyzing, and discussing the justice or injustice of resorting to war. Walzer does not substantially develop the categories of legitimate authority, likelihood of success, proportionality, last resort, and right intention in his work. In the preface to the second edition of *Just and Unjust Wars*, Walzer explains his reason for not developing proportionality or last resort: "because they did not seem to me in 1977 (nor do they seem to me today) to help much in making the crucial moral distinctions."[7] Walzer argues that proportionality "isn't going to make for useful discriminations in a great number of cases."[8] It is useful in only the obvious and extreme cases, such as the Soviet Union's 1968 invasion of Czechoslovakia; in this case, it was obvious that the United States should not have attempted to intervene.[9]

Because the major criterion Walzer is focused on is the presence of just cause in the form of aggression, his framework yields a general prohibition on offensive war and presumptive approval of all wars of self-defense. Walzer's framework is not ideally suited to the twenty-first century, where inter-state aggression is no longer the main worry. In addition, spirals of mutually antagonistic behavior between states can also make it difficult to identify who is the unjust aggressor in international conflicts. I argue that using all of just war theory's traditional categories of restraint in a comprehensive framework provides a better alternative.

The revised framework, including a more explicit treatment of all of the traditional *jus ad bellum* categories of restraint, and incorporating insights from the international relations literature as well as the traditional just war theory literature should be useful for analysis, discussion, decision-making, and judgment. I suggest that public discussion and debate about war might be best served by utilizing this broader framework, which I call the "comprehensive framework" as opposed to "Walzer's framework." I aim to convince the reader that the comprehensive framework yields a more satisfactory tool-kit for discussion, deliberation, and judgment about the justice of particular wars.

The primary purpose of just war theory is not to operate as a rigid formula for generating decisive judgments. It is not like a mathematical formula into which one might input data and expect to generate a precise and dichotomous result: "just war or unjust war." Rather the primary purpose of just war theory is to provide a language and a framework by which decision-makers and democratic citizens can organize, think through, and articulate their arguments about the justice of particular wars. Since just war theory is a language, it would be most useful if participants in the debate used the terms with consistent meaning and significance.

The first major objective of this book is to set out and problematize Walzer's views of non-intervention and just cause. The second objective is to develop a new theoretical justification for non-intervention. Third, the book aims to set a stable, universally acceptable threshold for just cause (including just cause for humanitarian intervention.) The fourth objective is to clarify, refine, and in some cases expand on Walzer's understanding of the other *jus ad bellum* categories. The fifth and last objective is to show the significance of the differences between the frameworks in a case study on Kosovo. In the next several paragraphs, I will elaborate on what the reader will find in each of the six chapters to follow.

Chapter summaries

My book is in six chapters:

1 a summary of Walzer's theory;
2 critical analysis of Walzer's treatments of just cause and non-intervention;
3 a new formulation of non-intervention;
4 an argument for a stable, universally acceptable threshold for just cause, including for humanitarian intervention;
5 restatement of the other *jus ad bellum* categories; and
6 a case analysis of Kosovo and the 1999 NATO intervention.

4   Introduction

Chapter 1: in the first chapter of the book, I summarize Walzer's arguments about justice and the resort to war, which Walzer articulates mainly in terms of just cause. As noted above, Walzer's view is generally that virtually all defensive wars are just, and almost all offensive wars are unjust and constitute crimes of aggression. Walzer makes a few exceptions to the rule about offensive wars: in the case of massive human rights abuses; counter-intervention in a civil war; and with respect to secessionist movements under certain circumstances. Walzer's view sets the threshold for humanitarian intervention very high at genocide, massacres, and official enslavement or ethnic cleansing.

Chapter 2: in the second chapter, I aim to show that Walzer's threshold for intervention is too high and that his doctrine on counter-intervention effectively works out to a form of realism. I draw upon older sources within the just war theory tradition and contemporary critics of Walzer to argue that sometimes offensive war is justifiable, and sometimes defensive war is not. Walzer also develops a new doctrine on non-intervention into civil wars, drawing on John Stuart Mill's essay, "A Few Words on Non-intervention." Walzer's new doctrine takes no view on the justice of either side's position, but solely on likelihood of success, which he takes as evidence of self-determination. Finally, Walzer develops a unique threshold for just cause and creates new and specific prohibitions against humanitarian intervention with his argument for a "wide gulf" between genocide and the "ordinary brutality of authoritarian regimes."

In Chapter 2, I also summarized some early and important critiques of Walzer's view, including arguments made by Charles Beitz, Gerald Doppelt, David Luban, and Richard Wasserstrom. The essence of their critiques is that Walzer's doctrine of non-intervention privileges individuals' rights to a historic community above all other human rights, without a sufficient reason for doing so. The critics argue that Walzer's theory "is conservative, and what it conserves are tyrannical regimes."[10] I also set out a summary of Walzer's responses and the critics' rejoinders. In the last section of the chapter, I offer my own comments on the debate between Walzer and his critics, and I also set out new critiques of Walzer's arguments.

Chapter 3: having argued that Walzer's articulation of the non-intervention rule rests on unstable foundations, I build a framework for analysis and judgment about non-intervention that builds on *The Responsibility to Protect* and avoids the problems in Walzer's view. I articulate a new and more stable non-intervention rule consistent with the emerging norms of responsibility to protect and sovereignty as responsibility.

This view is compatible with Walzer's observation that the barrier to intervention ought to be correlated with the usefulness of a state to its people, but it disagrees with Walzer on how to measure that usefulness. My view is that only capable and responsible states are owed the duty of non-intervention. I explain and defend this view in the first part of Chapter 3.

Chapter 4: in Chapter 4, I elaborate a new framework for thinking about just cause, including a new threshold for AHI. I am in substantial agreement with Walzer on many elements of just cause: self-defense, pre-emptive self-defense, and collective self-defense or defense of a neighbor. However, the new view on intervention, which I call the Atrocity Standard, diverges from Walzer's view. Walzer sets the bar for intervention at what he terms "massive" human rights abuses: enslavement, ethnic cleansing, widespread massacres, or genocide. I follow Walzer in arguing that a reasonable threshold for AHI would correspond to crimes that shock the conscience of mankind. A set of crimes that shock the conscience of mankind has been specified in Articles 6, 7, and 8, of the Rome Statute of the International Criminal Court, and I endorse and defend the suggestion made by David Little that these atrocity crimes might correspond to a reasonable threshold for just cause for AHI. Walzer's massive human rights abuses are among the crimes that shock the conscience of humanity enumerated in the Rome Statue; international consensus is evident in the language of the statute that all atrocity crimes shock the conscience of mankind. They ought to be stopped wherever possible, by force if necessary (if such resort to force is justifiable within the bounds of the entire *jus ad bellum* framework); and the perpetrators of these crimes ought to be brought to justice. In Chapter 4, I aim to convince the reader that the Atrocity Standard threshold is the best answer to Walzer's question, "How bad do things have to be?"

The Atrocity Standard is distinct from Walzer's threshold and also from the views of other theorists. In the second part of Chapter 4, I summarize a series of views about just cause along a spectrum of least permissive to most permissive, with Walzer at the least permissive end of the continuum. The Atrocity Standard finds just cause for intervention in a greater number of cases than either Walzer's view or John Rawls' as expressed in *The Law of Peoples*. The threshold for intervention, it could be said, is lower, and the level of responsibility demanded of the state to earn the right to non-intervention, is higher. Fernando Teson's view is more permissive than the Atrocity Standard. Although my view is in substantial agreement with Teson's, his view is slightly more permissive insofar as he argues that intervention might be permitted to establish democracy where it has been overturned, or to punish regimes for atrocity crimes that are no longer ongoing.

In the third part of Chapter 4, I anticipate and refute a series of possible objections to my view. In this section, I summarize and explain why I do not endorse Rawls' view as expressed in *Law of Peoples*, or the view of Fernando Teson. I also consider and refute objections from realism, international law, moral hazard, and anti-paternalism. I also consider the arguments that respect for human rights cannot be taught by force of arms and that pre-emptive humanitarian intervention is equivalent to punishing a state for something it has not done yet.

Chapter 5: I show how Walzer's focus, which is mainly on just cause and *jus in bello*, leads him to under-value some of the significance, relevance, and implications of the other *jus ad bellum* categories (beyond just cause). When overt aggression or another just cause is present, Walzer holds that there is a presumption in favor of military resistance. Last resort is assumed to be satisfied, and Walzer thinks that *ad bellum* proportionality and likelihood of success are only helpful in the very obvious cases. Walzer does not develop comprehensive presentations on legitimate authority or right intention. As a result of this, his framework can yield a different evaluation of the justice of particular wars from the evaluation generated by the comprehensive framework combined with the Atrocity Standard threshold for just cause.

Chapter 5 is in several sections. First, in the introductory section, I explain why the other *jus ad bellum* categories are so important in the comprehensive formulation. I have included a section on each of the *jus ad bellum* categories beyond just cause: last resort, right intention, competent authority, proportionality, and likelihood of success. In each section, I summarize Walzer's view on the category of restraint. Then I describe the category of restraint as it is understood by some of the important theorists in the early just war tradition. Finally, for each category of restraint I critique and expand upon the canonical formulation, adding several elements to the understanding of the significance and implications of the categories. A significant concern about Walzer's presentation is that in any case where a just cause exists, even wars that are likely to be disproportionate, or to fail at great cost, are held to be justifiable.

Walzer does not believe that the proportionality or the last resort constraints are very useful, and his formulation does not rely on them: "It is our abhorrence of aggression that is authoritative here, while the maxims of last resort and proportionality play only marginal and uncertain roles."[11] One reason this is worrisome is because a just cause may be overstated or misrepresented; it is especially important in cases like these that the cautionary principles of the additional *jus ad bellum* categories be utilized as tools of analysis. In Walzer's presentation of the aggressor–defender view, this additional layer of analysis is not as important; there is not a robust safety net of additional restraints on the recourse to war.

Chapter 6: I analyze the Kosovo conflict through the lenses of Walzer's just war theory and the comprehensive framework. The case study highlights the significance of the differences between the two views. The different applications of just war principles yield very different analyses. By showing how the two different frameworks yield different judgments about the justice of that particular war, the Kosovo chapter illustrates the consequences and significance of the differences between the frameworks.

Assumptions and limitations of the book

This book is limited to *jus ad bellum*. I do not engage the difficult question of whether sometimes the *jus in bello* might be legitimately set aside; I assume that the *jus in bello* must be upheld. Respect for the *jus in bello* is incorporated in the *jus ad bellum* categories of proportionality and right intention. If grave harm to civilians is anticipated, resort to war may fail the test of proportionality. Right intention requires that belligerents must fight in accordance with the laws of war, so as to preserve the prospects for achieving a just peace. If a war cannot be won by fighting within the laws of war, the war should not be commenced because it cannot be conducted in line with right intention.

Where war crimes are committed, the Atrocity Standard finds just cause for other actors to intervene to stop the war crimes, provided they can do so within the limits of the *jus ad bellum* and while respecting the laws of war (the *jus in bello*). I do not address the question of supreme emergency, and I do not address *jus post bellum* in a significant way.

This project is within the just war tradition. Unlike pacifists, I assume that some resort to war may be justifiable. Unlike realists, I also assume that it is possible to limit war, and that moral discussion about war is not absurd.

1 Walzer's formulation of just cause

Walzer elaborates his formulation of non-intervention and just cause across four broad categories: national self-defense, collective self-defense, pre-emption, and exceptions to the non-intervention rule. I'll summarize his views on each of those four categories here, highlighting the underlying reasons he gives for his positions.

National self-defense

Walzer's conception of just cause is among those threads of the tradition sometimes referred to as the aggressor/defender paradigm. In Walzer's formulation, offensive war (war for any purpose other than defense) is always wrong. Defensive wars are assumed to be justified, except the defensive wars of societies engaged in massive human rights violations (genocide, enslavement, and widespread massacre).[1] One element of Walzer's view is the idea that "no war, as medieval theologians explained, can be just on both sides."[2] In Walzer's understanding, all offensive war, or any armed attack on the political independence or territorial integrity of a sovereign state is a crime of aggression. "Nothing but aggression can justify war," Walzer writes. "Nothing else warrants the use of force in international society."[3]

> Aggression is the name we give to the crime of war. We know the crime because of our knowledge of the peace it interrupts – not the mere absence of fighting, but peace-with-rights, a condition of liberty and security that can only exist in the absence of aggression itself. The wrong the aggressor commits is to force men and women to risk their lives for the sake of their rights. It is to confront them with the choice: your rights or (some of) your lives! ... Aggression is remarkable because it is the only crime that states can commit against other states.... Aggression is a singular and undifferentiated crime because, in all its forms, it challenges rights that are worth dying for.[4]

The "rights worth dying for," according to Walzer, are the rights of individuals to a community: "the rights of contemporary men and women to live as members of a historic community and to express their inherited culture through political forms worked out among themselves."[5] Walzer does not require that these historic communities exhibit any particular characteristics except that they are not subject to foreign coercion, and in that way they are "self-determining."

He extends the right of self-defense (and the right to non-intervention) to severely repressive regimes: "Domestic heresy and injustice are never actionable in the world of states. Hence, again, the principle of non-intervention."[6] Walzer does make an exception to this rule; it's not absolutely true for him that domestic injustice is *never* actionable in the world of states. Walzer holds that states are normally, but by no means always, the institutional arrangements by which people work out their community lives. He recognizes:

> If no common life exists, or if the state doesn't defend the common life that does exist, its own defense may have no moral justification. But most states do stand guard over the community of their citizens, at least to some degree: that is why we assume the justice of their defensive wars.[7]

In other words, any first use of force (except justified pre-emptive self-defense) is aggression, and therefore, unjust. The party who retaliates is acting in self-defense, and this is almost always unconditionally justified for Walzer (except in the case of a slave society defending slavery or a genocidal government aiming to continue its genocide). The other *jus ad bellum* categories are assumed to be met if the situation is grave enough to say there is a just cause for war. I will say more about this in due course in Chapter 5, where I distinguish Walzer's views from my own views on last resort, proportionality, reasonable hope of success, legitimate authority, and right intention. In this chapter, I am focusing on Walzer's view of just cause.

There are wars where there is justice on neither side, "because justice doesn't pertain to them or because the antagonists are both aggressors, fighting for territory or power where they have no right."[8] As a case in point, Walzer cites Lenin's hypothetical example of such a conflict, between "a slave-owner who owned 100 slaves warring against a slave owner who owned 200 slaves for a more 'just' distribution of slaves."[9] Walzer thinks there is no right of self-defense on the part of a genocidal or slave state. However, all other states possess a right of self-defense against aggression. In Walzer's formulation, aggression includes wars of humanitarian intervention against tyrannical regimes if the regime's crimes do not rise to the level of genocide, widespread massacre, enslavement, or ethnic cleansing.

Collective self-defense: wars of law enforcement

Walzer writes, "Aggression justifies two kinds of violent response: a war of self-defense by the victim and a war of law enforcement by the victim and any other member of international society."[10] If one state is a victim of aggression, other states are entitled to join in its defense. There is a "presumption in favor of military resistance once aggression has begun" according to Walzer, because future would-be aggressors ought to be deterred, and the rights of states to political independence and territorial integrity ought to be maintained.[11] Walzer's view is that the victim of aggression fights back not only in his own defense, but in defense of the international order and the rights of all members of international society (states) to political independence and territorial integrity. An attack on one member of international society is an attack on the rights of all states and upon the international legal order. Any member of the international society, therefore, is entitled to defend that order, and thereby the stability of the international states-system. Although third-party states are entitled to join in the defense of the victim of aggression, they are not bound to do so; all states have a right to remain neutral.[12]

One important quality to note about Walzer's view of collective self-defense is that it is not motivated by charity, compassion, or the duty to assist a neighbor as such. It is the norm of non-intervention that is being defended as much as the state under attack. The entitlement of the third-party state to intervene is generated by the attack on the norm against aggression. It is the attack on the system, and its generation of insecurity for the third-party state and all other states that unanswered aggression poses, that generates this right of response by the third-party state.

Pre-emption

Pre-emption, in *Just and Unjust Wars*, is a form of self-defense in which the victim of aggression defends itself with a first strike. For Walzer, pre-emption is justified "under sufficient threat," which is "conceptually between 'preventive war' and 'pre-emptive strike in response to imminent threat.'" Under sufficient threat means, according to Walzer, that three criteria are met:

> First, there is a manifest intent to injure, made clear by some evidence; second, there is a degree of active preparation that makes that intent a positive danger, and third, a general situation in which waiting, or doing anything other than fighting, greatly magnifies the risk.[13]

Walzer's concrete example of such a situation is the three weeks immediately prior to the Israeli pre-emptive strike in the Six-Day War of 1967.[14] In this case, Egypt responded to a false report of Israeli troops massing on the Syrian border by placing Egyptian troops on "maximum alert," massing their troops in the Sinai, expelling the United Nations from the Sinai and the Gaza Strip, and closing the Straits of Tiran to Israeli shipping on May 22, 1967 – this closure itself a *casus belli*. By the end of May, the Egyptian President Gamal Abdel Nasser had announced that "if war came, the goal would be nothing less than the destruction of Israel"; Jordan, Syria, and Iraq announced their alliance with Egypt against Israel during the next two weeks. Diplomacy seemed to be useless. Israel pre-emptively launched attacks in what Walzer calls "a clear case of legitimate anticipation." Israel, against most expectations, won that war in six days.

In response to more recent events, noting that the "old arguments did not take into account weapons of mass destruction," Walzer has taken a slightly different view, but he has not fully elaborated a new doctrine. "Perhaps the gulf between preemption and prevention has now narrowed so that there is little strategic (and therefore little moral) difference between them."[15] Walzer's discussion of preemption in *Just and Unjust Wars* does not include any mention of pre-emptive collective self-defense or pre-emptive humanitarian intervention.

Interventions

Generally speaking, for Walzer, the right to non-intervention and national self-defense is possessed by all sovereign states. Under normal circumstances, "Any use of force or imminent threat of force by one state against the political sovereignty or territorial integrity of another constitutes aggression and is a criminal act."[16] Walzer does, however, make three exceptions to this general rule. The three exceptions are in the cases of secession, counter-intervention in a civil war, and humanitarian intervention. I will discuss each of these rules of disregard in detail below, along with a fourth exception Walzer has added more recently, the case of failed states.

Walzer argues that the non-intervention norm may be disregarded in the following circumstances (the first three rules of disregard are elaborated in *Just and Unjust Wars*, the fourth in more recent work):[17]

1. when the particular set of boundaries clearly contains two or more political communities, one of which is already engaged in a large scale military struggle for independence; that is, when what is at issue is secession or "national liberation";
2. when the boundaries have already been crossed by the armies of a foreign power, even if the crossing has been called for by one of the parties in a civil war, that is, when what is at issue is counter-intervention; and
3. when the violation of human rights within a set of boundaries is so terrible that it makes talk of community or self-determination or 'arduous struggle' seem cynical and irrelevant, that is, in cases of enslavement or massacre.[18]
4. Intervention in the case of a less than fully capable state; this is acceptable either to aid the individuals inside the state or in self-defense. Intervention is permissible in a failed state to stop widespread suffering and death due to state collapse and the ensuing chaos. Intervention is also within the borders of a state that is incapable of controlling the population within its borders (for example, Walzer made this argument about Hezbollah in Lebanon and Hamas in Gaza[19]).

Exception 1: secessions

In his discussion of secessionist movements in *Just and Unjust Wars*, Walzer distinguishes between legitimate and illegitimate secessionist movements by what he calls the "test of self-help."[20] The test of self help applies to governments, revolutionary movements, and secessionist groups: if the government, movement, or group can fight its own internal war successfully, it has met the test of self-help.

Intervention is permitted to aid the government against the rebels until such time as the secessionist movement can garner sufficient support to meet the test of self-help. After that, intervention on the part of either side is prohibited. Foreign powers must stay out and let the local balance work out on its own; such a fight is part of the process of self-determination. If foreign powers do not stay out, a counter-intervention is permitted on behalf of the other side, to restore the balance of forces to what it would have been, had the first, unjust intervention not occurred. Counter-intervention (not an initial intervention) is only permitted to aid a secessionist movement if the movement would have had sufficient support among the people to win a war against its government, and it is not permitted if it does not.

First, if the movement could win its freedom without external interference because a sufficient portion of the people is willing and able to fight, the movement meets the "test of self-help." In such a case, foreign governments are no longer allowed to provide military assistance to the government; a strict rule of neutrality is now in force.[21] Where a secessionist movement could win a revolt on its own without external assistance, Walzer's theory is permissive in allowing foreign support, even military assistance, for the revolt. When the movement is strong enough to win on its own, Walzer's theory endorses the movement's claim to a self-determining political community. Its ability to fight its own war, successfully, is evidence that the movement represents the historic community's self-determination.

For secessionist movements that cannot win a war of secession without foreign assistance, the rule of disregard does not apply. There is not a right to intervention (on the part of foreigners) to assist a secessionist movement, unless such assistance would not be necessary for the group to win in the absence of external force being brought to bear. There is not a right of intervention to assist the secessionist movement, even if it has met the self-help test, unless another foreign power has already intervened on behalf of the government. Walzer holds that if the movement is truly a legitimate movement, with standing among the people, it will succeed on its own. If it cannot succeed, it is because the people do not want it or perhaps because they think it is imprudent to rebel. Walzer makes no moral distinction between these two reasons. Whatever the people's reasons, foreigners must respect their decision, as it is evidenced in practice by the strength or weakness of their movement. Walzer argues that freedom, to be meaningful, must be arrived at by a people in their own way, if they can achieve it. If they cannot achieve it, they are not fit for it, or they do not want it. There is no right to be rescued (or to rescue) from a bloody repression.[22] To be freed by foreigners is not to be freed, but to be conquered. Walzer interprets John Stuart Mill's essay, "A Few Words on Non-intervention," to say that because of what freedom is, it necessarily must be earned by the people; freedom cannot be won for them by outsiders. A people get the government for which they are fit. Mill, according to Walzer, says a people must fight for their own freedom, just as an individual must cultivate his own virtue.

Walzer applies the self-help test to regimes as well as to secessionist movements: If the regime cannot compel its citizens to obedience, it is an illegitimate regime; if the regime is capable of repressing internal secessionist or revolutionary movements, the government passes the self-help test, and it is legitimate.[23] "A legitimate government is one that can fight its own internal wars."[24] Such a regime possesses rights to non-intervention and to national self-defense.

If a secessionist movement garners sufficient local support that the movement becomes capable of overthrowing the regime, the secessionist movement is legitimate, and an external force would be justified in assisting it. Although no external force would be necessary for the secessionists' victory, external intervention is permissible (*because* it is unnecessary). Walzer writes, however, that sometimes even a legitimate secessionist movement will not be justified in actually seceding if doing so "would remove not only land but also vitally needed fuel and mineral resources from some larger political community."[25]

That was Walzer's position in *Just and Unjust Wars*. However, we have an indication that he may recently have reversed his position on this question. He has at least indicated a different position in one interview. In a 2004 interview in the *Harvard International Review*, Walzer gives three conditions under which foreign support for a secessionist movement is permissible. First, as in the *Just and Unjust Wars* formulation, there must be a secessionist movement that commands material support among the people it is claiming to liberate. Second, he adds the very different qualification that "the movement cannot be helped by any form of assistance short of war, and it will certainly be defeated without some external use of force." Third, the intervention must be likely to succeed at a less than "terrible" cost.[26]

Exception 2: counter-intervention

In the case where a revolutionary or secessionist movement challenges an established government, Walzer permits intervention to aid the government against the rebels. "After all, [the government] is the official representative of communal autonomy in international society." Intervention is permitted to aid the government, but not a nascent rebel group. If the rebels have a measure of success, and gain control over territory and population, they become "equal in status" with the established government, and neutrality is required. Once the parties are "equal in status," foreigners are neither permitted to continue (or start) aiding the government, nor are foreigners permitted to aid the rebels.[27]

If neutrality is not respected and either side is aided by a foreign force, Walzer permits a counter-intervention.

> Self-determination is the right of a people 'to become free by their own efforts' if they can, and nonintervention is the principle guaranteeing that their success will not be impeded or their failure prevented by the intrusions of an alien power.[28]

If an alien power is assisting a secessionist movement, foreign counter-intervention is permissible to aid the government. "Counter-intervention is morally possible only on behalf of a government (or a movement, party, or whatever) that has already passed the self-help test."[29]

After the rebel movement has met the test of self-help by gaining control over substantial territory and population, if a foreign army is aiding the government, a counter-intervention would be permissible to aid the rebels. Walzer does not permit a counter-intervention to be decisive, but to restore the balance to what it would have been without the initial, unjust, intervention. The counter-intervention should restore the balance, to prevent the initial, unjust intervention from "establishing a sovereign, or a form of government, which the nation, if left to itself, would not have chosen."[30] Imagine a fistfight broke out between two brothers, and a friend of one of the men came to his aid or came to restrain the other brother. In Walzer's formulation, the first intervention would have been impermissible, but it would be permissible for a fourth party to intervene to restore the balance between the first two belligerents – to remove the first intervener and let the brothers "duke it out." There is no judgment made about which of the brothers is in the right, or about who started the fight. The only justifiable aim for the intervener is to restore the balance of forces to what it would have been had the first unjust intervention not taken place: "The goal of a counter-intervention is not to win the war."[31] The counter-intervention must only aim to restore the balance of forces between the government and the rebels, not to turn the tide. Such intervention ("to turn the tide" rather than to restore the balance) would constitute a denial of self-determination.

Exception 3: humanitarian intervention

Walzer's third rule of disregard grants that unilateral humanitarian intervention is permissible in the case of massive human rights violations – in *Just and Unjust Wars*, this meant widespread massacre, official enslavement, or genocide. In a 1980 follow-up article to *Just and Unjust Wars*, Walzer added what we might now call ethnic cleansing:

> I think that I would now add to massacre and enslavement the expulsion of very large numbers of people (not simply the retreat of political opponents after a revolution or the transfer of populations that sometimes follows upon national liberation struggles – though these can be brutal enough).[32]

In 1994, Walzer added the category of humanitarian intervention to rescue people in a failed state.[33] Although he is a passionate advocate of humanitarian military intervention under these circumstances, he is strongly opposed to intervention under any other circumstances.

In the case of massive human rights violations (genocide, widespread massacres, enslavement, or ethnic cleansing), Walzer says that the test of self-help does not apply. It is the victims' inability to help themselves and the horror of their situation that allows foreign armies to cross the outlaw state's border. Walzer says "the standard in the old law books[34] was that [outsiders] had a right to intervene when there was a crime that 'outraged the conscience of mankind.'"[35] In the preface to the third edition of *Just and Unjust Wars*, Walzer approvingly cites the Tanzanian intervention to remove Idi Amin in Uganda, the Vietnamese intervention in Pol Pot's Kampuchea, the Indian intervention in East Pakistan, and the NATO bombardment over Kosovo: "there were horrifying acts that should have been stopped," by foreign intervention if necessary.[36]

In an article written just after the Rwandan Genocide in 1994, "The Politics of Rescue," Walzer writes a moving defense of humanitarian intervention in the case of widespread massacre, genocide, enslavement, or ethnic cleansing. In this article, Walzer expands the cases in which intervention is permissible to include failed states that cannot provide for the security of their people, and he defends the idea of protectorates and trusteeships as possibly the best way to secure decent conditions of life for people who have been the victims of genocide, massacre, ethnic cleansing, and the chaos of failed states (in particular, reference to Somalia and Rwanda):

> I don't mean to abandon the principle of non-intervention – only to honor its exceptions. It is true that right now there are a lot of exceptions. One reads the newspaper these days shaking. The vast numbers of murdered people; the men, women, and children dying of disease and famine willfully caused or easily preventable; the masses of desperate refugees – none of these are served by reciting high minded principles. Yes, the norm is not to interfere in other people's countries; the norm is self-determination. But not for these people, the victims of tyranny, ideological zeal, ethnic hatred, who are not determining anything for themselves, who urgently need help from outside. And it is not enough to wait until the tyrants, the zealots, and the bigots have done their filthy work and then rush food and medicine to the ragged survivors. Whenever the filthy work can be stopped, it should be stopped. And if not by us, the supposedly decent people of the world, then by whom?[37]

Humanitarian intervention, where it is permissible (that is, in the cases of genocide, widespread massacre, enslavement, or ethnic cleansing) is allowed (unilaterally) to any state that has the capability to stop the violence. In the absence of an international institution capable of acting swiftly enough to stop the bloodshed, "a plausible maxim for humanitarian intervention is 'who can, should.'"[38]

Walzer has recently begun to argue that when "oppression carried out by the rulers reaches massacre and forced resettlement, then intervention is not merely right, it is morally required."[39] Someone should intervene, but the duty does not fall on any one country or institution in particular; nor does Walzer specify how the agent should intervene.[40] This argument seems inconsistent with his affirmation that even when genocide is occurring, all states individually retain their rights to neutrality, "even if its assertion seems ignoble."[41] The assertion of the right of neutrality is more ignoble in the case of genocide, widespread massacre, or ethnic cleansing, for Walzer, than it is in the case of other types of wars. The reason Walzer gives is that we can predict, in advance, the result of standing by while genocide occurs, but the consequences of staying neutral in the case of other types of wars is often less clear.[42]

Exception 4: intervention in a failed or less than fully capable state

In his recent work, Walzer has also approved of interventions to stop widespread loss of life in cases of state failure. He has also approved of limited intervention in cases where the state has not collapsed completely but where sub-national actors such as terrorist groups cannot be controlled by the state and pose a hazard to neighboring states.

First, Walzer allows unilateral intervention to stop bloodshed in circumstances of state failure, although he "won't have much to say about it."[43] He approves of "what the Nigerians did in Sierra Leone: they reduced the number of killings, the scope of the barbarism."[44] In the absence of global institutions to care for people's needs, people need a decent and effective state.[45]

Second, Walzer's doctrine permits cross-border anti-terrorist raids and targeted killings in a state that cannot control all of the population on its territory. Imagine a case where a state cannot control its territory and where a terrorist group is taking refuge or launching attacks from within its borders. The victim of the attacks has the right to cross the border of the state hosting the terrorist group, to conduct limited operations to kill the terrorists, and then leave.[46] These targeted killings are legitimate when states do not have control over all their territory, such as in Lebanon or Pakistan. One example of justified targeted killing that Walzer gives is the American hellfire missile attack on several suspected Al-Qaeda operatives in the Yemeni desert in late 2001:

> It isn't a war zone, but it also isn't a zone of peace – and this description will fit many, not all, of the 'battlefields' of the 'war' against terrorism. In large sections of Yemen, the government's writ doesn't run; there are no police who could make the arrests (14 soldiers had already been killed in attempts to capture the Al Qaeda militants) and no courts in which prisoners could expect a fair trial. The Yemeni desert is a lawless land, and lawlessness provides a refuge for the political criminals called terrorists. The best way to deal with the refuge would be to help the Yemini government extend

its authority over the whole of its territory. But that is a long process, and the urgencies of the 'war' against terrorism may require more immediate action. When that is true, if it is true, it doesn't seem morally wrong to target Al Qaeda militants directly – for capture, if that's possible, but also for death.[47]

The limits of the rules of disregard

For Walzer, the "presumption against intervention is strong; we (on the left especially) have reasons for it, which derive from our opposition to imperial politics and our commitment to self-determination."[48] The occasions for intervention are limited to genocide, official enslavement, widespread massacre, ethnic cleansing, and failed states. Short of this limit, Walzer insists that the justice or injustice of a state's domestic institutions has no bearing on its right to non-intervention. Alongside his support for humanitarian intervention in extreme cases, Walzer insists upon a "wide chasm" between genocide, systematic massacre, forced resettlement, and the failed state on the one side, and what he calls "common nastiness" or the "ordinary brutality of authoritarian regimes" on the other.[49] "Ordinary brutality" includes routine, widespread political imprisonment, or murder, repression, and denial of political rights like free association, movement, and speech – anything except for genocide, widespread massacre, and forced resettlement. "Domestic tyrants are safe."[50] Walzer believes that foreign intervention is wrong in the case of "ordinary brutality" because such intervention denies the people living inside the state to work out their own way of living together.

Walzer also cites prudential reasons not to intervene:

> The common brutalities of authoritarian politics, the daily oppressiveness of traditional social practices – these are not occasions for intervention; they have to be dealt with locally, by the people who know the politics, who enact or resist the practices. The fact that these people can't easily or quickly reduce the incidence of brutality and oppression isn't a sufficient reason for foreigners to invade their country. Foreign politicians and soldiers are too likely to misread the situation, or to underestimate the force required to change it, or to stimulate a "patriotic" reaction in defense of the brutal politics and the oppressive practices. Social change is best achieved from within.[51]

The state must not commit massive human rights abuses, and it must maintain enough control over its territory that chaos does not result in harms similar to genocide, massacre, and forced resettlement. It must also maintain enough control over its territory that terrorists cannot hide out there or launch attacks from its territory into neighboring states. Beyond those limitations, Walzer argues that outsiders must regard the regime as if it is legitimate, and they must respect the state's political independence and territorial integrity. The reason Walzer gives is not that the state is in fact legitimate with its own people. The state may have no standing with its own people, and it may perpetrate systematic abuses of human rights. But for Walzer, this domestic illegitimacy does not translate into international illegitimacy. Foreigners are bound to stay out.

2 Walzer's innovations

Walzer's theory is innovative, in contrast to the older tradition, in five areas relevant to my argument about just cause. Walzer's theoretical contributions to the just war category of "just cause" include new arguments in support of the aggressor–defender paradigm, a new doctrine of pre-emption, new arguments about the underlying justification for defense of a neighbor (Walzer calls this collective self-defense), new formulations about the circumstances when intervention in civil wars is permissible, and new restrictions on the occasions for humanitarian intervention. Walzer himself does not always make clear where his theory of aggression is innovative and where he is endorsing traditional doctrine. Although he makes use of traditional just war sources, he does not comprehensively engage them as he elaborates his own theory of aggression. Walzer touches upon Emerich de Vattel, Francisco de Vitoria, Francisco Suarez, and Hugo Grotius, so I will look to these theorists in particular to show more clearly how Walzer's theory departs from theirs.

There are additional elements in Walzer's theory that are innovative in other areas of the *jus ad bellum* and (especially) *jus in bello*, but I will only focus on just cause for this section. In this section, I will contrast Walzer's five innovations (to just cause) against other important voices in the tradition in the following order:

a   Aggressor–defender paradigm upheld and strengthened by Walzer;
b   Underlying motivation for collective self-defense is self-interest (it is in the self-interest of states to maintain an international order free of inter-state aggression) not love of a neighbor;
c   Walzer's pre-emption doctrine is more restrictive than the older prevention doctrine;
d   Rationale for whether and when intervention in a civil war is permissible takes no view on the justice of either side's position, but solely on likelihood of success, i.e. self-determination;
e   New specific prohibitions on humanitarian intervention: the wide gulf between genocide and "ordinary brutality" is new and relies upon a reformulation of the concept of self-determination.

Aggressor–defender paradigm

Walzer's formulation of the aggressor–defender paradigm includes the idea that offensive war is always unjust and defensive war is always just (Walzer makes exceptions, but accepts the rule – thus the "exceptions"). I will argue in Chapter 3 that sometimes there is just cause for offensive war. In this sub-section, however, I aim merely to show that Walzer's view (that offensive war is always wrong) is not a traditional just war view, and it is also not endorsed by some of Walzer's contemporaries.

Walzer is explicit in his limitation of just cause to self-defense, pre-emptive self-defense, collective self-defense, and intervention under limited circumstances. Early expressions of the idea of just cause were not aligned so strictly with defense. Offensive war on account of some fault or to redress some wrong done was permitted in the just cause formulations of Augustine, Aquinas, Vitoria, Suarez, Gentili, and Grotius.[1] We can see the development of the notion of just cause from the churchly and secular origins of the medieval doctrine and the modern doctrine, which began to develop in the sixteenth and seventeenth centuries (the modern doctrine developed into secular[2] international law).[3] Vitoria, Suarez, Gentili, and Grotius explicitly connected just war to natural law in an effort to "discover universally applicable ethical criteria – standards which would be normative for all men and nations in all times and places."[4] In this time period of the tradition's development, the use of force was justified "not only by self-defense but also by the moral imperative to punish wrongs and protect the innocent."[5]

Augustine suggested that a just war "avenges wrongs, when a nation or state has to be punished for refusing to make amends for the wrongs inflicted by its subjects or to restore what it has seized unjustly."[6] Aquinas interpreted this to mean that resort to war could only be justified when "those who are attacked deserve it on account of some fault."[7] Faults rising to the level of just cause for war according to Vitoria, Suarez, Gentili, and Grotius included denial of free trade or interference with the freedom of the sea, the practice of piracy, injury to the reputation or honor of the prince or the state, harming an ambassador, and certain crimes against nature such as cannibalism or human sacrifice. Extension of empire or the so-called "natural slavery" or inferiority of "primitive" or "uncivilized" peoples did not constitute a just cause for war. Self-defense in case of an actual armed attack was only one of many just causes for war, including wars to "rescue the weak from the clutches of the wicked"[8] according to Aquinas[9] and also affirmed by Vitoria and Grotius, as I will discuss below under "humanitarian intervention."

Walzer was not the first person to identify offensive war with unjust war;[10] the aggressor–defender paradigm was an expression of the minority voice in just war thinking prior to Walzer, but Walzer is arguably its most influential contemporary exponent, and it is his formulation to which I will refer throughout the book. Among his contemporaries Paul Ramsey, A.J. Coates, C.A.J. Coady, James Turner Johnson, and G.E.M. Anscombe, Walzer's view that defensive war is (almost always) the only just war is unique. For Coates, "the problem with the aggressor–defender paradigm is its moral sterility.... Aggression does not consist in the use of force as such (regardless of whether the use be offensive or defensive) but in the unjust use of force."[11] Paul Ramsey suggests that the ban on offensive war is a direct (but insufficient) response to the massive destructive capability of nuclear weapons. It was a direct response insofar as the "unshootable" nature of nuclear weapons seemed to make any resort to war automatically disproportionate. The doctrine is insufficient though, as it simply trades just war theory for a ban on war that Ramsey finds (along with the aggressor–defender paradigm generally) to be theoretically untenable. Aggression is ill-defined, according to Ramsey, in the aggressor–defender paradigm. For Ramsey, starting the injustice that eventually makes war necessary is not the same thing as being the first to use force. The presumption is against injustice, and against threatening the security of other states or threatening the laws of peace. The aggressor–defender paradigm cannot capture this complexity: war is permitted in defense of justice, but "it is plain that [allowing wars] 'to repress injustice' may easily burst the bonds of the aggressor–defender terminology."[12] Anthony Coates makes a similar point, that in some sense all just wars are defensive, but a "much less literal and more critical understanding" of aggression is required: "wars that are fought to commit a wrong rather than to right one."[13]

Coady writes, "The call for humanitarian war harks back to the older tradition and challenges the paradigm of outlawing all aggression of states against other states."[14] James Turner Johnson advises:

> The attempt to render just cause in the contemporary terms of an aggressor–defender dichotomy does not escape the ambiguity that, in an earlier age, led to the concept of simultaneous ostensible justice and the connected concern that all participants in a war scrupulously observe the principle of restraint – in case their own cause was, after all, unjust. There is a second problem with the aggressor–defender *jus ad bellum* of recent international law as viewed from the standpoint of just war tradition. Rather than concentrating solely on defense as the only allowable just cause for war, perhaps it is necessary to keep in mind what Augustine saw clearly: that it is a moral duty for those who possess power to protect those who are relatively impotent when they are being threatened by others more powerful than they.[15]

Finally, Anscombe writes, "The present-day conception of 'aggression,' like so many strongly influential conceptions, is a bad one. Why *must* it be wrong to strike the first blow in a struggle? The only question is, who is in the right?"[16]

Collective self-defense and defense of a neighbor: self-interest versus love

In traditional just war theory, the type of just cause that Walzer terms "collective self-defense" was sometimes referred to as "defense of a neighbor." Paul Ramsey argues that there is a discernable origin of the idea of just war in the idea of the primacy of love. Augustine first justified forceful defense of another person in danger, not violent self-defense. Explaining the change-over from pacifism to just-war thinking first formulated by Ambrose and Augustine, Ramsey explains that the same love of neighbor that disapproved the use of force (in pacifism) did not change its character as love, it merely changed its tactics (to just war):

> Love for neighbors threatened by violence, by aggression, or tyranny, provided the grounds for admitting the legitimacy of the use of military force. Love sometimes had to resist evil.... The root reason for engaging in public defense most likely was not self-preservation.[17]

Walzer's justification for collective self-defense is the preservation of the stability of the system of sovereign states, thus it is indirectly a form of self-defense. However, the permissibility of coming to the aid of a neighbor threatened by violence certainly pre-existed the Westphalian order and the sovereign states-system. This is somewhat peripheral to my main argument about intervention, but it is not entirely peripheral. Walzer's complete abandonment of the earlier understanding of "love of neighbor" as a justification for war in favor of the "defense of the stability of the system of states" rationale is consistent with the corresponding lacuna in Walzer's theory of intervention. The reason for collective self-defense in Walzer's articulation of the theory is not neighbor love, but the protection, by the state, of the state's own interest in maintaining the stability of the system of nation states. The shift to "defense of the stability of the states-system" as a just cause is one root of Walzer's less permissive theory about intervention. The ignobility (in Walzer's theory) of a state asserting its right to neutrality and declining to assist another nation that has been attacked arises from the idea that the neutral state acts as a free-rider, getting benefits from the stability of the states-system, but not defending it, rather than from any sense of duty to aid a neighbor out of charity (love) or duty.

The distinction I want to make between "love of neighbor" and "preservation of the states-system" as rationales behind just cause might also reflect a shift to the "world of states" after Westphalia, where states have become the primary actor and unit of analysis. A self-regarding interest in the stability of the states system is not inconsistent with the other-regarding desire to promote human security for all people. Self-interested and charitable motives may be present together. The shift I propose now is from the "world of states" to something more like the "world of men" where human security is the primary value, and state security is valued insofar as it contributes to the preservation of human security.

Pre-emption and prevention

Walzer's pre-emption is more restrictive than some voices in the earlier tradition. Alberico Gentili, for example, argued that preventive war might sometimes be just: "one might sometimes anticipate that the trend of events will lead to a situation of extreme necessity; in such cases one is fully justified in taking preventive action."[18] Gentili was not only writing about pre-emption of imminent attack; he meant that force was sometimes justifiable to prevent the formation and consolidation of "probable and possible" threats as well:

> One ought not to delay, or wait to avenge at one's peril an injury which one has received, if one may at once strike at the root of the growing plant and check the attempts of an adversary who is meditating evil. ... A defense is just which anticipates dangers that are already meditated and prepared, and also those which are not meditated, but are probable and possible.[19]

Grotius also allows that wars may be justly undertaken to prevent wrongs not yet committed,[20] but Grotius' endorsement is not an endorsement of the early kind of preventive war allowed in Gentili's construction. By "wrongs not yet committed," Grotius explicitly means that the danger must be immediate, not merely a "supposed intention."[21] In the passage below, he seems to be referring to Gentili's argument: "the danger must be immediate which is one necessary point. ... But they are themselves much mistaken, and mislead others, who maintain that any degree of fear ought to be a ground for killing another, to prevent his supposed intention."[22]

Grotius says leaders should take heed of Cicero's counsel that many wrongs are done through fear. In that discussion he approvingly quotes Livy who writes, "Great infamy redounds to those who by anticipation perpetrate the criminal act which they fear."[23] In the event of a conspiracy and a planned attack, Grotius insists that there is no right of preventive self-defense until the attack is otherwise unpreventable.

Walzer, in a formulation quite compatible with that of Grotius, requires "a manifest intent to injure, a degree of active preparation that makes that intent a positive danger, and a general situation in which waiting, or doing anything other than fighting, greatly magnifies the risk."[24] The danger must also be imminent; it must be hours, days, or weeks – not months or years – away. I endorse this view and further extend its logic to pre-emptive humanitarian intervention (also endorsed by the International Commission on Intervention and State Sovereignty).[25] Walzer rejects extending this pre-emption doctrine to interventions; pre-emption is limited to self-defense.

Walzer requires that outsiders take no view on justice of civil conflict.

In distinction to Walzer's view that we can judge the legitimacy of secessionist or revolutionary movements only by their relative strength (relative to the government), Vattel's formulation ignores relative strength entirely. Instead, Vattel's formulation *requires* external judgments about the justice of the domestic political institutions and, thereby, about the justice of the cause of each side in a civil war.

> When a people, from good reasons take up arms against an oppressor, it is but an act of justice and generosity to assist brave men in the defence of

their liberties. Whenever, therefore, matters are carried so far as to produce a civil war, foreign powers may assist that party which appears to them to have justice on its side. He who assists an odious tyrant, – he who declares for an unjust and rebellious people, – violates his duty.[26]

Grotius believed that non-involved states were:

> under obligation to determine the just cause of every war and to discriminate in their treatment of the just and unjust sides. Only when the justice of the cause was seriously in doubt did Grotius countenance non intervention.[27]

As noted earlier, Walzer's theory requires that foreigners recognize the party who has sufficient force capability to win the war as the side that may legitimately be assisted, no matter what that party stands for, substantively, because by its strength it has proven itself to be representative of the local will: "Foreign states can't join a civil war simply because they admire the principles of the party that has invited them in, or even because they believe that that party would win a free election." Instead, only a force mobilization sufficient to make the rebels' victory certain, and thereby make intervention "superfluous," would make it justifiable for a foreign government to assist a revolutionary or secessionist movement.[28]

Armed intervention by foreign actors to come to the aid of subjects of another political entity, what we now call humanitarian intervention, is a very old concept. Likewise the newly coined terms "sovereignty as responsibility" and "responsibility to protect" have deep roots in very old ideas and debates. Francisco de Vitoria (1486–1546), a Spanish theologian and Professor at the University of Salamanca, affirmed a right of outsiders to "defend the innocent against tyranny" and he also spoke publicly in favor of the right of so-called primitive peoples to be left unmolested by potential colonizers. Vitoria argued that these principles were derived from the universal laws governing all of humanity, including the idea that nature has decreed a kinship among men and the law referred to in the proverb, "Do as you would be done by."[29]

For Vitoria, defense of a neighbor did not only mean defense of a neighboring state, but also it meant defense of an individual from

> tyrannical and oppressive laws ... and from any nefarious custom or rite. The proof is that God gave commandment to each man concerning his neighbor. The barbarians are all our neighbours, and therefore anyone, especially princes, may defend them from tyranny and oppression. A further proof is the saying: 'deliver them that are drawn unto death, and forbear not to deliver those that are ready to be slain' (Prov. 24:11). This applies not only to the actual moment when they are being dragged to death; they may also force the barbarians to give up such rites altogether. If they refuse to do so, war may be declared upon them ... their masters may be changed and

new ones set up. ... It makes no difference that all the barbarians consent to these kinds of rites and sacrifices, or that they refuse to accept the Spaniards as their liberators in the matter.[30]

Vitoria argued here about the rites of human sacrifice as practiced by the North American Indians. He did not affirm the right of the Spaniards to impose Christianity by force on the Indians, nor did he accept arguments that the Indians were natural slaves or unfit for self-government. Vitoria did not allow that lesser violations of natural law, such as bestiality or homosexuality, ought to be causes for war; nor did he think that religious difference was a just cause for war. The *casus belli* was not the difference of religion, but the violation of the natural right to life of the barbarians – jeopardized as it was by the "nefarious practices and rites" of cannibalism and human sacrifice. Vitoria further argued that the Indians' refusal to allow safe passage of missionaries through their territories was a violation of the natural law of hospitality, and a just cause for war. Vitoria derived this construction of just cause from what he called the "universal natural law binding all men." At the same time, Vitoria was careful to limit circumstances under which universal law may be upheld by force (human sacrifice and cannibalism, but not lesser deviations such as "sexual immorality" which Vitoria attributed to differences in education and habits).[31]

Walzer writes in the preface to the third edition of *Just and Unjust Wars* that "ever since the Spaniards conquered Mexico in order to stop the Aztec practice of human sacrifice (among other reasons) the term [humanitarian intervention] has evoked mostly sarcastic comments."[32] We should also note that the theorists who wrote in support of the Spaniards' right of intervention also condemned the Spaniards' abuses. Vitoria wrote that "no business shocks me or embarrasses me more than the corrupt profits in the Indes. The very mention of them freezes the blood in my veins."[33] Vitoria, Suarez, Gentili, and Grotius all sternly forbade territorial aggrandizement or empire building as a just cause for war, and insisted that fighting such a war (or abusively profiteering from it) under the veil of a war of rescue would be a crime. All these theorists recognized the likelihood that princes might wage wars ostensibly to defend the innocent against tyranny, but with a hidden intention of self-aggrandizement.

Bartholome Las Casas (d. 1566) and Francisco Suarez took similar positions to Vitoria's and spent several years bravely and vociferously defending the Indians with arguments supporting their natural rights against the oppression of the Spaniards. A defense of humanitarian intervention did not entail a defense of the conquerors' abuses.

"Turning savagely on the people" was condemned in the earlier tradition, whether it was the people's own state that turned on them or the intervening state. "Turning savagely on the people" encompassed more offenses than Walzer's enslavement, genocide, widespread massacre, and forced resettlement. For Grotius, it included the torture and killing of political prisoners,[34] and war was sometimes permissible to rescue an oppressed people from the yoke of a brutal regime. Grotius advocated armed force as justified to protect Christians from persecution, but he did not do so merely for Christians; he also argued to that barbarians ought to be protected from oppression at the hands of Christian rulers. To "rescue the weak from the clutches of the wicked" was a just cause, as was a war to depose rulers who violently mistreated their political adversaries.[35] A humanitarian intervention to defend subjects of another state (without the victims' invitation) against injury from their own sovereign is permissible according to Grotius, in cases where the injuries are "very atrocious and very evident."[36]

> Though it is a rule established by the laws of nature and of social order, and a rule confirmed by all the records of history, that every sovereign is supreme judge in his own kingdom and over his own subjects, in whose disputes no foreign power can justly interfere. Yet where a Busiris, a Phalaris, or a Thracian Diomede provoke their people to despair and resistance by unheard of cruelties, having themselves abandoned all the laws of nature, they lose the rights of independent sovereigns, and can no longer claim the privilege of the law of nations. Thus, Constantine took up arms against Maxentius and Licinius, and other Roman emperors either took, or threatened to take them against the Persians, if they did not desist from persecuting the Christians.[37]

Here Walzer has reversed Grotius' doctrine. For Grotius, the people never have a right to rebellion, but outsiders have a right (perhaps even an obligation) to rescue them from tyranny:

> Admitting that it would be fraught with the greatest dangers if subjects were allowed to redress grievances by force of arms, it does not necessarily follow that other powers are prohibited from giving them assistance when labouring under grievous oppressions. For whenever the impediment to any action is of a personal nature, and not inherent in the action itself, one person may perform for another, what he cannot do for himself, provided it is an action by which some kind service may be rendered. Thus a guardian or any other friend may undertake an action for a ward, which he is incapacitated from doing for himself.[38]

For Walzer, the formulation on rebellion is exactly the opposite; the people always possess a right of revolution, and outsiders have no right to pre-empt the people's decision to rebel (or not to rebel) by intervening on their behalf.

The term "sovereignty as responsibility" has only recently been coined, but the phrase names a very old concept. Emerich de Vattel was one of the fathers of the modern notion of sovereignty. Though Vattel plainly affirmed the autonomy of the sovereign state, particularly the equality of small and weak states against large and powerful ones,[39] he attached duties and responsibilities to sovereignty. Vattel puts it this way:

> if the prince, by violating the fundamental laws, gives his subjects a legal right to resist him, – if tyranny, becoming insupportable, obliges the nation to rise in their own defence, – every foreign power has a right to succour an oppressed people who implore their assistance.[40]

Grotius, like Vitoria, knew that princes would have a tendency to wage war in self-interest, and they anticipated it would be likely princes might pretend a humanitarian motive when territorial aggrandizement, empire-building, or simple greed was their actual motive.[41] These complications notwithstanding, Grotius like Vitoria affirmed the justice of a true war of rescue:

> Pretexts of that kind [rescuing the oppressed] cannot always be allowed, they may often be used as the cover of ambitious designs. But right does not necessarily lose its nature from being in the hands of wicked men. The sea still continues a channel of lawful intercourse, though sometimes navigated by pirates, and swords are still instruments of defence, though sometimes wielded by robbers or assassins.[42]

Samuel Pufendorf (d. 1694) is in agreement with Grotius, Vitoria, and Vattel as to the permissibility of humanitarian intervention in limited circumstances. However, hoping to overcome the theoretical difficulty posed by the likelihood of rulers to undertake wars for self-interested purposes, Pufendorf and Vattel (unlike Vitoria and Grotius) restrictively insist that the victims of the oppression must invite the assistance: "Otherwise any man might make war upon any man upon such a pretense."[43] Whether the party ostensibly to be assisted by the intervention requests the interference has no place in Walzer's theory.

Another distinctive element of Walzer's view in contrast to these historical examples is Walzer's "wide chasm" between the ordinary brutality of an authoritarian regime (where intervention is not permissible) and cases of genocide, widespread massacre, enslavement, and ethnic cleansing (where it is). Vitoria, Grotius, Vattel, and Pufendorf did not posit any such threshold. Vitoria thought intervention was permissible to stop "nefarious rites or customs," a formulation Walzer would reject on anti-paternalist grounds. Grotius used the example of torturing subjects (as Phalaris did with his brazen bull); Walzer also rejects widespread torture as a sufficient reason to resort to war on the grounds that this type of intervention denies the victims their right to self-determination or their right to revolution.

Why did Walzer make these innovations?

Walzer's innovations are rooted in his communitarianism, his anti-paternalism, anti-imperialism, and his experience in the anti-war movement of the 1960s and 1970s. Walzer explicitly attributes his inspiration for writing *Just and Unjust Wars* to his experience as an anti-war activist during the Vietnam War; his book was meant to recapture, for the ordinary citizen, the moral language of what Charles Beitz has called "one of the few ideas to have attained substantial development in the tradition of international thought – the just war."[44] Walzer was especially concerned with the ideas of restraining international aggression and allowing for national self-determination. The idea of foreign intervention for the good of the people of the target state (especially where intervention might not be welcomed by such people) fell into serious crisis in the post-colonial era, particularly after the American involvement in Vietnam from 1945–1975 and the French involvement in Algeria. Walzer developed a belief that the right to self-determination supercedes other rights, and without a community free of foreign interference, political rights are meaningless.[45] On the ordinary liberal view, it makes more sense to say that without political rights, the right to a community free from foreign intervention is of dubious meaning. Perhaps this difference in valuation is explained by Walzer's communitarian approach. Walzer resists the label communitarian,[46] but the label fits insofar as communitarianism can be taken to mean placing a high value upon community integrity and understanding attachments, values, and perspectives to be determined locally and only understandable insofar as they exist within one's own community.

The label communitarian was attached to Walzer's 1983 critique of John Rawls' idea of "justice as fairness" as formulated in *Theory of Justice*. Responding to Rawls' idea that universally acceptable ideas about the nature of social justice can be abstracted from specific communities' values, Walzer argued that meaningful criticism of social arrangements could only be derived from within communities of actual people, living in specific times and places. This view informs Walzer's arguments in *Just and Unjust Wars*. I do not mean to attribute to Walzer an endorsement of the "second-wave" version of political communitarianism represented by Amitai Etzioni and others.

Walzer argues that values and ideas about justice are sensible to people only locally, within local mores. Algerian mores might affirm different values than French mores, and so an Algerian government might look unjust to a French eye, although it is perfectly Algerian. The fact that it is Algerian means that it is the embodiment of Algerian historic community, and its justice or injustice is insensible to (meaning that it cannot be understood by) an outsider with different mores and a sense of justice determined by his own historic community. Justice only makes sense as interpreted locally and expressed in self-determination.

Walzer speaks of political communities made up of the people and their government as a cohesive unit, and ascribes them communal integrity. Walzer says that to invade a country to protect human rights denies "the rights of contemporary men and women to live as members of an historic community and to express their inherited culture through political forms worked out among themselves."[47] These rights, as Walzer constructs his formulation, are to be construed as individual rights to a community, rather than a community's rights over its members. States rights, and community rights, are nothing more than the aggregate of the rights of individuals who make up the community.

An interventionist war against a repressive government is a crime, Walzer argues, because it forces people to fight for their right to a historic community that they have worked out on their own. Walzer accepts some rights as self-evident and universal, such as the right to a historic community arrived at through self-determination, the right not to be enslaved or to be a victim of genocide, and the right against ethnic cleansing. The presumption against non-intervention is overridden when the rights against enslavement or genocide are infringed, because this kind of radical coercion cannot allow for self-determination.

The highest political right of individuals is their access to a self-determining political community. This view privileges those rights over other rights that might plausibly also be held to be self-evident, such as the right to be free from torture or arbitrary arrest, the right to bodily integrity, and free movement. Walzer thinks that outsiders cannot know enough about the politics, the history, and the culture of a people to "form concrete judgments of the conflicts and harmonies, the historical choices and cultural affinities, the loyalties and resentments"[48] because they are not members of the same community from which those sensibilities have arisen and within which they have their existence. Repressive governments on this view are not seen as an impediment to self-determination, but as an expression of the self-determination process.

Walzer's early critics, Walzer's response to them, and the critics' rejoinders

An early chorus of critics responded to Walzer's book with arguments that his theory sheltered tyrannical or domestically illegitimate regimes that should not be protected against foreign intervention. Walzer did not deny that his theory protects such regimes, but he defended his reasons for doing so in a "response to critics" article. In this section I will summarize the arguments of four of Walzer's early critics: Gerald Doppelt, Charles Beitz, David Luban, and Richard Wasserstrom. I will then set out a summary of Walzer's response to these critics, and the critics' rejoinders.

Gerald Doppelt makes three major arguments in his 1978 article "Walzer's Theory of Morality in International Politics." First, Doppelt identifies a confounding paradox in Walzer's theory of aggression: Walzer's definition of the crime of aggression is "to force men and women to risk their lives for the sake of their rights." What rights, Doppelt asks, does Walzer mean? If they are "individual rights to life and liberty," as Walzer says on page 51, this would be a plausible view; but for Walzer, a government only forfeits "its rights of political sovereignty only when it engages in the enslavement or massacre of its own citizens."[49] Doppelt reasons that "denial of individual rights to life and liberty" can be perpetrated by a tyrannical regime, without reaching the level of genocide and massacre. Tyrannical regimes, not only foreign aggressors, can commit the moral wrong of forcing men and women to risk their lives for the sake of their rights.[50] Building on this point, Doppelt argues that a tyrannical government cannot derive a right against aggression in the name of protecting its citizens' right to life and liberty, when by its tyranny, it is already denying those rights itself. The paradox is that on Walzer's definition of aggression, it seems as though a tyrannical state would have no right against a humanitarian intervention aimed at helping the citizens of the state "gain a free state – one in which they would *not* be forced to risk their lives for the sake of their rights."[51] For Doppelt, Walzer makes the paradox explicit when he writes, "Though states are founded for the sake of life and liberty, they cannot be challenged in the name of life and liberty by any other states."[52]

Second, Doppelt argues that Walzer spuriously values independence from external military intervention above any other value in international morality and above any other value in domestic political life. For Walzer, people laboring under an oppressive government must, "even if they are seeking to better their lot, maintain their strict independence from external military intervention (or assistance) above all else, even it the alternative is continuing oppression." Doppelt finds that it's a "strange conception of international morality which thus abstracts from the moral character of the states whose independence is so prized."[53]

Finally, Doppelt objects to Walzer's understanding of self-determination. He offers Walzer's doctrine on counter-intervention as a proof. As I summarized in Chapter 1, Walzer does not permit counter-intervention to be decisive, but only to restore the balance to what it would have been without the initial, unjust, intervention. The counter-intervention should restore the balance, to prevent the initial, unjust intervention from "establishing a sovereign, or a form of government, which the nation, if left to itself, would not have chosen."[54] Doppelt writes:

> To my mind, this doctrine of counter-intervention reveals the least plausible dimension of Walzer's conception of self-determination as the highest good of international morality. If Walzer values a nation's development of the political capacity to govern itself, how can he justify a foreign nation's right of counter-intervention on behalf of a tyrannical status quo which may in fact block this development on the mere basis of superior force? Indeed if the outcome of a political struggle in a nation reflects nothing but the balance of internal military might, I see no more reason for calling this process one of "self-determination" (in a positive moral sense which gives the victor rights of sovereignty) than I do for denying that it is self-determination on the mere basis that foreign troops have played some role in it.[55]

A second critic, Charles Beitz, in his 1979 book *Political Theory and International Relations*, rejects what he calls Walzer's "communal integrity thesis" – the idea that states, analogous to persons, have a right to be respected as autonomous entities. Beitz finds that this idea, which Walzer refers to as the domestic analogy, "brings a spurious order to complex and conflicting moral considerations. The idea is neither fundamental, nor adequate as a justification of the supposedly derivative principles of nonintervention and self-determination."[56] Beitz argues that non-intervention and self-determination are grounded in more basic principles of justice, and that state autonomy should not be respected in some obvious cases, contrary to Walzer's communal integrity thesis. For example, strict observance of the autonomy and non-intervention principle in situations "involving colonialism would, in effect, protect colonial powers against demands for colonial self-determination."[57]

In his 1979 book review in *International Organization* entitled "Bounded Morality: Justice and the State in World Politics," Beitz criticizes Walzer's "right to a historic community" justification for states' rights to sovereign territorial integrity with an argument quite similar to Doppelt's second point, above:

> The justification that Walzer advances simply cannot be construed so that its premise (that there is some sort of right to build a common life) both has a meaning worthy of our adherence and clearly supports so sweeping a conclusion. The idea that the rights of states are based on the rights of their citizens is plausible only if the rights of citizens are given a definite moral content, but any definite moral content will require a limitation in the scope of the principle protecting the rights of states to those states which satisfy the corresponding moral criteria.

Beitz also disputes Walzer's view (adopted from Mill) that "the members of a political community must seek their own freedom, just as the individual must cultivate his own virtue."[58] Beitz notes that Walzer provides no empirical evidence for the Millian claim that free institutions will not survive unless they arise locally, from among the people who will be governed by them. According to Beitz, evidence is needed because "the conclusion that the generalization is supposed to justify is so nearly absolute."[59] Beitz further notes that even if the empirical assumption were correct, the view would nevertheless fail to support a general ban on interventions, because the Mill–Walzer view only offers an argument about why an intervention to support the development of free institutions would necessarily fail. This "leaves open other paternalistic justifications for intervention, of which many can be imagined, ranging from satisfaction of a people's material needs to establishment of one or another type of economic system."[60] Beitz argues in essence that Walzer's non-intervention doctrine both goes too far and does not go far enough – the doctrine is not based in empirical evidence, so its conclusions go further than the empirical evidence can support; and even if that problem was absent, the doctrine does not offer an argument against paternalistic interventions not aimed at setting up free political institutions, so it does not go far enough to be a thorough doctrine against intervention. I think Beitz's criticism of the domestic analogy is convincing, and that this is his most powerful criticism along with his note that empirical evidence is lacking for the claim that free institutions set up by foreigners will not be maintained by those they would liberate.

David Luban, in his article "Just War and Human Rights," first takes aim at rights of sovereignty that are insensitive to the question of domestic legitimacy. For Luban, "a legitimate state has a right against aggression because people have a right to their legitimate state."[61] If this is true, he writes:

> we should be able to define *jus ad bellum* directly in terms of human rights, without the needless detour of talk about states. If the rights of states are

derived from the rights of humans, and are thus in a sense one kind of human rights, it will be important to consider their possible conflict with other human rights.[62]

Luban admits that a people, or a nation, have a right to a self-determining political community, but he finds that Walzer and the legalist paradigm "systematically and fallaciously confuses a nation and its state, granting illegitimate states a right to which they are not entitled."[63] A nation has a stronger claim to make to being a "historic community" than a state, which is merely the present government, whether it is representative of the nation or the peoples within it, or not. Luban thinks Walzer's arguments might have a certain plausibility if they were applied strictly to nation-states, but since that is not Walzer's project, Luban rejects the view that tacit consent has been given (in states) on social contract grounds.

Walzer seems to adopt the view he attributes to Mill, that the people must want their tyranny, or they would not have it. Luban goes on to say:

> somehow oppression of domestic vintage carries a prima facie claim to legitimacy which is not there in the case of foreign conquest. It seems that Mill suspects that the state would not be there if the people did not secretly want it. This seems to me to be an absurd, and at times even obscene view, uncomfortably reminiscent of the view that women are raped because secretly they want to be.[64]

Walzer thinks that the people must want their tyranny, because otherwise they would throw it off. Luban rejects that argument, because "such struggles do not always succeed, and after each bloody repression the possibility of another uprising grows less. Heart and flesh can only bear so much."[65] Luban's first revision to Walzer's *jus ad bellum* is that sometimes intervention is justified, even in the absence of massacre, enslavement, or genocide. Luban claims that Walzer concedes this point, quoting Walzer out of context: "a state (or government) established against the will of its own people, ruling violently, may well forfeit its right to defend itself even against a foreign invasion."[66] Walzer does write this in a footnote, but he goes on in the next chapter to clarify his position explicitly; a state loses its right to defend itself in cases where massive rights abuses are present (genocide, massacre, enslavement). It is unclear why Luban takes this point out of context, but the footnote taken alone does not represent Walzer's considered and fully articulated view in *Just and Unjust Wars*.

Luban makes a second revision to Walzer's formulation of *jus ad bellum*; he rejects the ban on offensive war. Luban writes that the ban on offensive war is just a legal rule that forecloses the discussion about when war is justifiable; as such it may be a legal rule, but it cannot be a principle grounded in justice. It is no longer a theory of just war. "By giving absolute primacy to the world community's interest in peace, [the ban on offensive war] does not really answer the question of when a war is or can be just, it simply refuses to consider it."[67]

Richard Wasserstrom pursues a related argument. He rejects the aggressor–defender paradigm and insists that defensive war is not always just. Additionally, Wasserstrom presents a view similar to Luban's and Doppelt's view that

> it is unclear [in *Just and Unjust Wars*] why the rights of individuals do not justify more in the way of intervention and less in the way of commitment to the desirability of the nation-state.... The rights of states come to enjoy an exalted, primary status.[68]

The "rights of individuals" on which Walzer bases his doctrine of non-intervention, Wasserstrom argues, work out in fact to be reduced to "the solitary individual 'right' to a civil society of almost any sort. And this is at least an uninspiring, constricted theory of individual rights."[69] Worse, one morally unattractive implication of Walzer's theory is that "where a state can reduce its citizens to obedience, it is a legitimate state."[70] To clarify, Walzer does not say the state is legitimate, but that outsiders must act as if it is legitimate. Nevertheless, the effect is the same; the oppressive state enjoys a right to non-intervention. The strength or weakness of internal resistance against an oppressive regime is the indicator, for Walzer, of whether the resistance is legitimate and may be aided from the outside. This seems plainly wrong to Wasserstrom, who argues that it is very "unrealistic to suppose that a modern state cannot control its citizens effectively without genuine consent."[71] Widespread acceptance of the government's rule may be as much a testament to the government's thoroughgoing oppression and the personal danger to dissenters as to any sort of domestic legitimacy. I think Wasserstrom is correct in his estimation. That the strength of resistance is such an important indicator of legitimacy in Walzer's formulation is very troubling, because the strength of resistance may have to do simply with power and force, and nothing to do with the actual preferences, loyalties, and aspirations of the people living in the state.

Walzer's reply to his critics and my comments on the debate

Walzer replied to his critics in a 1980 article in *Philosophy and Public Affairs*, entitled "The Moral Standing of States: A Response to Four Critics," in which he expanded and clarified his argument from *Just and Unjust Wars*. Walzer amended the circumstances under which humanitarian intervention was permissible from "genocide, widespread massacre, and enslavement" to also include "mass deportations and forced resettlement" in this article, in response to a misunderstanding by Gerald Doppelt who misconstrued Walzer's use of the term "enslavement" in *Just and Unjust Wars* to mean "ethnic cleansing."[72] Although Walzer's original intention was not to include "ethnic cleansing," he amended his argument in "The Moral Standing of States" to include it. This is, however, the only change Walzer made to his theory in response to the arguments from these four critics. The rest of his response is a re-statement, expansion, and clarification of the same principles he articulated in *Just and Unjust Wars*. Walzer does not, to my mind, successfully refute his critics' main arguments; some he does not engage, and some he dismisses without a clear rebuttal.

I think many of the critics' points are correct, and they convincingly destabilize Walzer's non-intervention doctrine by problematizing its foundations. Walzer does not rebut his critics' arguments directly. Instead, in his response, Walzer restates and clarifies his original position. The consensus reached by his critics, according to Walzer, is that "a) the theory protects states that should not be protected against intervention, and b) it does so on grounds that are either inadequate or incoherent."[73] To address these criticisms, Walzer "enlarges upon the argument of the book, and at one or two points, amends the argument, but the basic position remains intact."[74]

One issue raised by the four critics is: What exactly are the rights Walzer is referring to when he speaks of aggression, the crime of which is to "force men and women to risk their lives for the sake of their rights?" Walzer's response, in my view, moves his doctrine onto shakier, not more solid, ground. Walzer clarifies "individual rights of men and women" to mean just one right, "the right to a historic community."

Doppelt and Wasserstrom suggest that if a government deprives citizens of their rights already, an attack narrowly aimed at that government cannot deprive the people of rights (that have already been taken away by the government). Walzer replies with an argument that the people's right to revolution (or not to have a revolution) should not be taken away by foreigners:

> the tyranny of established government gives rise to a right of revolution, of which they cannot be deprived. When invasions are launched by foreign forces, it is entirely plausible to say that the rights of citizens have been violated. Their "slowness" has been artificially speeded up, their "aversion" has been repudiated, their prudential calculations have been rejected – all in favor of someone else's conceptions of political justice and political prudence.[75]

In response to the criticism that Walzer's concept of sovereignty is insensitive to domestic political legitimacy, Walzer denies that it is. He makes two points on this topic: first, he reiterates that his theory allows outsiders to intervene on behalf of secessionist or revolutionary movements when they have commanded sufficient resources and support to shake off the de facto regime on their own. Second; Walzer says that his critics all make the same mistake by insisting that the theory of just and unjust wars requires Walzer to call tyrannical states legitimate. Walzer disputes this, arguing that in fact his theory does not require outsiders to actually believe that states are legitimate, merely to "act as if they are legitimate, that is, must not make war against them"[76] unless the citizens actually living there muster enough resources to wage a successful campaign for change on their own. I do not find this response convincing, for several reasons. First, Walzer explicitly specifies that "a legitimate government is one that can fight its own internal wars";[77] he believes that if they were not domestically legitimate, they would not exist. His theory is tautological, as Wasserstrom argued. In any event, it is unclear how "acting as if" yields a morally different outcome than "believing" that a state is legitimate.

For Walzer, almost nothing a tyrant does can justify outsiders' depriving the right of the people to revolution and self-determination. It is the people's right to choose whether it is prudent to revolt. If they have decided it is imprudent, outsiders have no right to foist rebellion onto them from outside. Walzer elaborates further, in response to Wasserstrom's observation that Walzer's understanding of legitimacy appears to be "a government that can reduce its people to obedience."[78] Walzer accepts this characterization, and clarifies it further by arguing that if the local people wanted to revolt, they would. If they do not think revolt is prudent, that is because the local government enjoys sufficient support that their revolt would fail. If the local government enjoys this much support, it is evident that the local government must be representative of the collective will of the local people. Walzer explicitly means to preserve the possibility, the arena, in which peoples *might* be self-determining. If there is a gang of thugs that is ruling in their own interests (as opposed to the people's), then it is up to the people to overturn it. If they cannot or do not wish to, for whatever reasons, outsiders are bound to respect their reticence, their aversion to change, or their prudence.[79] In other words, "it is not a gang of rulers acting in its own interest, but a people governed in accordance with its own traditions."[80] The important thing for Walzer is that it is *their* inability, *their* failure, and they can call the resulting community *their own*. Therefore, even if they are severely repressed, it is a self-determining sort of repression, because it is merely local repression and the locals are not able, or do not wish, to muster enough resources to overthrow it. This repression, according to Walzer, could be shaken off by locals if it was not representative of their wills because the police, the soldiers, and the officials of the state are all compatriots. This seems very odd to me. Consider being a witness to a mugging. If the victim was exercising his prudential judgment (and self-determination as an individual) by not fighting off the mugger, it does not seem like a reasonable conclusion that it would be wrong to assist him on the grounds that one should not interfere with his choices or his self-determination.

The convictions and preferences of the people are:

> likely to be bound up with, and partly explanatory of, the form and character of their states. That's why states objectively illegitimate are able, again and again, to rally subjects and citizens against invaders. In all such cases, though the fit between government and community is not of a democratic sort, there is still a fit of some sort, which foreigners are bound to respect.[81]

Walzer ends his response with the Swedish magic water thought experiment mentioned earlier. Consider, he says, that in Algeria a group comes to power with a promise of a democratic, secular state, with equal rights for all citizens. Instead, the group creates a military dictatorship creates a:

religious republic, without civil or political liberties, and brutally repressive ... women have been returned to their traditional religious subordination to patriarchal authority.... It is clear that this regime has deep roots in Algerian history, although its popularity has never been tested in a democratic way; but there is no doubt it is an Algerian regime.[82]

Walzer asks his readers to imagine that there is a special magical water that could be introduced safely into the Algerian water supply that would turn all of the Algerians into Swedish style social democrats, leaving them with no sense of loss about the change in their political views. He asks whether that "Swedish magic water" should be used, and answers himself "emphatically not," because this regime, although it denies the Algerians their rights, is an *Algerian* regime, and that is what they *really* have a right to and the only style of regime they are likely to call their own.[83]

A legitimate government does not have to be a democratic government; if the local people want a democratic government, they will institute one. If they cannot, Walzer insists, it is because a large enough portion of them do not want to do so. No local government, Walzer argues, invoking the Sandinistas in Nicaragua, can keep a people in subjection who do not wish to be in subjection. I do not find this idea compelling for at least two reasons. First, as Walzer's critics suggest, it is implausible to imagine that a modern state, particularly a dictatorship, could not control its people. As Luban notes, each failed insurrection would decrease future chances of success by disheartening the potential rebels;[84] it also might provide an excuse and an inspiration for more ruthless oppression on the part of the state enforcement apparatus. Second, in *Just and Unjust Wars*, Walzer grants that it is permissible for outsiders to intervene on behalf of the state against internal resistance, and this often happens in the real world. This is inconsistent with Walzer's idea that resistance groups would succeed if they were popular enough, because they face only domestic oppression. If the government is being aided by outsiders, as Walzer says is permissible until such time as the rebels have passed the test of self-help, it does not seem plausible to suggest that the resistance faces merely domestic oppression.

Critics' rejoinders

Doppelt, Beitz, and Luban replied to Walzer's essay with short, colorful, impassioned rejoinders (Wasserstrom did not write one). Doppelt, in "Statism Without Foundations," makes the point that there are states where there is no viable secessionist movement, no civil war, and no widespread massacre, genocide, or enslavement, and yet where "it would be straining to the point of incoherence to say that a majority of its people enjoy the right 'to express their inherited culture through political forms worked out among themselves.'" Doppelt notes that the form of government expressing "traditions of illiteracy, ignorance, depoliticizing material deprivation, political intimidation and incapacity" are inherited cultures that support small, powerful classes ruling in their own interests, and Doppelt rejects the idea that it can make sense to think of this process as "self-determination."[85] Doppelt also rejects Walzer's argument that the presence of a form of government is evidence of its acceptance by the people living under it.

Finally Doppelt, like Luban, asks what reason there is to hold the right to a historic community as more basic than other human rights in international morality. Doppelt denies that "the individual right to national autonomy is more basic than other human rights, such as freedom from terror, torture, material deprivation, and suppressed speech."[86]

Beitz's begins his rejoinder with the "obvious objection that the absence of fit is far more pervasive than Walzer allows."[87] Beitz's more subtle criticism is that he does not believe Walzer's communal integrity thesis is supportable. Beitz also finds Walzer's Swedish Magic Water example illuminates a different principle than the communal integrity principle Walzer tries to defend with the example. The Swedish Magic Water is a special magical chemical that could be introduced safely into the Algerian water supply and turn all the Algerians into human-rights affirming, Swedish-style, social democrats. Beitz argues, convincingly in my view, that it is not the communal right that is violated by using mind-control of this sort, it is the individual right to autonomy and free thought of the individual persons that would be violated. Those are exactly the same rights that are also violated by the Algerian *junta* in the example.

Luban, in "The Romance of the Nation-State," insists that basic rights are universal, and he is extremely troubled by Walzer's acceptance of nationalism. Luban finds that Walzer's insistence that foreigners treat dictators "as if they are legitimate" glosses over many evils. On Walzer's notion that "there is a fit of some sort," Luban observes:

> if there is a union of people and government, why are the jails so full? Surely all those strapped to the torture table are not misfits in their own culture. ... The government fits the people the way the sole of a boot fits a human face: after a while the patterns of indentation match with uncanny precision.[88]

Luban is convinced that the "violence of modern nationalism and its indifference to basic human rights arises from the conviction that the only right that matters is the right to a unified nation-state." He is disturbed by Walzer's endorsement of this conviction. Luban calls this view "the Romance of the Nation-State." This view focuses on historic community, emphasizing common tradition, culture, and history, and it "glosses over class conflict, turmoil, violence, and repression; these it represents as the reflection of inscrutable processes akin to national destiny. In place of respect for people it sets respect for peoples; in place of universalism, relativism."[89] Luban argues that Walzer's historic community concept leads him "to a deficient account of human rights and a blindness to the threat physical repression poses to political processes." Members of a national or religious group might be so severely repressed they cannot "work out social arrangements on their own and live in the way they would like," and so

Walzer's non-interventionism, in the face of internal threats, endangers the very community rights he wishes to protect from foreigners.[90]

My comments on the debate, and some new points

I will make six new points in this section. These points are not necessarily related to each other; they are additional, freestanding critiques of Walzer's argument.

First, the neutrality requirement comes into force too late to guarantee self-determination, even on Walzer's terms. This point addresses an inconsistency in Walzer's argument. Walzer says that foreigners should not intervene to assist revolutionary movements, even if they are invited, because if the movement represented the will of the people, it would be able to win on its own. If foreigners intervene to help a group that cannot win on its own, they will be assisting a group that does not reflect the will of the people. Walzer argues that a domestic tyranny could not overpower a people who really want to be rid of it; the domestic tyranny needs social support to stay in power.

> "Armies and police forces are social institutions; soldiers and policemen come from families, villages, neighborhoods, classes. They will not fight cohesively, with discipline, or at length unless the regime for which they are fighting has some degree of social support."[91]

Walzer claims that the rebel group, if they have social support, should be able to overcome merely domestic oppression. However, this is not only blind to the superior coercive power of the modern authoritarian state and to the power of the state to shape popular ideas, it is also inconsistent with Walzer's assertion of that external aid to the de facto regime is permissible. Until rebel groups gain a substantial foothold, Walzer's theory permits outsiders to prop up the repressive regime: "After all, it is the official representative of communal integrity in international society."[92] Until such time as the rebels gain a significant foothold, the state, but not the rebels, may receive outside assistance. Rebel groups must gain (without external assistance) a significant foothold against a regime that enjoys the privilege of asking for external assistance. This does not seem to me to reflect an internally self-determining political community, according to Walzer's own understanding of self-determination. If the regime is being aided by foreign forces, it is not merely domestic oppression that the rebels face, and Walzer's reason for saying the people must want their oppression or they could throw it off (because all their oppressors are compatriots) falls apart.

The problem I see with the Walzer–Mill doctrine is that it does not distinguish between legitimacy of states where free institutions do not exist because they are not wanted by a majority of the people and states where free institutions do not exist because the government is too brutally oppressive and the people cannot successfully resist. The Walzer–Mill doctrine instead takes the existence of the status quo as evidence of its legitimacy. The reason the people cannot successfully resist is taken to be that they do not want free institutions badly enough, or not enough of the people want them. Walzer describes this doctrine in two different ways, saying on the one hand that he only means outsiders must "act as if it is legitimate and refrain from making war on it"[93] and on the other hand saying that any government "that is able to fight its own internal wars" is actually legitimate.[94] Neither formulation is attractive, not least because neither takes sufficient account of the possibility of coercion by the state's enforcement apparatus – the police, the military, and so on.

Second, Walzer's formulation does not take account of individuals who do not identify themselves primarily as members of articulate groups with self-determining or nationalistic aims. Walzer says that "the citizens of a sovereign state have a right, insofar as they are coerced and ravaged at all, to suffer only at one another's hands."[95] It seems unreasonable to assume that all people living within the state would value that right more than the other kind of rights Walzer acknowledges when he talks about *jus in bello*, the rights not to be murdered or raped at all.[96] Walzer accepts the primacy of natural rights in *jus in bello*. It is inconsistent for him not to accept the same in the context of *jus ad bellum*.

Third, Walzer uses the domestic analogy and compares the state to an individual. There are some things we cannot do to an individual, even for his own ostensible good. This analogy could perhaps be helpfully revised by thinking of the state as analogous to a household with several members rather than an individual. An individual has only himself and his own shortcomings to contend with while cultivating his virtues, and if he is really to be rid of his shortcomings, he must be the one to wage that battle. It is an internal affair. If he does not overcome his defects, nobody else can do it for him. If a state was like an individual, it would seem to follow that non-intervention is almost always the best policy. However, a state is not like a single individual; a state, like a household, is comprised of different, separate individuals. There are strong and weak ones in the house, and the stronger ones generally bear the responsibility to protect the weaker; at least they are obliged to do them no harm. If the strong ones instead attack the weak ones, we do not say that the weaker ones must overpower the stronger – we do not say that whatever happens inside the house cannot be judged by those outside. We affirm a right of families to privacy and self-determination, but it is subject to limitation. We do not insist that defenseless children, brutalized spouses, or abused elders meet any requirements of self-help before we interfere. We do not wait for murder to be underway before we consider neighborly unilateral interference permissible.[97] It seems odd to think that a state/country, where the bonds and commitments between ruler and ruled are *less intimate* than the bonds between husbands and wives or parents and children, would be entitled to *more privacy*.

Fourth, perhaps, in some cases, an elite clique or a minority "gang of thugs" is not running the country in its own interests, but a repressive or tyrannical majority is ruling. Although it might be representative of the majority will, its dominance does not represent legitimacy but might, or a favorable (to it) brute power balance. Even if it is true that the majority of people favor the repressive rule, and the state is capable of fighting its own internal wars, which is Walzer's test for political legitimacy,[98] this permits a tyranny of the majority. This kind of legitimacy is hard to distinguish from a doctrine of "might makes right." This is the wrong test for political legitimacy. Fernando Teson summarizes the point I wish to make here beautifully:

> The trouble with accepting majority preference rather than a minimal standard of human rights as the indicator of state legitimacy is that a majority of the people may benefit from the oppression of the minority. Only the victims have a right to refuse assistance.[99]

Fifth, Walzer's reading of Mill is selective. Mill permits intervention in the case of tyrannical or uncivilized regimes to improve conditions so that people may become fit for self-government, but Walzer dismisses Mill's exceptions about intervention to rescue peoples from "incompetents and barbarians" with a footnote: "Whatever plausibility such arguments had in the nineteenth century, they have none today."[100] Furthermore, the idea that "the members of a political community must cultivate their own freedom, just as the individual must cultivate his own virtue. They cannot be set free, as he cannot be made virtuous, by any external force" is only a partial representation of Mill's point. Mill recognized that some peoples "cannot be improved without a prior change in government" – meaning that the cultivation of civic virtue might be impossible under an incompetent or abusive regime.

Mill writes in language that is distasteful to the post-colonial ear, to be sure, of "barbarians" and "the uncivilized." Without wishing to endorse Mill's commitment to colonialism, I do think that Mill's definition of an uncivilized people is very similar to what we now might call a less-than-fully-capable and responsible state. Mill's use of the terms "barbarian" and "uncivilized" might productively be understood in terms of their meaning as given/defined by Mill himself, instead of the meaning they have taken on in the post-colonial era. Walzer's reading of Mill is especially curious because Walzer does support intervention in the case of a failed state, although he does not define what he means by failed state. In his essay entitled "Civilization," Mill writes in language that could plausibly describe failed and indecent/ineffective states of today, if we set aside our post-colonial response to his use of the words "savage" and "civilized":

> In savage life there is little or no law, or administration of justice; no systematic employment of the collective strength of society, to protect individuals against injury from one another; every one trusts to his own strength or cunning, and where that fails, he is without resource. We accordingly call a people civilized, where the arrangements of society, for protecting the persons and property of its members, are sufficiently perfect to maintain peace among them; i.e. to induce the bulk of the community to rely for their

security mainly upon the social arrangements, and renounce for the most part, and in ordinary circumstances, the vindication of their interests (whether in the way of aggression or of defense) not by their individual strength or courage.[101]

According to Mill, civic virtue cannot arise in a state that meets the description given above, which fits failed and collapsed states like Somalia and also indecent and ineffective states (including Zimbabwe and Burma) that possess too little capacity, too little responsibility, or both. Walzer's reading of Mill's anti-interventionism is too sweeping. That prohibition (in Mill) only applies to states that cannot be described by the above quotation. Many states that are not genocidal and not failed or collapsed would still be described as barbarous by Mill; because civic virtue cannot arise in them, liberal states have a right to intervene until such time as the people are fit for self-government (according to Mill). I do not necessarily wish to endorse Mill's argument in all its implications, only to raise the point that Walzer's reading of Mill is selective.

Finally, even if Walzer is correct that all values and all experience are local, I do not believe that outsiders do not know and cannot understand or say anything about the values of a foreign people. We know there are some things that we can say, even as foreigners, for at least three reasons:[102]

First, almost all states are signatories to international human rights agreements, and by these agreements they have indicated to the rest of the world community that they uphold these values and pledge to respect them. We do not have to make judgments about their loyalties and resentments, they have indicated to the international community that they do hold certain values by signing agreements affirming human rights. Perhaps they signed the agreements hypocritically, without truly affirming them. Nevertheless, outsiders are justified in reminding all signatories of the commitments they have made and holding parties responsible for their obligations under international agreements, whether the agreements were made in good faith or not.

Second, there are some things all humans have in common, just as human beings, and those common needs and capabilities are the same for all human beings across all borders.[103] It is also possible to reach an overlapping consensus between world religions, cultures, and peoples on elemental questions of human value.[104] The content of this overlapping consensus is the subject of some disagreement, but we can say that some minimal set of commonalities exists.

Finally, Walzer is in essence saying that "outsiders ought to leave historical communities alone because those communities know better than outsiders what form of living is best for them." He thinks this because he fundamentally respects the right of others to live lives that have meaning and value to them. But strict adherence to Walzer's doctrine could sometimes require respect for the preference of some persons to abuse some others. In that case, the requirement of withholding interference with local arrangements and respecting them as legitimate just because they are of local origin and possess sufficient capacity to maintain their dominance loses much of its appeal.

So, we can say some things on the issue of the "fit" between rulers and public in non-democratic states. It is possible to draw a continuum in which citizens in some cases will rally to support their government in times of war (e.g. Soviet citizens in response to the Nazi invasion) in contrast to those in which the "social contract" is either completely broken or never existed; and it is also possible to distinguish between cases where citizens support their government because they are forced to do so (literally, at the barrel of a gun) as opposed to where they genuinely support their government. It is also true that citizens may genuinely support their government against an adversary who would like to impose a tyrannical regime even worse than the current government, but the citizens would not support the government against a humanitarian intervention. Walzer does not accept any of these distinctions; his view is that "if citizens can be expected to defend their state" for whatever reason, there is a fit. It does not matter to Walzer why we expect them to fight; I think this position does not answer the question of justice but refuses to consider it.[105]

I would like to make very clear from the outset that while expanding the conditions for "just cause" beyond those identified by Walzer, I am also presenting a more substantial elaboration of the other restraining criteria in *jus ad bellum* that Walzer either brushes over or leaves rather loose and indeterminate; that is, the check on excessively permissive interventionism in my argument comes by focusing on all the other restraining criteria for a just war.

If Walzer's defense against the objections raised above is unconvincing, we are left with the unattractive spectacle of a destabilized non-intervention rule, and in Walzer's formulation at least, we have an incomplete picture of the other restraints against intervention. Walzer largely glosses over or does not elaborate on the other just war restraints, right intention, last resort, proportionality, likelihood of success, and legitimate authority. Walzer's statism is shown by his critics to be insufficiently qualified, or as Doppelt argues, "without foundation." The next task of this book is to rebuild foundations for non-intervention on more stable grounds than Walzer's, and, thereby, to build a qualified, limited statism and a new non-intervention doctrine. The new doctrine will specify the duty of non-intervention as being owed to capable and responsible states, and I will set out the details of such a doctrine in Chapter 3. The second task of the book is to set a new threshold for just cause, which I will do in Chapter 4. In Chapter 5, I will provide a richer account of the other traditional *jus ad bellum* categories, and fill out some gaps in Walzer's account in this way. In Chapter 6, I will show how Walzer's framework leads to a different analysis than a more comprehensive approach would yield through an examination of the Kosovo case (NATO's 1999 "Operation Allied Force").

3 Stable grounds for the non-intervention norm

Introduction

In the first part of this chapter, I shift the grounding for the non-intervention rule to a new foundation. My claim is that the purpose of the non-intervention rule is to secure the international and domestic benefits provided by capable and responsible states. Along the way, I will explain what I mean by "capable and responsible" in contrast to states which are either incapable, irresponsible, or perhaps both. Weak but responsible states lack capability but are willing to accept foreign assistance; wicked states possess capability but not responsibility, so they use their capability for objectionable ends. Failing and failed states usually have neither capability nor responsibility. States can also be partially capable and responsible. Leaders may attempt to govern responsibly, but lack the capability to do it. States like this can sometimes remediate their incapacity by asking for outside assistance, but there may be some problems that remain beyond the capability of the state to solve immediately. This does not necessarily mean the state cannot be called responsible. For example, harmful traditional practices such as honor killing in Jordan and widow immolation in India persist and are accepted and glorified by some parts of the population, in spite of these states' legal efforts to eliminate the practices; states' attempts at enforcement may be resented and actively resisted.[1] It is important to note that while responsibility and capacity are often correlated, there are some cases when states will be partially capable.

In the second part of the chapter, I suggest that the threshold criteria for just cause, particularly in the case of AHI, should be revised to include all the atrocity crimes[2] (crimes against humanity and war crimes) specified in the Rome Statute of the International Criminal Court. In the third section of this chapter, I will answer some likely objections to my views on non-intervention and on just cause.

This chapter deals only with the just cause category of *jus ad bellum*; I will elaborate on the other categories of restraint in Chapter 4. I would like to state from the outset that satisfaction of the just cause criterion alone is not sufficient evidence that the actual resort to military force is justifiable, acceptable, or desirable. In my view, resort to war can only be called just if the other *jus ad bellum* restraints – last resort, proportionality, likelihood of success, right intention, and legitimate authority – are satisfied as well. Just cause is a necessary but insufficient condition for us to consider when we evaluate the justice of a particular case of resort to military force. A more comprehensive and complex approach is required in order for just war theory to fulfill its main function, "organizing the debate."[3]

My view's insistence on this holistic or comprehensive approach is distinct from Walzer's view. Walzer's view holds that all defensive wars are just and all offensive wars are unjust, with certain exceptions for emergencies. The case by case judgments are made based on the justice of the cause alone, with minimal emphasis given to the other categories of restraint. In this paradigm, just cause and *jus in bello* are the critical criteria for judgment.

The non-intervention norm

Walzer begins his book with a critique of realism, but then he adopts the central assumption of realism, that states are the most important actors in international relations. Sovereignty and non-intervention become nearly absolute principles. Walzer does acknowledge exceptions, including that the non-intervention norm may be unilaterally set aside in the case of massive human rights abuses, because the rule no longer seems to serve the purpose for which it was created.[4] I agree with Walzer that the non-intervention norm may be unilaterally set aside when it no longer serves its purpose. However, my position differs on the purposes the non-intervention rule is meant to serve, and, therefore, when it can be set aside. In my view, the reason we ought to value the non-intervention rule is because non-intervention and respect for state sovereignty tends to promote international peace and security, which we value because it promotes human security. Non-intervention is properly valued insofar as it promotes human security, in my view. Walzer is also concerned with the security of the state, and the protection of state sovereignty. Walzer values the security of the state because it is presumed to protect the life of the historic community living within the state. My view takes the protection of human security, not the protection of historic communities, to be the primary purpose the non-intervention rule is meant to serve.

In my view, the fundamental reason we value international peace and security is that the absence of war promotes human security. When the non-intervention norm is in conflict with the preservation of human security, the non-intervention norm loses its foundation. If human security is not served, the non-intervention principle gives way to the more fundamental value of human security. For my purposes, I will adopt the definition of human security worked out by the International Commission on Intervention and State Sovereignty. In its report, the Commission defines human security as "physical safety, economic and social well-being, respect for the dignity and worth of human beings, and the protection of their human rights and fundamental freedoms."[5]

Satisfaction of the just cause criterion alone is insufficient to trigger intervention. Generation of such a right (to military intervention) would require that all the *jus ad bellum* criteria were met, in addition to just cause. Just causes for war are national self-defense, collective self-defense, pre-emptive self-defense, pre-emptive collective self-defense, AHI to remediate genocide, ethnic cleansing, crimes against humanity or war crimes, and pre-emptive humanitarian intervention. By crimes against humanity, I mean those crimes specified in Article 7 of the Rome Statute of the International Criminal Court. Hereafter I will sometimes refer to all these crimes including genocide, ethnic cleansing, other crimes against humanity, and war crimes, by the unifying shorthand term suggested by David Scheffer, "atrocity crimes."[6]

Where atrocity crimes are present or where the state in question otherwise manifestly fails to provide the benefits expected to be provided by a capable and responsible state, either internationally or domestically, the non-intervention rule does not apply. However, resort to military force would not be permissible unless there is a just cause for war and all the other *jus ad bellum* categories of restraint were satisfied as well.

Walzer finds unilateral military intervention in defense of human security to have been permissible in Sierra Leone, because the state was not "decent and effective" (presumably defined as decent and effective in meeting the needs of its people). If that is a just cause for intervention, then subject to the other *jus ad bellum* criteria, intervention should also be permissible in places like Burma and Zimbabwe for the same reason; these states are also not "decent and effective" in meeting the needs of their people. Walzer disagrees with this last point; in recent writings he reaffirms his insistence on the "wide chasm between genocide and the ordinary brutality of authoritarian regimes."[7] However, it is difficult to see a moral reason to distinguish between a state that does not serve its people because it does not possess sufficient capacity (like Sierra Leone, where Walzer endorses intervention) and an authoritarian state that uses its capacity for morally objectionable ends (like Burma and Zimbabwe, where he would not endorse intervention).

Capable and responsible states are states with capacity and the inclination to appropriately apply it – this is what it means to be a "decent and effective state." "Indecent and/or ineffective states," or "incapable and/or irresponsible states" do not provide the benefits that generate the right to non-intervention. The "brutal authoritarian regime" does not generate these benefits, so it has no rights-claim to non-intervention.

I have argued that Walzer's definition of a legitimate state as "one that can fight its own internal wars"[8] is inadequate; it amounts to equating legitimacy with mere capacity. If we reject the state capacity definition of legitimacy in favor of the "decent and effective" or "capable and responsible" definition, it is appropriate to ask what sort of new test for legitimacy we have in mind, and how we justify that test. From here forward, I will be consistent in using the language "capable and responsible states" as synonymous with "states owed the duty of non-intervention" or "states bearing the right to non-intervention."

My view is compatible with the re-characterization of sovereignty from "sovereignty as control to sovereignty as responsibility."[9] "Sovereignty as control" refers to the idea that a government could claim sovereign rule if it was able to exert its authority to control its territory and population. I do not hold that governments must be able to control all of what happens within their borders. The crucial element is that if they lack capacity to control, they must be responsible – they must be willing to ask for and accept outside help. States must be responsible in order to claim the right to non-intervention. If they lack capacity, they can remedy that by asking for outside assistance.

I will not generally employ the term sovereignty, because that term has a scope beyond what I mean to specify. Sovereignty carries a legal connotation compared to the phrase, "entitled to non-intervention," and my thesis is mostly concerned with that particular element of sovereignty. States that are not owed the right to non-intervention continue to exist as states. However, such a state can no longer claim the right to non-intervention in the area of its affairs where non-intervention does not serve the purposes for which it is intended. Such states may regain the right to non-intervention if they become capable and responsible. I am limiting my discussion of sovereignty to addressing circumstances under which states can no longer claim the right to non-intervention.

It is also true that when it does serve its good purposes, the non-intervention rule is in force. Those purposes are, generally speaking, to reduce the frequency of inter-state wars and to allow states to function securely, so they can fulfill the proper functions of states, providing both domestic and international dividends in human security. Non-intervention as a general rule works to allow a state's capable and responsible functioning – free from foreign aggression, the capable and responsible state can devote its resources to the provision of the domestic and international benefits for which it is valued.

The domestic and international benefits of capable and responsible state functioning are often identical, because many international threats have their origins in domestic circumstances that threaten human security. Capable and responsible states are the actors most able of cooperating to address these threats.[10] Capable and responsible states are the structures/sets of institutions through which many urgent problems are solved. States are often the actors that organize and execute basic infrastructure projects, transportation, and utility networks, and public health systems. Environmental threats can be addressed by local enforcement. A good public health system is obviously good for a state's people, but it is also a matter of international public health security. A society that is respectful of human rights is similarly obviously good for its own people, but it is also good for international peace and security – it won't generate de-stabilizing flows of refugees and asylum seekers. One of the benefits of non-intervention in the affairs of capable and responsible states is to support self-determination of political communities. Free of foreign domination and enjoying basic political rights, individuals and communities living within capable and responsible states can work out among themselves the best ways of living together that suit their preferences, aspirations, histories, and cultures.

A state cannot be said to be providing the benefits of capable and responsible functioning if that state poses a threat to international peace and security. In its

2004 report, *A More Secure World: Our Shared Responsibility*, the United Nations Secretary-General's High-level Panel on Threats, Challenges and Change defines threats to international peace and security in this way: "Any event or process that leads to large scale death or lessening of life chances and undermines States as the basic unit of the international system is a threat to international security."[11] The report identifies six clusters of threats: economic and social threats, including poverty, infectious disease and environmental degradation; inter-state conflict; internal conflict; nuclear, radiological, chemical and biological weapons; terrorism; and transnational organized crime.[12] States can cooperate to contain these threats. The emergent understanding of "international peace and security" is not simply the absence of war and refugee flows, the security of state borders, per se. It includes a robust understanding of human security at the individual level, including health, social and economic security, and environmental security. The High-level Panel arrived at this new understanding by "literally going around the world and asking people 'What threatens you?'"[13]

Negligent or less-than-fully capable states can threaten international peace and security without aggressive aims or repressive regimes. For example, when a state responds irresponsibly and ineffectively to an infectious disease outbreak, the threat is not only domestic, but it is also international.[14] The state is either irresponsible or incapable, or perhaps it is both. In either case, it threatens international public health (international peace and security). Imagine the case of a government that is very irresponsible in the way it handles the HIV or drug-resistant tuberculosis epidemics. This mismanagement is a threat to international peace and security as understood by the High-level Panel. It would be permissible under United Nations rules[15] that the threat be brought under Article 99 by the Secretary-General to the Security Council. The Security Council could order a quarantine to be enforced militarily from outside the offending state's borders. This is an example of a "threat to international peace and security"[16] in the new understanding and a potential, though limited, military response (as opposed to the old understanding of "threat to international peace and security" where aggression was the main worry).[17]

A state that cannot maintain order nor meet the basic needs of its citizens for economic and social opportunity and security might also pose a threat to international peace and security by creating refugee flows. Additionally, terrorist or other international criminal organizations may operate with impunity in a weak state's territory.

Although a state may not be wicked, if it is weak, its incapacity prevents it from containing threats to human security. Although a state's national government may have formal legislative protections for its people, in a country where the national government's law enforcement capability does not reach all corners of the country, the people living outside its reach are at the mercy of the local balance of power. Threats to personal security exist to some extent for everyone, of course, but where the state cannot provide resources to enforce formal legislative protections, personal insecurity is an especially serious issue.

Working states provide extremely important benefits, both domestically and internationally. The International Commission on Intervention and State Sovereignty says the following about the advantages of a system of capable and responsible sovereign states:

> It is strongly arguable that effective and legitimate states remain the best way to ensure that the benefits of the internationalization of trade, investment, technology and communication will be equitably shared. Those states which can call upon strong regional alliances, internal peace, and a strong and independent civil society, seem clearly best placed to benefit from globalization. They will also be likely to be those most respectful of human rights. And in security terms, a cohesive and peaceful international system is far more likely to be achieved through the cooperation of effective states, confident of their place in the world, than in an environment of fragile, collapsed, fragmenting or generally chaotic state entities.[18]

Non-intervention into the affairs of capable and responsible states serves purposes that are useful domestically and internationally by preserving international peace and security, and by setting a stage on which state actors can cooperate effectively. I endorse this view and extend it by arguing that the right of non-intervention is grounded by the dividends it pays in each particular case.

For a state to claim the right of non-intervention, the people in that state and the people in the international community must benefit from non-intervention in that particular case. There is a direct relationship between a state's capable, responsible functioning and the strength of its claim is to the right of non-intervention. Where a state can claim the right of non-intervention, this means that other states owe the duty of non-intervention to that state; and outsiders are bound not to intervene militarily in its internal affairs. Where a state cannot claim the right to non-intervention, or can claim it only weakly or partially, because it is not providing the benefits of a capable and responsible state, the duty of non-intervention on the part of other states is consequently less binding.

A state that is owed the duty of non-intervention must aim for the basic needs of its people to be met; if it cannot achieve this aim, it must be willing to accept outside assistance. Further, it must not obstruct its people from exercising their capacities and possessing basic capabilities. I will take a moment to clarify my usage of the terms capacities[19] and capabilities as they refer to human beings and to states. By capacities of human beings, I mean that a set of possibilities that all human beings have like walking, eating, worshipping, thinking, talking, working, and having emotional attachments, intellectual curiosity, and spiritual beliefs. When I am referring to capabilities of human beings, I will follow the usage coined by Amartya Sen. Capabilities are "what people are actually able to do and to be."[20] People's capabilities depend on their access to resources and their political freedoms, so they differ across countries and across groups within countries, and across individuals within groups. "Capabilities" can be thought of as a shorthand expression meaning for "rights plus resources," or "opportunities plus goods."

Another important distinction is between capabilities and functionings. Capabilities are what people are actually able to do and to be, and functionings refers to the subset of capabilities that people actually do and are (the capabilities they actually exercise).[21] I will generally not use the term capacities hereafter when referring to people. I will use the term capabilities, meaning capacities plus the rights and resources necessary to exercise/meet/achieve/fulfill them.

If the state is a kleptocratic state, hoarding the resources and thereby lessening the life chances of its citizens, it would not be entitled to non-intervention. It is true that capabilities require resources, and we can say that foreigners have liberty to provide assistance to help alleviate poverty in order to support the development of capabilities. A state cannot claim a right to keep outsiders from assisting in the case of a famine, for example. If a state's action is the impediment to the positive liberty, for example, if the regime is hoarding the resources, or persecuting some group within the state by denying them access to resources, the state would not be supporting its citizens' abilities to exercise their capabilities.

I am not engaging the vitally important question of distributive justice here, and whether poor people have a right to assistance (entailing a duty of assistance on the part of others). I am confining my argument to liberty rights; the state should not interfere with its citizens' development of and exercise of their capabilities, except where exercising the capabilities infringes on the similar exercise of capabilities by others.

I do not take a position on whether intervention, where it is permissible, is obligatory; I only address the question of when it is permissible. Carla Bagnoli, Michael Walzer, Kok-Chor Tan, and Allen Buchanan have argued that where humanitarian intervention is permissible, it is obligatory; but they disagree as to who bears the responsibility and how it arises. Walzer's maxim is "Who can, should." In his view, the duty of intervention is an imperfect duty, falling on nobody in particular.[22] Bagnoli and Tan argue against this position.[23] Instead, they claim, the duty falls on everyone, and it is a perfect duty. The fact that it is difficult to discharge does not make it less of a duty. Buchanan argues that states are obligated to fix the existing international institutions so they might successfully meet their responsibility to protect.[24] Bagnoli and Buchanan argue that these obligations do not arise from charity, but they are duties that arise out of the Kantian principle of respect. Terry Nardin applies this argument to the case of famine and disease, and finds that outsiders have a perfect duty to intervene to help persons suffering without sufficient resources to help themselves.[25] All of these arguments build on Kant's ideas about respect for human beings *qua* human beings.

When discussing capabilities or capacities of states, I follow the general usage found in international relations literature, especially as used in the *Report of the International Commission on Intervention and State Sovereignty* (2001) and in the Report of the United Nations Secretary-General's High-Level Panel on Threats, Challenges, and Change (2005). This is distinct from my use of the term capabilities as they refer to people, as defined above. If its people are unable to meet their basic needs or exercise their basic capabilities because the state lacks capacity (resources, infrastructure) to assist them, outsiders possess the liberty to assist, and the state should be willing to ask for and accept outside assistance.

Non-intervention is valuable because we value a life of peace with rights, as Walzer says. The benefits of capable and responsible states could be summed up in the phrase "the protection of peace with rights"[26] or the "promotion of domestic and international peace and security" although these terms themselves must be further defined if they are to illuminate. As I argued in Chapter 2, "rights" possessed by citizens of a state must mean more than "the right, insofar as they are to be coerced and ravaged at all, to suffer only at one another's hands."[27] I argued in Chapter 2 that a people can be aggressed by its own government as well as by foreigners. It is also possible that other powerful elements in society (including rebel groups) might commit widespread or systematic atrocity crimes against some segment of a population.[28] It is the insecurity this brings (whether its source is foreign or domestic) that denies "peace with rights."

I understand "peace with rights" to refer to a more substantial domestic set of rights than Walzer does. Because "peace with rights" and "life and liberty" are open to various interpretations, I will specify precisely what I mean. At a minimum, the goal of a capable and responsible state should be to maintain law and order, and to create the conditions whereby all individuals in the society can meet their basic needs and exercise their basic capabilities, which I mentioned before and will enumerate shortly below. The non-derogable rights may not be infringed upon for any reason by the state or with the acquiescence of the state. By non-derogable rights, I mean those rights agreed upon in the major human rights conventions to be non-derogable for any reason, even in times of national emergency. Those rights are: to be free from arbitrary deprivation of life; to be free from torture and other ill-treatment; freedom from slavery; freedom from imprisonment for debt or the application of retroactive laws; recognition before the law; and freedom of thought, conscience, and religion.

Persons may not be denied any of the other rights enumerated in the Universal Declaration of Human Rights on the basis of religion, sex, race, ethnicity, nationality, or political view. If a state upholds all the rights enumerated in Articles 1–20 of the Universal Declaration of Human Rights and does not deny any rights on prohibited grounds, this seems to me to be a reasonable threshold for a state to claim that it respects human rights enough to deserve the right to non-intervention. If these rights are affirmed by a state, its people will not be blocked by the state from enjoying sufficient freedom to exercise their basic capabilities. The state must also not be kleptocratic. Formal affirmation of freedoms will not translate into decent and effective government if the state leadership is hoarding the resources and blocking the exercise of capabilities in this way. I will say more about this toward the end of Chapter 4, in the section on rights and capabilities.

My argument is not meant to be "anti-statist." It is meant to develop a qualified statism derived from the provision of benefits (the effects of capable and responsible state functioning) both within and without state borders. People need a political association like a state to enforce contracts, to provide security, and thereby to provide conditions under which basic infrastructure can be developed and function so basic needs can be met. The state is generally the venue where people work out their way of living and create and manage institutions that meet their needs and allow them to flourish as they see fit (by flourishing, I mean that they exercise their human capabilities as they choose as far as such exercise doesn't hinder their compatriots from likewise exercising their capabilities). Human security is provided for; basic needs are met – currency is exchanged, the police protect property and physical security, water is purified and distributed, electricity is produced, mail is delivered, people engage in commerce and industry, and the people are protected from foreign invasion.[29]

A norm against international aggression is a great good because it reduces inter-state violence and its attendant suffering. When non-intervention preserves international peace and security, it preserves a society of states where diplomacy can take place and conflicts can be resolved – a set of institutions where cooperation can take place between representatives of peoples.[30] However, in this section I have argued that to earn the right of non-intervention, a state must capably and responsibly fulfill the proper functions of a state.

I have revised the foundation for non-intervention from a "state capacity"- to a "state capacity plus state responsibility"-based structure. Walzer says a legitimate state is one that can fight its own internal wars. I argued in the section "Collective self-defense: wars of law enforcement" in Chapter 1 that this formulation works out to a problematic "might-makes-right" or state capacity-based justificatory structure, although Walzer would contest this, because he thinks the state capacity is evidence of at least tacit consent, as noted in the last chapter.

In my new formulation, a capable and responsible state must aim to protect its people from foreign invasion and domestic crime. Furthermore, the state itself must not be the source of insecurity; people are to be free from arbitrary arrest and torture, and fundamental rights are to be respected. The state must also maintain a set of institutions within which all its people are free from persecution on political, racial, ethnic, national, cultural, religious, or gender grounds. Free from persecution and buoyed by capable and responsible institutions, people can exercise their basic capabilities. When some groups of people are persecuted the state cannot say it is fulfilling its proper function. If the state does not function effectively either due to incapacity or irresponsibility, the purposes of non-intervention is no longer served.

In my view, whether a state has a right to non-intervention (or whether other states owe the duty of non-intervention to a particular state) is not a question of making exceptions to a general rule. Non-intervention is owed to all states that function capably and responsibly, both domestically and internationally. In capable and responsible states, non-intervention serves the purpose for which it is intended. Where the capable and responsible functioning is absent, the right/ duty of non-intervention is not generated.

The determination of whether a state is owed the duty of non-intervention is a separate judgment than whether just cause exists for AHI. Although it is true that whenever there is a just cause, there is no duty of non-intervention, the reverse is not always true. It is not always true that where there is no duty of non-intervention, there is a just cause for war. There may be all kinds of things wrong with the state such that we cannot say it serves all the purposes a capable and responsible state should serve, but these flaws may exist without constituting harms that rise to the level of just cause. For example, say that some segment of society was discriminated against and not allowed to vote on the basis of race, religion, sex, political view, or ethnicity; but this discrimination did not lead to large-scale lessening of life chances. This is the case in Rawls' hypothetical Kazanistan. In my formulation as specified above, the denial of any of the rights enumerated in the Universal Declaration on discriminatory grounds means that the state is not securing the domestic benefits for its people. In this case the rights being denied on prohibited grounds are the rights enshrined in Article 21, the rights to take part in one's own government and to equal suffrage. However, this discrimination is not severe; it has not led to a large-scale lessening of life chances. It has not risen to the level of persecution. This means that the state is not owed the duty of non-intervention, on the grounds that it is denying some rights on prohibited grounds; but there is no just cause for AHI. I will say more about crime of persecution in the section "The Atrocity Standard" in Chapter 4.

If there is no duty of non-intervention, there is some failure on the part of the target state that warrants assistance, influence, or interference from the outside; it is not necessarily the case that there is just cause for war. If the state in question cannot claim a right to non-intervention, the correlative duty of non-intervention (on the part of other states) is not generated.[31] The mere absence of the duty of non-intervention does not generate a corresponding right to intervene, however. There must be a *just cause* for outside influence, interference, or intervention. Furthermore, just cause alone is insufficient to justify any action. Justification for militarily intervention would require that all the other *jus ad bellum* criteria were met, including last resort, right intention, proportionality, likelihood of success, and competent authority.

4 Just cause

I presented Walzer's view on just cause in Chapter 1, and in this chapter I will set out my own view. I will not repeat Walzer's view here in its entirety, although I refer to it as I distinguish my own view from his. The most significant area of disagreement between Walzer's view and mine is on the questions of AHI and intervention in civil wars.

I want to insist from the outset that the aim of any intervention must be limited to rectifying the specific dysfunction of the state, which is the just cause for intervention, i.e. the harm done either internationally or domestically that warrants a response from outsiders. It is not the case that because a state is irresponsible in one area, the entire government may be thrown out – the remediation of the problem is limited to the just cause.

By "intervention," I mean military intervention. I will refer to other, non-military, methods by which outsiders seek to change state behavior by acting within the borders of another state as "interference" (more intrusive and coercive) and "influence" (less intrusive and coercive). Non-military activities with a direct effect on material conditions inside the target state such as economic sanctions, funding of local opposition groups or NGO's, or delivery of material assistance to local actors, I will call interference. Other outside pressure, if it is limited to non-material pressure, I will call influence – in this category is so-called "naming and shaming." Influence aims to persuade, but it does not coerce with physical or material force.

There is a continuum of outside pressure that can be exerted on states. The continuum ranges from non-intrusive, non-coercive influence, through more coercive interference such as economic sanctions, all the way through coercive military force. Even if a just cause is present, resorting to force is never permissible if some less destructive method might remedy the just cause. I will discuss this continuum in more detail in this chapter under the headings of "Last resort" and "Likelihood of success."

Walzer, in his Preface to the third edition of *Just and Unjust Wars*, asks:

> What is the value of sovereignty and territorial integrity to the men and women who live within a particular state's territory? The answer to this question establishes the moral barrier to intervention: the greater the value, the higher the barrier.[1]

This is exactly my thesis on the barrier, and if this line represented all Walzer had to say on the topic, I would have no argument with his position at all.

However, Walzer simultaneously insists on a "radical break, a chasm, with nastiness on one side and genocide on the other."[2] By this he means that until the chasm is crossed, outsiders must stay out; they may attempt to influence, but only from across the border: they "are to hold open the possibility of domestic politics."[3] My view holds with Walzer's that the strength of a country's claim to the right of non-intervention is directly related to the usefulness of non-intervention to all the individuals who live there, but my view rejects the wide chasm. A failure to function capably and responsibly, for example, by perpetrating systematic or widespread rights violations, suggests that there would be just cause for some kind of outside action – influence, interference, or intervention.

There are many other important barriers to the resort to force (for any just cause, including self-defense as well as intervention). For the resort to force to be justified, all the other restraints of the just war doctrine – proportionality, likelihood of success, last resort, competent authority, and right intention – must be satisfied. Even in the case of genocide, self-defense, or defense of a neighbor, the comprehensive framework cannot automatically sanction the resort to force. We might be able to say there is just cause for the use of military force, but the other categories must still be met before we can say the resort to war is "just."

I endorse and defend the suggestion by the International Commission on Intervention and State Sovereignty that pre-emptive humanitarian military intervention is justifiable when harm is "imminently apprehended."[4] If pre-emptive self-defense is a just cause, then pre-emptive defense of a neighbor or pre-emptive humanitarian intervention is also a just cause. As the International Commission on Intervention and State Sovereignty observes: "Without this possibility of anticipatory action, the international community would be placed in the morally untenable position of being required to wait until genocide begins, before being able to take action to stop it."[5] I agree with Walzer insofar as self-defense, collective self-defense, and exceptions for humanitarian intervention are appropriate criteria for just cause. I disagree with his standard about when humanitarian intervention or intervention in a civil war is allowable. I depart from Walzer's threshold for humanitarian intervention and adopt instead the Atrocity Standard as has been suggested by David Little.[6] The Atrocity Standard adopts some of the principles of the Rome Statute of the International Criminal Court.

I should note that the International Criminal Court exists to prosecute individuals. Its charter is explicitly *not* meant as a legal justification for intervention. The Rome Statute does not address the question of legal (or moral) justification for AHI. Nevertheless, the negotiated character of the instrument and the broad international consensus on the idea that the enumerated crimes "shock the conscience of mankind" is striking. Because of this consensus, we can be sure that the condemnation of these atrocity crimes is not distinctly western or liberal.

The Atrocity Standard

I argued that Walzer's threshold for AHI is too restrictive. I'm suggesting that his threshold be amended to include genocide, crimes against humanity, and war crimes as enumerated in Articles 6, 7, and 8 of the Rome Statute.

Genocide, which is part of Walzer's threshold, is included in the Atrocity Standard, and it is enumerated in Article 6 of the Rome Statute. Almost no just war theorist would disagree that genocide, ethnic cleansing, or enslavement is just cause for intervention. However, international lawyers do point out that unilateral military intervention for humanitarian purposes, even in the case of genocide, is illegal without authorization from the United Nations Security Council.[7]

Walzer's threshold also includes ethnic cleansing and enslavement, which are elements of the Atrocity Standard as well, enumerated in Article 7 of the Rome Statute. My view is distinct from Walzer's in that other crimes against humanity, when either widespread or systematically committed, are just cause for AHI in my view but not in Walzer's. "Crime against humanity" in Article 7 of the Rome Statute refers to any of the following crimes when committed as part of an ongoing course of actions against a civilian population:

a murder;
b extermination;
c enslavement;
d deportation or forcible transfer of population;
e imprisonment or other severe deprivation of physical liberty in violation of fundamental rules of international law;
f torture;
g rape, sexual slavery, enforced prostitution, forced pregnancy, enforced sterilization, or any other form of sexual violence of comparable gravity;
h persecution against any identifiable group or collectivity on political, racial, national, ethnic, cultural, religious, gender, or other grounds that are universally recognized as impermissible under international law;
i enforced disappearance of persons;
j the crime of apartheid;
k other inhumane acts of a similar character intentionally causing great suffering, or serious injury to body or to mental or physical health.[8]

In this section, I elaborate on definitions of enforced disappearance, apartheid, and persecution. I do not elaborate on the definitions of all the other crimes because they are well-understood. Enforced disappearance is a name for the crime committed when persons are abducted, detained against their will, or otherwise deprived of their liberty by either government officials or private individuals working with or for the government or with the government's consent, followed by official refusal to disclose the fate or whereabouts of the persons concerned, with the intention of placing such persons outside the protection of the law for a prolonged period of time. Under Walzer's standard, this is not a just cause for humanitarian intervention; it is deplorable and brutal to be sure, but it is on the other side of the wide gulf from genocide. Disappearance is among the ordinarily brutal tactics of authoritarian regimes. Under the Atrocity Standard, enforced disappearance of persons constitutes just cause for external influence, interference, or intervention.

Apartheid is defined in the Rome Statute as "crimes against humanity committed in the context of an institutionalized regime of systematic oppression and domination by one racial group over any other racial group or groups and committed with the intention of maintaining that regime." I would support expanding the definition of apartheid to say "an institutionalized regime of systematic oppression and domination by one political, racial, national, ethnic, cultural, religious, gender group over any other group or groups and committed with the intention of maintaining that regime"; however, the Rome Statute does not do so in the context of apartheid.

It is possible to imagine systematic oppression and domination by one religious, ethnic, or gender group of another. When such oppression and domination is severe and intentional, leading to large-scale lessening of life chances, this amounts to the crime of persecution, about which I will say more below. Although such societies are not called "apartheid societies" but "persecuting societies," such persecution is a just cause for AHI. It would be a strange doctrine indeed that condemned racial domination and oppression but allowed political, national, ethnic, cultural, religious, or gender domination and oppression.

Genocide and ethnic cleansing are extreme examples of persecution, and in those cases, Walzer's standard and the Atrocity Standard overlap. However, the crime of persecution includes other acts that do not constitute just cause according to Walzer's standard. "Persecution" means the "intentional and severe deprivation of fundamental rights contrary to international law by reason of the identity of the group or collectivity." This does not help us enough, however; we need a clearer understanding of both "intentional and severe deprivation" and "fundamental rights."

The question will naturally arise, how bad do the human rights abuses have to be? As a definitional matter, let us say "severe" means "leading to widespread or systematic lessening of life chances." Nor does the statute define "fundamental rights." Do these rights encompass the full panoply of liberty and claim rights enumerated in the Universal Declaration of Human Rights, including the aspirational economic, social, and cultural rights? We can investigate the jurisprudence of the International Criminal Tribunal for Yugoslavia, which has interpreted the Rome Statute in its judgments.

The judgment of the International Criminal Tribunal in Yugoslavia in the Tadic case makes clear that persecution does not have to entail a separate inhumane act; it is the discriminatory nature of the offense that makes it inhumane. An infringement of rights becomes an inhumane act when the infringement is severe, intentional, and committed on prohibited grounds.

> Persecution is a form of discrimination on grounds of race, religion [gender] or political opinion that is intended to be, and results in, an infringement of

an individual's fundamental rights. It is not necessary to have a separate act of an inhumane nature to constitute persecution, but rather, the discrimination itself makes the act inhumane. The Trial Chamber held that the crime of persecution encompasses a wide variety of acts, including, *inter alia*, those of a physical, economic, or judicial nature that violate an individual's basic or fundamental rights. The discrimination must be on one of the listed grounds to constitute persecution.[9]

However, the language in the judgment does not specify which rights are basic or fundamental. We can say that the fundamental rights must include at least those rights that are agreed by widespread international consensus to be non-derogable even in the case of national emergency. Those ultra-fundamental rights are: the right to equal dignity as a human being and equal treatment before the law; right to life; freedom from torture; freedom from enslavement; freedom of thought, conscience, and religion; freedom from retro-active penal laws; and freedom from imprisonment for debt. Any attack on these rights on political, racial, national, ethnic, cultural, religious, or gender is certainly persecution.

The next set of rights is not quite as fundamental as that, because these rights might be limited in case of emergency, or in order to ensure the functioning of a society where everyone's rights are preserved. The right to free expression, for example, might be limited to ban "fighting words" as it is in the United States, with a reasonable defense. We can also imagine limitations on free assembly, such as limiting times and places where large crowds might gather, or requiring permits. The other civil and political rights enumerated in the declaration include freedom from arbitrary arrest, detention or exile; the rights to effective judicial remedy, a fair trial and public hearing by an independent and impartial tribunal, and to be presumed innocent until proven guilty; freedom from arbitrary interference with privacy, family, home, or correspondence; freedom of movement and residence; the right of asylum; the right to a nationality; the right to marry and to found a family; and the right to own property. If members of identifiable groups are intentionally and severely denied these rights for reasons of political, racial, national, ethnic, cultural, religious, or gender identity, this is persecution.

In fact, there is no reason to believe that there is any defensible reason to limit any rights specified in the Universal Declaration of Human Rights on prohibited grounds in a severe and intentional way. I want to be very clear that haphazard denial of these rights, or reasonable limitations of the rights for sound reasons, is not just cause for war. To rise to the level of just cause, persecution must be an intentional and severe infringement of rights on prohibited grounds, leading to widespread or systematic lessening of life chances for the victims.

A list of "fundamental rights" has not been agreed upon by interpreters of the Rome Statute. The courts have resisted specifying a clear list of possible infringements, referring to the logic against enumerating specific tortures. If all tortures are enumerated, then it would serve merely as an incentive for torturers to create new methods. In paragraph 623 of the Kupreskic decision, the court explains:

The Trial Chamber does not see fit to identify which rights constitute fundamental rights for the purposes of persecution. The interests of justice would not be served by so doing, as the explicit inclusion of particular fundamental rights could be interpreted as the implicit exclusion of other rights (*expressio unius est exclusio alterius*). This is not the approach taken to crimes against humanity in customary international law, where the category of "other inhumane acts" also allows courts flexibility to determine the cases before them, depending on the forms which attacks on humanity may take, forms which are ever-changing and carried out with particular ingenuity. Each case must therefore be examined on its merits.[10]

One argument, from quarters wishing to interpret these rights narrowly, is that the use of the word "fundamental" might imply that only some rights qualify. If some rights are called fundamental, some rights must not be fundamental, this argument goes. Otherwise, the wording would have simply been "an individual's rights," not "an individual's basic or fundamental rights."

An opposing argument might be that the Universal Declaration of Human Rights explicitly says that no right can be traded away for any other right, suggesting they are all equally inalienable. In determining exactly what constitutes persecution, it would be helpful to explore what the courts have understood the terms "persecution" and "fundamental rights" to mean. Additionally, persecution contains within its definition a qualification that rights deprivations must be "intentional" and "severe." It is not the case that any deprivation of fundamental rights on prohibited grounds constitutes persecution. However, like "fundamental rights," the modifiers "severe" and "intentional" are not precise terms. In the course of its work, The International Criminal Tribunal for Yugoslavia interpreted the meaning of persecution. The judgment written in the case of *Prosecutor v. Kupreskic* et al. is worth quoting at length. In the Kupreskic judgment, the court looks to the jurisprudence of international military tribunals for a precedent on the meaning of persecution:

> The International Military Tribunal commenced [its discussion of persecution] with a description of the early policy of the Nazi government towards the Jewish people: discriminatory laws were passed which limited offices and professions permitted to Jews; restrictions were placed on their family life and rights of citizenship; Jews were completely excluded from German life; pogroms were organized which included the burning and demolishing of synagogues; Jewish businesses were looted; prominent Jewish businessmen were arrested; a collective fine of 1 billion marks was imposed on Jews; Jewish assets were seized; the movement of Jews was restricted; ghettos were created; and Jews were compelled to wear a yellow star. According to the IMT, "these atrocities were all part and parcel of the policy inaugurated in 1941 [...] But the methods employed never conformed to a single pattern.[11]

It is clear from its description of persecution that the IMT accorded this crime a position of great prominence and understood it to include a wide spectrum of acts perpetrated against the Jewish people, ranging from discriminatory acts targeting their general political, social and economic rights, to attacks on their person:

> 598. This broad interpretation of persecution was upheld in subsequent cases. None of the courts endeavored to define persecution but the term was generally used to describe the treatment suffered by the Jews and other groups specifically targeted by the Nazis. Persecution was a central allegation in several of the cases brought before Military Tribunals under Control Council Law No. 10. The Tribunals held that in persecuting Jews and other groups, the accused had infringed a wide variety of rights.
>
> 599. The Tribunal described the progression of infringement of rights, which started with the deprivation of rights of citizenship; rights to work and education; economic and property rights; and then led to arrest and confinement in concentration camps; beatings, mutilation and torture; deportations; slave labor and "finally over six million were murdered." The US Military Tribunal did not purport to find a common definitive element in the wide variety of acts it illustrated.[12]

Where there is a severe and systematic denial (the ICTY has used the words "gross and blatant"[13]) of any of the rights affirmed by international consensus on human rights, on political, racial, national, ethnic, cultural, religious, or gender grounds, this is persecution. The cumulative effects of the acts of discrimination can be weighed to see if together they rise to the level of persecution. A good test for this is whether the discrimination leads to widespread or systematic lessening of life chances. A society may discriminate without persecuting. Cases must be judged individually.

Persecution is a threat to human security. In the new understanding of international peace and security, threats to human security constitute a threat to international peace and security.[14] Severe and intentional denial of fundamental rights, when it leads to widespread lessening of life chances, is cause for intervention according to the Atrocity Standard. The Atrocity Standard, therefore, is compatible with the old standard of "threat to international peace and security" if such threats are understood as they have been defined in the report of the UN Secretary-General's High-level Panel on Threats, Challenges, and Change.

No matter how significant or compelling the just cause, there may be no just recourse to the use of armed force if the other *jus ad bellum* restraints are not met. The criterion of just cause only accounts for the type of offense, not the extent of its severity or scope. Persecution has, as part of its definition, severe consequences to its victims. I do not want to say that a certain number of people must have been killed, or that life expectancies are reduced by a certain number of years, for just cause to be met. Such a threshold would have the effect of folding in considerations of proportionality into the category of just cause.[15] If the destructive effect of the persecution is small, intervention would be ruled out by considerations of proportionality. If the destructive effect of the persecution is large, it is more likely that the intervention might satisfy the proportionality restraint.

Persecution as defined above constitutes just cause whether it satisfies proportionality or not. The question of whether the persecution is causing more harm than would be caused by armed humanitarian military intervention is a separate question, to be handled under the proportionality criterion, which I will discuss in Chapter 5. These questions are not relevant to just cause. Although there is some disagreement on this among just war theorists, in my view just cause is most useful conceptually if it is limited to describing the type of problem to be addressed by force of arms. Speaking of this approach, Jefferson MacMahon observes:

> [j]ust cause says *nothing* about considerations of scale or magnitude, but functions entirely as a restriction on the *type* of aim or end that may legitimately be pursued by means of war. It does not require that there be a great deal of good to be gained from war; nor does it imply that if there *is* a great deal of good to be gained, there is therefore a just cause.[16]

Persecution constitutes a just cause for interference, influence, or intervention. In cases where persecution can be stopped with the assistance of the regime in power, it would be premature to resort to war. However, if the state refuses assistance, or where the state itself is the impediment to the exercise of fundamental rights, this constitutes a just cause for outsiders to assist by means of influence, interference, or, if all the influence and interference options have been exhausted and all the other *jus ad bellum* criteria are met (meaning it is the last resort, likely to succeed at proportionate cost, rightly intended, and so on), even by military intervention.

War crimes also constitute atrocities. If a conflict is ongoing and war crimes are being committed, outsiders have a just cause for intervention to stop the atrocities. It must be reiterated that just cause is only one of the criteria that must be satisfied for resort to war to be justified. If an intervention would cause more destruction than it would prevent, proportionality concerns would trump the just cause.

Walzer's view certainly is concerned with war crimes as part of his highly developed *jus in bello*. As concerns just cause, however, war crimes are not an element of Walzer's threshold. Walzer permits AHI in the case of genocide, massacres, ethnic cleansing and enslavement. Walzer's view on just cause for intervention in civil wars does not address whether one side or the other is perpetrating war crimes short of the threshold already mentioned. Walzer's threshold entails the self-help test for secessionist movements, and it permits only counter-intervention in civil wars. According to the Atrocity Standard, if one or both sides in a civil war are committing atrocities, a just cause would exist for external intervention to stop the atrocities and protect the victims of war crimes, whether they are soldiers or civilians.

We can sum up the new threshold for just cause for AHI in this way: Atrocity crimes correspond to the acts forbidden under Articles 6–8 of the Rome Statute of the International Criminal Court.[17] These crimes include genocide, ethnic cleansing, other crimes against humanity, and war crimes. Crimes against humanity include all of the enumerated crimes above, and other inhumane acts.[18] Just cause exists for AHI into any state that perpetrates, is complicit in, or fails to stop these atrocity crimes from occurring within its borders.

Failed states

When states are incapable of maintaining law and order and so pose both a domestic threat to human security and an international security threat, the international community is justified in crossing the border, subject to other *jus ad bellum* constraints, if intervention is necessary to remedy the threat.

For Walzer, in the case of intervention in a failed state, "the goal is to create a political agency that can maintain law and order and provide basic services."[19] I accept Walzer's view on intervention in the case of failed states. The just cause we wish to rectify in the case of a failed state (absence of a political agency that can maintain law and order and provide basic services) is very similar to the just cause we wish to rectify in all humanitarian intervention. The difference is again in the "capacity" versus "capacity plus responsibility" formulation – "a political agency that can maintain law and order and provide basic services" versus "a political agency that can *and will* maintain law and order and provide basic services." For Walzer, a state that could maintain (decent) law and order and provide basic services but does not do so, like Zimbabwe, is "safe" from intervention; it is only when a state cannot, as in the case of Sierra Leone, that outsiders are free to intervene.

Civil war and secession

Walzer has apparently changed his position on the case of secession. In *Just and Unjust Wars,* Walzer argued that intervention must not be necessary to the secessionist movement's success, if such intervention is to be justified – the secessionist movement must meet the test of self-help – it must be capable of setting itself free, without external assistance. Walzer has said exactly the opposite in 2004:

> If people are not prepared to give their time and energy to the movement, to put their wealth at its service, to risk even their lives, they cannot expect foreigners to come to their aid. That kind of support is the first condition of any military intervention. The second condition is necessity: that the movement cannot be helped by any form of assistance short of war and that it will certainly be defeated without some external use of force, like the intervention that the French undertook in 1781.[20]

62 *Just cause*

We must be careful about weighing his comments in an interview as heavily as we weigh his carefully crafted text in *Just and Unjust Wars*. In either case, it seems to me that whether the movement is capable of fighting its own battle should not be a factor in the determination of just cause. Whether the movement is capable of victory on its own depends entirely on the force capacity of each side; it is a question of might, not right. Just cause determinations are a question of right, not might. Proportionality and likelihood of success are determinations where a consideration of might is crucial. When a state is not capably and responsibly serving its people, resistance is permissible subject to all the *jus ad bellum* criteria, and likewise foreign assistance is permissible to a justified resistance, but military intervention is only permissible if all the *jus ad bellum* criteria are satisfied.

Wars of secession are generally asymmetric. The favored techniques of the weak often include guerrilla war. A frequent tactic for guerrilla fighters is to hide themselves among the civilian population, and to launch attacks from the cover of a village full of non-combatants. Sometimes guerrillas hide themselves among encampments of refugees attempting to flee the fighting. If the state responds to such a tactic by indiscriminately attacking civilian areas or refugee camps in the hopes of killing the guerrillas as well, an intervention might be justified to protect non-combatants from the state's indiscriminate attacks or to try and bring the conflict to an end, even if we cannot determine as outsiders whether the state or the secessionists have justice on their side.

In many civil wars, combatants target civilians and relief workers with impunity. Beyond direct violence, deaths from starvation, disease and the collapse of public health dwarf the numbers killed by bullets and bombs. Millions more are displaced internally or across borders. Human rights abuses and gender violence are rampant.[21]

It is generally (though not universally)[22] thought that just cause can exist only on one side in a conflict; but it is equally well-understood that both sides very often believe they have justice on their side.[23] James Turner Johnson explains simultaneous ostensible justice in this way:

> Beginning with Vitoria the possibility is admitted that, while one side may actually be in the right in a given war, the other side may, because of invincible ignorance, believe itself to be in the right also. In such cases only God could know who really was fighting justly. As for the belligerents, they should be chastened by this realization that both sides might seem equally to be in the right, and so they should be especially scrupulous in observing the *jus in bello*, the rules of war. The doctrine of simultaneous ostensible justice thus was intended to affect the conduct of war, not the resort to war. But princes who had read Machiavelli as well as Vitoria and Grotius applied this doctrine another way. Any resort to war could be justified, they argued, because invincible ignorance clouded men's minds and made all concerned in a dispute think they were right. This is the root of the doctrine of *competence de guerre*, which says that

every sovereign has the power to make war on his judgment that his nation's interests require it.[24]

Although both sides may think they are justified in making war, objectively speaking there cannot be a preponderance of justice on both sides. Aquinas argued that we should follow our conscience, even though it might be wrong. However, human discernment is limited, and it is often likely that there is some justice and some injustice on each side of a conflict.

I detailed Walzer's threshold and his rationale in Chapters 1 and 2. Walzer finds just cause for AHI only in cases of genocide, ethnic cleansing, massacres, and enslavement. I will elaborate the argument for the Atrocity Standard in the next section, where I contrast it with Walzer's, Rawls', and Teson's thresholds. First, I will briefly introduce the thresholds endorsed by Walzer, Rawls, and Teson, then proceed to a more thorough discussion of the rationale for choosing the Atrocity Standard over any of these alternatives.

Rawls has affirmed Walzer's views about the justice of war generally.[27] Rawls thinks AHI may be justified in grave cases, when outlaw states deny human rights and when the denials are egregious and sanctions are of no use.[28] By human rights, Rawls means the "special class of urgent rights, such as freedom from slavery and serfdom, liberty (but not equal liberty) of conscience, and security of ethnic groups from mass murder and genocide."[29] Rawls' view is slightly broader than Walzer's view. Walzer denies that denial of liberty of conscience, on its own, would constitute a *casus belli*. By denial of liberty of conscience, Rawls means compelling or preventing thought or belief or worship, not discrimination on the grounds of religion.

Table 4.1 Thresholds for just cause for Armed Humanitarian Intervention

	Walzer	Rawls	Rome	Teson
Just cause threshold	Genocide, ethnic cleansing; enslavement; widespread massacres	Grave cases of denial of the special class of urgent rights: freedom from serfdom and slavery; liberty (but not equal liberty) of conscience; and security of ethnic groups from mass murder and genocide[25]	Atrocity crimes as enumerated in the Rome Statute.	To overthrow severe tyranny; to restore democratic institutions; to punish a regime for past atrocities; to spread democracy[26]

Rawls endorses Walzer's general view on just cause, and he also gives an original example of when AHI might be called for. He asks us to imagine a society like the Aztecs. It is not aggressive internationally, but "it holds its own lower class as slaves, keeping the younger members available for human sacrifice in its temples."[30] If such a society did not respond to sanctions, and the violations of human rights were egregious (enslavement, genocide, ethnic cleansing, and preventing or compelling religious belief), Rawls notes that humanitarian intervention might be justified.

I endorse the Atrocity Standard, which I elaborated in the previous section. This view understands a broader "special class of urgent rights," to borrow Rawls' phrase, but it would not find just cause for AHI in the absence of ongoing atrocity crimes. The Atrocity Standard, therefore, is more permissive than Walzer's formulation, but less permissive than Teson's.

"Humanitarian imperialism" is associated with the thought of Fernando Teson, who was given the label by Terry Nardin. Teson accepts the moniker on his own terms: "If being a humanitarian imperialist means advocating that the hegemon use its might to advance (by appropriate moral means) freedom, human rights, and democracy, then I am a humanitarian imperialist."[31] Teson would sanction intervention in all the cases the Atrocity Standard would, and he goes beyond that standard by expanding just cause to include restoring democracy where one has been overthrown and punishing regimes for past atrocities.

It might be helpful at this point to provide an example of a case in which the Atrocity Standard and Teson would find just cause for AHI, but Walzer's standard and Rawls' would not. In many countries, severe and intentional discrimination on prohibited grounds such as gender and religion is widespread. In some of these cases persecution would constitute a just cause according to the Atrocity Standard, but not for Walzer or Rawls. One example that may be useful can be found in the case of Afghanistan under the Taliban. Walzer supported the US war against the Taliban regime as a war of self-defense because of the Taliban's partnership with Al-Qaeda. The war was justified for Walzer as a response to the attacks of September 11, 2001, but not as a humanitarian intervention. Although the Taliban's policies were brutal, they were on the "ordinary brutality" side of Walzer's wide chasm between genocide and nastiness.

Rawls would not have considered Afghanistan under the Taliban to be a decent hierarchical society. However, that is not the standard Rawls requires for non-intervention. Rawls permits wars of self-defense against outlaw states on the part of well-ordered and decent societies as well as benevolent absolutisms. Rawls endorses Walzer's standard for non-intervention, including exceptions in the case of egregious violations of human rights (such as enslavement and human sacrifice). Rawls makes clear, however, that it would be preferable to find "a tactful approach that could make them cease these practices" and make them realize that a system of cooperation would benefit them.[32] The atrocities in Afghanistan did not include genocide or enslavement, and there is nothing in *Law of Peoples* that suggests clearly that Rawls would have supported an intervention in Afghanistan to oust the Taliban for humanitarian reasons. However, Rawls' framework does allow wars of self-defense against aggressive outlaw states, which the Taliban–Al-Qaeda partnership in Afghanistan arguably was. Rawls endorses Walzer's just war theory generally, and the *Law of Peoples* framework would have endorsed the war against the Taliban after September 11, 2001, on self-defense grounds.

The Atrocity Standard would find just cause for war against the Taliban, as would Teson's standard, even if the attacks of September 11 had never happened. Official policies of the Taliban regime intentionally denied many fundamental rights to Afghans on prohibited grounds contrary to international law. Equal religious liberty and equal dignity for all persons did not exist. The rights to freedom of expression, association, and assembly; the right to work; the right to education; the right to freedom of movement; the right to be free from torture, degrading, cruel, or inhuman treatment; and the right to health care were all severely and intentionally denied:

> [In 1999,] Taliban officials continued to beat women on the streets of Kabul for dress code violations and for venturing outside the home without the company of a close male relative. In Kabul, girls were not permitted to attend school, although primary schools for girls were permitted in other parts of the country. Women's employment remained severely restricted and was generally limited to health care. To ensure that religious practices were strictly enforced, Taliban police continued to arrest [Muslim] men for having beards that were too short, for not attending prayers, and for having shops open during scheduled prayer times.
>
> As in previous years, the Taliban enforced its laws according to its interpretation of Islamic Sharia, with weekly public executions, floggings, and amputations in Kabul stadium and other cities under its control. Several men accused of sodomy were punished by having walls pushed on them by a tank. In one case, a man who survived the ordeal after being left under the rubble for two hours was reportedly allowed to go free.[33]

These deprivations were carried out in both a systematic and a widespread manner, resulting in widespread lessening of life chances. Women's health care was massively impacted. Women without a male relative to support them were nevertheless forbidden to seek employment and were reduced to begging in the streets for alms. Human Rights Watch observed in 2001 that "the discrimination is cumulative and so overwhelming that it is literally life threatening for many Afghan women."[34]

In cases where the atrocity crimes enumerated in the Rome Statute are underway, as in the case of Afghanistan as described above (persecution), the Atrocity Standard asserts just cause for AHI. Foreigners possess a right to seek to influence, to interfere, and if the other *jus ad bellum* restraints are met, to intervene with military force. If AHI is not permissible, the reason will be that all the other *jus ad bellum* restraints cannot be satisfied. If all the other *jus ad bellum*

66 *Just cause*

restraints are satisfied, I see no reason, it would be impermissible for outside actors to remedy the just cause through AHI.

Fernando Teson would also find that there was just cause for humanitarian intervention in Afghanistan to liberate the people there from the rule of the Taliban. Teson's just cause threshold includes all that the Atrocity Standard endorses, as well as finding just cause for intervention to restore a democracy where one has been toppled, intervention to punish a regime for past atrocities, and intervention to spread democracy and free markets.

Likely objections to my view

In this section, I will try to further specify the details of my view on just cause in contrast to the views of Walzer, Rawls, and Teson. I will also make clear the rationale for choosing the Atrocity Standard over the alternatives by engaging some powerful countervailing views and likely objections: the objection that my view is too strong, too distinctively liberal, or that it does not allow space for non-liberal but decent hierarchical peoples; the objection that my view is too weak; the moral hazard objection; the objection that respect for human rights cannot be taught by means of violence; the objection that pre-emptive AHI is punishing a state for something it has not done; the objections from descriptive and prescriptive realism; the objection from international law; the might makes right objection; and the objection from anti-paternalism.

The objection that the Atrocity Standard is too strong

The objection is something like this:

> I agree that Walzer's wide chasm is not sustainable. However, this view you have presented is too strong. Allen Buchanan, for example, argues that we naturally prefer the whole panoply of liberal rights, but for an international norm, we don't want to propose that any failure would be sufficient to trigger intervention.[35] Why not leave decent societies alone, as Rawls has recommended?

This objector might also say we can imagine that a society might be rigidly patriarchal (for example) because it wants to be, and another society has no right to interfere. I will address these points in turn.

First, let me say that my view does not argue that any failure at all from the whole panoply of liberal rights is sufficient to trigger intervention; my view requires that states do not deny citizens' non-derogable rights on any grounds, and that they do not deny other fundamental human rights on prohibited grounds; however, intervention is not triggered unless these deprivations lead to death, imminent danger of death, or widespread or systematic lessening of life chances. My view does not require that the state provide the whole panoply of liberal rights. Democracy, for example, is not a requirement of a capable and responsible state. In fact, mere procedural or formal democracy can be problematic for human rights under certain circumstances, such as when the will of the majority might be to deny some rights to some group of citizens on ethnic, national, religious, gender, or other grounds. If democratic institutions such as elections are held in a country with no traditions of democracy or political structures that function to promote fundamental human rights, the election merely serves to crystallize the status quo or the power relationships, oppression, or discrimination already existing on the ground. Or, it might change the relationships but do so by installing new tyrannical majority rule. Local affirmation of fundamental human rights, including equal dignity and respect for all, is necessary before democracy can be viable. Formal democracy is not necessarily correspondent with respect for human rights; we can imagine a nominally democratic society where human rights are not respected and upheld, as I described above. We can also imagine a non-democratic society, like Rawls' benevolent absolutism, where human rights are respected (other than the right to full political participation). I will distinguish my view further from the "whole panoply view" in the next section, on "the objection that my view is too weak."

To address the second part of the objection, which asks "Why not leave decent societies alone?," let me first say that in some cases, decent hierarchical peoples would not pose a just cause for AHI. However, this will not be true in all cases. It would be helpful to summarize Rawls' conception of a decent hierarchical society and then explain under what circumstances such a society might present a just cause for AHI.

The decent hierarchical society, Kazanistan, described by Rawls in *Law of Peoples*, respects human rights enough that according to the Atrocity Standard, there would not be just cause for AHI. The state religion, Islam, is the final authority on many important matters of public policy, and senior positions in society are open only to Muslims. There is intentional denial of the right to equal treatment on the prohibited basis of religion; however, the discrimination does not meet the definition of persecution, because it is not severe. It does not result in the large-scale lessening of life chances. In Kazanistan, there is no just cause for humanitarian intervention. Although high public offices are not open to all, in Rawls' example, the discrimination does not rise to the level my threshold requires.[36]

However, the minimal set of rights that Rawls requires, that decent hierarchical societies respect (to be members in good standing of international society), is not substantial enough to guarantee that all such societies would satisfy the Atrocity Standard. Kazanistan is more respectful of human rights than Rawls requires all decent hierarchical societies to be. It is possible to imagine a society which would meet the standards Rawls specifies for a decent hierarchical society but where just cause for AHI would be satisfied according to the Rome Statute threshold.

Decent hierarchical societies affirm those rights enumerated in Articles 3–18 of the Universal Declaration of Human Rights, appended here (hereafter I will refer to Article numbers only). However, they need not honor the fundamental idea that all people are due equal respect as human beings (Articles 1 and 2), the full measure of freedom of thought, conscience, and religion (Article 18), and freedom of opinion, expression, and association (Articles 19 and 20.) A society that does not honor these rights could be so oppressive that there is a just cause for AHI, while still honoring the rights enumerated in Articles 3–18. (Decent hierarchical societies honor Article 18 insofar as they do not explicitly prevent or compel belief, but because discrimination is permissible on the grounds of religion, they do not affirm a full measure of freedom of thought, conscience, and religion.)

It would be helpful at this stage to specify further what is at stake if decent hierarchical peoples may not respect some fundamental rights and then to describe a society that might deny these rights while still affirming the "special class of urgent rights" enumerated in Articles 3–18.

Articles 1 and 2 are excluded from the set of rights Rawls requires decent peoples to affirm. Article 1 is a cornerstone of the Declaration, which lays out the foundation of equality: "All human beings are created free and equal in dignity and in rights." The fundamental right against discrimination is set forth in Article 2 of the UDHR, which states:

> Everyone is entitled to all the rights and freedoms set forth in this Declaration, without distinction of any kind, such as race, color, sex, language, religion, political or other opinion, national or social origin, property, birth or other status. Furthermore, no distinction shall be made on the basis of the political, jurisdictional or international status of the country or territory to which a person belongs, whether it is independent, trust, non-self-governing or under any other limitation of sovereignty.

Decent hierarchical peoples do not necessarily affirm that all citizens are equal in dignity or rights. Rawls believes that equal dignity is not a fundamental right, but a liberal aspiration.[37] Decent societies are not required to regard citizens as "free and equal."[38] Rawls also excludes the right against discrimination from human rights proper. Rawls' exclusion of this rule is the most central reason that decent hierarchical societies might sometimes be in conflict with the Atrocity Standard. The Atrocity Standard explicitly calls denial of fundamental rights on prohibited grounds the crime of persecution, and if it leads to large-scale lessening of life chances, there is a just cause for intervention under the Atrocity Standard.

Decent hierarchical societies admit a measure of freedom of religion and thought; persecution is not allowed, but discrimination on the grounds of religion is permitted.

Article 18 specifies:

> Everyone has the right to freedom of thought, conscience and religion; this right includes freedom to change his religion or belief, and freedom, either alone or in community with others and in public or private, to manifest his religion or belief in teaching, practice, worship and observance.

Decent hierarchical societies may not persecute religion as such, that is, they may not explicitly prevent or compel religious belief or observance. However, they may discriminate on the grounds of religion; for example, offices might not be open to non-believers. David Little explains the norms that guarantee freedom of conscience:

> [T]he set of human rights norms that guarantee "the freedom of religion or belief" ... are of two sorts: There are the articles enshrined in the international instruments that protect legitimate religious interests, such as freedom of belief and conscience, as well as the freedom to manifest belief in "teaching, practice, worship, and observance." In addition, there are the articles that prohibit discrimination based on religious belief or affiliation. The human rights to free exercise and to freedom from discrimination are elaborated in the first two articles of the of the UN *Declaration on the Elimination of All Forms of Intolerance and Discrimination Based on Religion or Belief*. The remaining six articles of that declaration further specify the protections and prohibitions that follow from these two fundamental rights.[39]

As innocuous as a little bit of discrimination sounds in Rawls' gentle voice and in his Kazanistan example, we can imagine a case where it would amount to persecution as that crime has been interpreted in international jurisprudence. In the Kazanistan example, it is only the top leadership posts in government that are closed to non-Muslims. In a society where such discrimination was more widespread throughout society, we can imagine a much more destructive effect on life chances. Aside from this harm, it might also be argued that such discrimination, by making it difficult to be a member of the out of favor religion, amounts to persecution as such, and to a roundabout attempt to "prevent or compel belief."[40]

Rawls' limitation of "freedom of thought, conscience, and religion" is especially troubling if we try and apply *Law of Peoples* to actually existing states. Rawls, of course, does not mean to say that "peoples" as he has described them actually exist; he is using "peoples" as a device of representation. In actually existing states, as with Rawls' peoples, the majority religious community often becomes hegemonic, but discrimination does not generally exist without persecution:

> Discrimination and intolerance in matters of religion and belief is a serious dimension of the catalogue of violation of human rights in the world including situations of gross violation. Religious persecution of minority faiths, forcible conversion, desecration of religious sites, the proscribing of beliefs and pervasive discrimination, killings and torture, are daily occurrences at the end of the twentieth century. Even in a world which has emerged from the paralysis of the Cold War, little, it appears, can be done for the victims. In 1995 the United Nations could not even afford to publish their complaints.[41]

Of course those crimes would not represent a decent hierarchical state; they do not torture or kill believers, nor do they force conversion. However, these societies could practice pervasive discrimination in ways that lead to large-scale lessening of life chances. It is possible that educational opportunities or work opportunities would be offered only to the favored group, and that out of favor ethnic, racial, religious, gender, or political groups would be excluded. Such arrangements, in actually existing societies, lead to large-scale lessening of life chances. For one example, consider discrimination on the basis of gender, which led to large-scale lessening of life chances for women living in Afghanistan under the Taliban. Discriminatory laws, which the government attempted to justify by appeals to religion and tradition, prevented women from working in many jobs, attending school beyond primary grades, or being treated by male physicians (among many other restrictions). As a result, many intelligent and able-bodied women without male caretakers had no alternative but to beg on the street for alms. As a result of laws restricting medical care for women, women's health care was extremely poor under the Taliban.

Allen Buchanan has observed:

> Rawls' list of human rights does *not* include the right to freedom from religious discrimination, but rather only the right to freedom from religious persecution, understood as the right to freedom of religious thought and to practice one's religion "without fear." Nor does it include a right to freedom from other forms of discrimination including systematic, institutionalized, public discrimination – on grounds of race, gender, ethnicity, nationality, or sexual orientation, beyond the rights to subsistence and a wholly unspecified right to personal property. So-called welfare rights of any kind are also absent. So it appears that for Rawls a society in which there is a permanent racial, ethnic, religious, or gender underclass hovering just above subsistence, systematically excluded from the more desirable economic positions, having a grossly inferior property rights, lacking access to education and health care services available to the dominant classes, unable to afford legal counsel and bereft of sophisticated due process protections available to others, would not be a society in which those who were thus disadvantaged could complain that their human rights were violated.[42]

Rawls' worry in *Law of Peoples* is to find an overlapping consensus that representatives of societies (corporate bodies, peoples, not representatives of the individual members of these societies) could agree upon. He calls this the second original position.[43] Parties in the second original position are not individuals living in an unknown country, but representatives of unknown peoples (not people). Each people would demand substantial latitude in interpreting its idea of the common good for itself in this second original position. While the formulation is attractive to those leaders of non-liberal hierarchical peoples who would fear liberal intervention into their affairs, it does not take into account the preferences of *individuals* for the kind of society in which they would like to live.[44]

Rawls' formulation seems to me to suffer from one of the same weaknesses as Walzer's formulation. Too much weight is given to the idea of communal integrity and communal identity and not enough weight to the worry of the dissenting citizen. Peoples are attributed a thoroughly shared, monolithic conception of the good in a way that does not seem analogous to the conceptions of the good held by persons in actually existing states, marked as they are by many different and often contesting groups within them. *Law of Peoples* bolsters international stability at the expense of the possibilities for dissenting individuals living under repressive regimes to choose, if they desire, to live according to a different light than the one held up by the community. Rawls' escape valve for dissenting members of peoples is a right of exit, which he acknowledges will not be meaningful if there is not a right of entry into other states.[45]

Rawls' category of "peoples" does not easily fit into just war thinking, because "peoples" are explicitly not states. For just war theory, it is clearer to maintain the language of states rather than peoples, nations, or societies, unless we are talking about sub-state or trans-state actors, which Rawls is not. However, if we were to talk about peoples as if they were states, just for the purposes of answering the objection above, I would like to be very clear that it is possible that some decent non-liberal peoples, like Kazanistan, could fit the category of capable and responsible states. In that case Rawls and I would have "arrived at the same place" by different routes, and Rawls would say "so much the better."[46] It is possible that a decent hierarchical society might satisfy the higher threshold that I have set; I agree with Rawls that liberal democracy is not a requirement for a state to be deserving of the right to non-intervention. Unlike Rawls, however, I claim that a state's exclusion of a group from political participation on prohibited grounds is a just cause for AHI if it rises to the level of persecution (which entails large-scale lessening of life chances), as was the case under the Taliban regime in Afghanistan.

Since Rawls wrote *Law of Peoples*, the idea of universal human equality in dignity and rights has been signed onto again (by all leaders of states in the *Outcome Document* referenced earlier). This unanimity gives reason to believe that we can justifiably argue that it should be honored by all peoples. We can now claim that Rawls was too cautious when he described "equality in dignity and rights" as a distinctively liberal aspiration. The exclusion of Articles One and Two is the central reason that Rawls' decent societies would not necessarily always be owed the right of non-intervention – it is possible that in a decent hierarchical society, a set of persons might be persecuted on prohibited grounds. (Persecution entails by definition severity; it leads to large-scale lessening of life chances.)

Another critic might worry that the substance of the overlapping consensus is the same thing as old fashioned natural rights; the critic would say something like "don't you see you are just masking comprehensive liberalism?" We are not smuggling in comprehensive liberalism because we are not insisting that any person or community adopt any particular functionings; I am only insisting that the state refrain from persecuting identifiable groups. My view is compatible with political liberalism, although not completely compatible with Rawls' *Law of Peoples*.

The third part of the objection is this question:

> What if a society shaped itself as rigidly patriarchal, as might be allowed to one of Rawls' decent hierarchical peoples; does another society have the right to interfere? What about an Islamic theocracy? They may have a version of human rights that is simply different from that proposed by the Atrocity Standard.

The Atrocity Standard holds that if a patriarchal society is not acting in a way that lessens the life chances of some of its members, there is no right on the part of foreigners to interfere. I am skeptical of the claim of any theocratic government that there is actually a unified faith and a monolithic version of that faith accepted by the entire society. Even an Islamic theocracy which claims to be a unitary state is not made up of people of identical faith. It is very unlikely that there are no dissenters. It is more likely that the loudest, most powerful, most aggressive, most numerous, or most intolerant members of the state have seized control of the state machinery and labeled their religious beliefs the state's official ones. We do not acknowledge a right of governments to discriminate against some citizens on the basis of religion. A right does exist, and has been affirmed unanimously by representatives of every country in the world, to freedom from discrimination and also to liberty of consciousness, thought, and religion.

However, if there is no apparent dissent within the society and no request for outside intervention, and the state is not blocking capabilities in such a way as to be causing widespread or systematic lessening of life chances, outsiders may reasonably attempt to influence and interfere, but they may not intervene with military force. Following Grotius, my formulation requires that military interventions must be welcomed by at least someone.[47]

If we imagine that it is true that the regime is just acting out what the society wishes, there is still the problem of adaptive preferences. The society may have patriarchal preferences, and we can imagine a repressive society where there were no (or at least very few) dissenting members. However, their preferences may have adapted in this way because the only alternative they can imagine is worse.[48]

Kok-Chor Tan has convincingly refuted the objection that an entire society might prefer a system of inequality:

> To be sure, we can imagine a hierarchical society in which all persons are content with their station and its duties in the social order, and hence there will be no visible dissent in the society. But one can reasonably suspect that such a society is not really a decent one but a successfully tyrannical one that has effectively stymied or stunted any opposing views members of that society would otherwise have through say religious or political indoctrination.[49]

State-sponsored gender discrimination may not generate audible dissent because there are no reliable or safe structures through which to voice dissent, or because the possible reward to be gained by dissent is outweighed by the likely punishment. In Saudi Arabia, for example, when women protested the law against women driving, the government responded by outlawing all future political demonstrations by women.[50]

There may be no dissent because of the "phenomenon of 'adaptation,' in which an individual's preferences are shaped to accord with the (frequently narrow) set of opportunities she actually has."[51] Amartya Sen argues that many young women's preferences are shaped in exactly this way; inequality becomes naturalized, and it seems appropriate.[52] Local acceptance of unequal treatment is not harmless, particularly in areas such as unequal access to education and health care. Unequal access to family resources such as money for food and medicine, as well as to public resources such as education and employment, lessens the life chances of women in these societies, literally shortening their lives, increasing female childhood mortality, and contributing to female infanticide.[53]

When a state's practices lead to widespread death or the lessening of life chances for some segment of its population, this is to be construed as a threat to human security within the state and a threat to international peace and security; and on that account the state cannot claim the right to non-intervention.

I'd like to emphasize that merely having a just cause does not warrant the resort to force. A locally accepted practice of persecution, say, honor killing, widow immolation, or female infanticide, is not likely to be successfully challenged by military intervention. These practices are best challenged from within. Outsiders can best help by lending support to those persons within the society who would challenge this tradition. However, this does not detract from the just cause. This is a barrier in the likelihood of success and proportionality categories of restraint; we should not attempt to change these practices by force of arms because it would not work or might be disproportionately costly.

The problem my view is concerned with is not to protect the rights of hegemonic religious, social, or cultural majorities inside states from unwelcome international influence, or from what might be understood as international paternalism. Freedom of religion and freedom from discrimination are affirmed in major human rights conventions, demonstrating widespread agreement on the primacy of these rights; no right exists for a hegemonic religious, ethnic, or other group to persecute non-believers or other un-favored groups.

The objection that the Atrocity Standard is too weak

A cosmopolitan critic might say, well, I agree with you that Rawls' "human rights proper" is too restrictive. However, your view is not strong enough. Why not embrace the view, say, of Fernando Teson? Why not say that liberal democracy is a universal human right, and denial of democratic institutions is, sometimes, a just cause for war?

Teson would endorse my view in part, I think, but he would say it does not go far enough for two reasons. First, Teson would add the just cause of "restoring democracy where it has been overthrown" even if no other human rights abuses have been committed; second, punishing perpetrators for past atrocity crimes that are no longer ongoing or imminent is a just cause for AHI for Teson.

Teson's position is distinct from the Atrocity Standard that I endorse: if a democracy is overthrown by an undemocratic regime, say a military *junta*, but the new regime was not committing crimes that rose to the level of atrocities as defined in the Rome Statute, there would not be a just cause for AHI. In my view, something rising to the level of an atrocity crime would have to be committed by the usurpers to trigger AHI to oust them. In practice, it is likely that such a regime would be carrying out such crimes, but this clarification serves to separate the theoretical positions.

Second, Teson would say that my view does not go far enough because it does not support punishment for atrocities that are not ongoing or imminent as a just cause for AHI. My view requires stopping atrocities to be the just cause. Reversing ill-gotten gains or punishing atrocity perpetrators will be part of the settlement of a just peace, and part of right intention, and as such it could arguably be part of the just cause; but the Atrocity Standard does not find punishment for past atrocities alone to be a just cause for war if atrocities are no longer ongoing.

For Teson, atrocities need not be ongoing. If a regime tortured people (in the past) and has now stopped, the previous torture remains a just cause to invade the country and overthrow that regime. Teson made this argument in response to Ken Roth of Human Rights Watch, who rejects Teson's defense of the 2003 Iraq war as a humanitarian intervention:[54]

> The argument by Human Rights Watch is that we didn't have ongoing atrocities, and that humanitarian intervention is only justified in such cases. Saddam was one of the worst dictators since the Second World War – whereas the war took place and Saddam was deposed after the atrocities had been committed. That standard is inadequate, because it creates a motivation for murderers to speed up the execution. All Hitler would have had to do to fend off a humanitarian rationale would be to exterminate all the Jews, so there are no more Jews to save. All Milošević would have to do is to exterminate all the people that he was trying to exterminate in the former Yugoslavia, or ditto the Pakistani army in Bangladesh in 1971, to fend off any justification based on the humanitarian-intervention doctrine as appropriate.

My view will overlap with Teson's on some cases. However, there are some cases in which Teson would find just cause where I would not, for example, where a democracy has been overthrown but no other rights violations are underway, or to punish a regime for past crimes without any presently occurring just cause.

The moral hazard objection

A serious problem is that a secessionist or other rebel group may intentionally endanger non-combatants by provoking massacres, with the aim of bringing international intervention to bear in their cause. As Alan Kuperman has argued, the Kosovo Liberation Army seems to have employed this strategy to bring NATO intervention to bear on its side.[55] Speaking more broadly, knowledge that international intervention may be forthcoming may trigger greater violence, having the opposite effect from the one desired by the intervener:

> The common wisdom underlying this emerging norm is that humanitarian military intervention reduces the amount of genocide and ethnic cleansing (forced migration), which together can be labeled "genocidal violence". However, this causal relationship has not been demonstrated, and there is some contrary empirical evidence and deductive logic suggesting that the intervention norm may at times actually cause genocidal violence. This is because the norm, intended as a type of insurance policy against genocidal violence, exhibits the pathology of all insurance systems by creating moral hazard that encourages risk-taking.... Specifically it encourages disgruntled sub-state groups to rebel because they expect intervention to protect them from genocidal retaliation by the state. Actual intervention, however, is often too late or feeble to prevent such retaliation. Thus, the norm causes some genocidal violence that otherwise would not occur.[56]

We can understand the moral hazard problem in two senses. First, if a norm of intervention to stop massacres would make victims expect to be rescued, it should also make perpetrators expect intervention. If they had this expectation, and a fear of intervention, rather than the expectation of impunity, this might deter some would-be genocidaires. Second, in Kuperman's view at least, a norm of intervention to stop massacres will encourage persons who would like to bring international intervention to bear in a case to provoke, or even perpetrate, massacres against themselves/their people. However, we should be clear that expecting rescue from genocide is not the same as provoking genocide.

Moral hazard is a powerful objection; most importantly, it highlights the requirement that the intervener must look closely at the potentially different sets of evidence on both sides of a conflict. However, I think Kuperman misses the root problem. Setting the threshold for AHI at massacres is not too low, as Kuperman thinks; the threshold is too high. The temptation to instigate massacres arises because in the current international legal context, intervention is always banned except in the most extreme cases, like genocide and ethnic cleansing. Imagine a shockingly persecuted group, denied many of the non-derogable rights on prohibited grounds. There is no freedom of religion, no freedom from torture, no equality before the laws. Fundamental rights such as freedom of movement and association, freedom of expression, the right to participate in one's own government, and the right to effective legal remedy are all denied on grounds of religious, ethnic, racial, political, or gender identity. Life chances for this persecuted group are severely truncated. The state has the weapons, so there is no possibility this group can liberate itself from its oppressors by force, and complaining about circumstances is punished. It does not look likely that the situation will change without outside intervention. There is no hope for intervention because the state's crimes do not rise to the threshold level of genocide, ethnic cleansing, or massacres. Under these circumstances, a rebel group might calculate that a massacre or two of its own people is worth the expected rescue intervention. Such a use of civilian suffering is condemnable; but we can see how the moral hazard problem arises. The solution is not to remove the possibility of intervention; the solution is to set the bar lower. If the threshold for outside intervention were set at atrocity crimes, as I suggest, the necessity for massacres to trigger outside help would not be an issue. A lower threshold such as the one I suggest would both remove the incentive to provoke massacres and serve to deter tyrants. Outsiders would have more leverage with which to pressure the state to respect the human rights of its people. In any case, it is not a tenable solution that intervention not be permitted to stop massacres. If massacres are provoked by extremists on one side and perpetrated by extremists on the other side, the non-combatant civilians need protection from both parties.

The moral hazard problem points to several other problems. First, there is the problem that outside influence, interference, and intervention often are not brought to bear early enough to prevent conflicts from escalating to the point that massacres are underway. Second, there is the problem that outsiders, if they do not become involved early, are vulnerable to manipulation by "insiders."

Knowing that the temptation exists for parties to a conflict to manipulate circumstances such that their cause appears just, international actors should preempt escalation and manipulation by being engaged on the ground in the conflict prevention process early. Lowering the threshold for influence, interference, and intervention means outsiders can be involved earlier and thereby be less vulnerable to confusion (or intentional obfuscation by the parties) about which party is responsible for which action. With international actors on the ground early, "disgruntled groups" will be less able to pull the wool over the eyes of the international community.

I will argue in Chapter 5 under proportionality and last resort for additional reasons why actors have a responsibility to gather information and take preventive action to resolve conflicts early. The moral hazard problem illuminates one important reason why, instead of waiting outside the borders for massacres to occur, international actors should become engaged earlier inside the borders – both to prevent situations from getting out of hand and so that later, international actors are armed with knowledge about each side's claims, grievances, and activities. In this way, outside actors can reduce some of their vulnerability to manipulation by parties in the conflict.

I have argued that intervention should be brought to bear to assist the side with the balance of justice, but the complexities of conflict situations, particularly after they have been allowed to develop over years or even decades, can make a determination of justice on one side or the other impossible. It is often likely that there is some justice and some injustice on each side. Nevertheless, if one side or both is committing atrocities, there is a just cause for AHI to stop the atrocities.

Just cause 77

To sum up my response to the moral hazard objection: first, if an emerging norm of permissibility of humanitarian intervention can be argued to embolden rebels to provoke massacres, it can also be argued to deter tyrannical regimes. The possibility of decisive intervention on behalf of the side on which the international community perceives to be on the side of justice might be expected to act as a lever to promote negotiation by all parties, toward a settlement in line with justice.

Second, the moral hazard objection assumes that rebel groups are willing to deliberately use civilian casualties as a means to their political goal of obtaining foreign intervention. Although this is sometimes true, it is not always the case. When it is so, this is an unjust tactic for the same reason that terrorism is unjust; civilians may never be used as means to military ends.

The high threshold for triggering AHI contributes to the moral hazard problem as well. If outside intervention were permissible without massacres being underway, rebel groups might not be inclined to resort to such sinister tactics. If rebel movements think their only option for obtaining outside help is to provoke massacres, it is true that there is an incentive for them to do so; but the existence of the incentive does not mean that the action will occur. The moral hazard objection yields insights that recommend early fact-finding and preventive action.

The objection that "you cannot teach respect for human rights by force of arms"

Even if a just cause is present, military intervention may not always be the most effective way to remedy the just cause. Jack Straw, at the time he was UK Secretary of State for the Foreign and Commonwealth Office, voiced a concern about the hope for instituting democracy in Iraq – whether democracy could succeed in a country with no habit or experience of democratic rule.[57] Straw's worry was similar to the concern expressed by Mill:

> But the evil is, that if they have not sufficient love of liberty, to be able to wrest it from merely domestic oppressors, the liberty which is bestowed on them by other hands than their own, will have nothing real, nothing permanent. No people ever was and remained free, but because it was determined to be so: because neither its rulers nor any other party in the nation could compel it to be otherwise. If a people – especially one whose freedom has not yet become prescriptive – does not value it sufficiently to fight for it, and maintain it against any force which can be mustered *within* the country), even by those who have the command of the public revenue, it is only a question in how few years or months that people will be enslaved. Either the government which it has given to itself, or some military, leader or knot of conspirators who contrive to subvert the government, will speedily put an end to all popular institutions unless indeed it suits their convenience better to leave them standing, and be content with reducing them to mere forms:

for unless the spirit of liberty is strong in a people, those who have the executive in their hands easily work any institutions to the purposes of despotism. There is no sure guarantee against this deplorable issue, even in a country, which has achieved its own freedom; as may be seen in the present day by striking examples both in the Old and New Worlds: but when freedom has been achieved *for* them, they have little prospect indeed of escaping this fate.[58]

I have already argued against the idea that being "unable to wrest liberty from merely domestic oppressors" indicates whether the people have sufficient love of liberty. Putting that question aside, the Mill–Walzer doctrine does hold an important insight. This insight is echoed in the worry of then-UK Foreign Minister Jack Straw in his 2002 memorandum to UK Prime Minister Tony Blair in preparation for Blair's visit to President George W. Bush's ranch in Crawford, Texas.[59] The memorandum questioned whether a link existed between Iraq and Al-Qaeda, whether an invasion would be legal, and put forward some post-war considerations under the heading "Consequences of Military Action":

> 10. A legal justification is a necessary but far from sufficient precondition for military action. We have also to answer the big question – what will this action achieve? There seems to be a larger hole in this than on anything. Most of the assessments from the US have assumed regime change as a means of eliminating Iraq's WMD threat. But none has satisfactorily answered how that regime change is to be secured, and how there can be any certainty that the replacement regime will be better.
>
> 11. Iraq has had NO history of democracy so no-one has this habit or experience.

This is the most important reason that foreigners should not attempt to spread respect for human rights by force of arms, where such respect is not locally affirmed. Foreigners especially should not spread democracy to those areas, by force. In such cases, the likely outcome might simply be eliminating the repression of one group in favor of repression of another; this is not the institution of a just peace. However, that is a very different (prudential) reason from the one Walzer gives (respect for local rights to historic community).

The proportionality concern that military intervention will have greater negative than positive effects is also a major "brake" on remediation of human rights by force of arms. Remediation of human rights would be a just cause. However, it seems to be true that when an election is held prematurely in a country with no habit of democracy or human rights, the election merely serves to crystallize the status quo or the power relationships/oppression/discrimination already existing on the ground or to institute new patterns of the same. We have seen this most recently in Afghanistan and in Iraq.

Just cause 79

This objection, therefore, is a strong "likelihood of success" objection but a weak objection on "just cause." Walzer seems to indicate that he is questioning the justice of the cause in the quotation below:

> The common brutalities of authoritarian politics, the daily oppressiveness of traditional social practices – these are not occasions for intervention; they have to be dealt with locally, by the people who know the politics, who enact or resist the practices. The fact that these people can't easily or quickly reduce the incidence of brutality and oppression isn't a sufficient reason for foreigners to invade their country.[60]

The brutalities of authoritarian politics might be countered successfully with military force, whereas the oppressiveness of traditional social practices probably cannot. Walzer errs in lumping these together. In each case, I would contend there is a just cause, but likelihood of success probably forbids attempting to remediate oppressive traditional social practices by force. Walzer also errs by lumping together the "people who enact or resist the practices." Brutality and oppression may be sufficient just causes for foreigners to invade, but likelihood of success and proportionality pose high hurdles.

The objection that pre-emptive humanitarian intervention is punishing a state for something it has not yet done

Because my view of just cause includes pre-emptive humanitarian intervention, when genocide or ethnic cleansing is apprehended or imminent, critics may object that this amounts to punishing states for things they have not yet done.[61] This is partially true, but not entirely. If genocide or ethnic cleansing is apprehended or imminent, the state is likely already doing something that merits stopping. Genocidal massacres are usually preceded by persecution and targeted killings or disappearances of moderates and elites. In addition, crimes of this magnitude usually arise in states that do not meet the criteria I lay out for a state to be owed the duty of non-intervention. These states tend to be repressive and to persecute members of identifiable groups on political, racial, national, ethnic, cultural, religious, or gender grounds as defined in Article 6, paragraph 3 of the Rome Statute; and on that basis they are already not owed the right of non-intervention.

Punishment was a just cause for war in some historical formulations, but it is no longer a just cause on its own; however, an element of *post bellum* justice is assumed under right intention, including righting the wrongs created by the just cause and preventing perpetrators of atrocities from keeping ill-gotten gains. Intervention to pre-empt genocide is intended to protect the targets of the genocidal state. Punishment is not the just cause for the war; the war will be the fought to stop atrocities, and to create a just peace. The conditions of a just peace might make possible war crimes trials, where punishment could be meted out as part of *jus post bellum*. To meet the threshold of just cause, the aim must be "stopping" atrocities, not simply punishing. My view is distinct here from Teson's view that past atrocities constitute just cause for intervention. Teson argues:

> [T]he requirement of imminent or ongoing massacres, genocide, or crimes against humanity is too strict. ... Under that standard, a genocidal regime has an incentive to speed up the killings. Once it stops it is protected against intervention, since according to Nardin (who adopts a line similar to that of Human Rights Watch) past atrocities are not legitimate grounds for intervention.

If a leader has committed atrocity crimes in the past but those are not ongoing, just cause exists for a limited raid to execute an international arrest warrant, but the threshold I have set for AHI is limited to stopping those crimes specified in Articles 6–8 of the Rome Statute.

Objections from descriptive realism

The descriptive realist holds that anarchy is the primary ordering principle in international relations and that states pursue their interests exclusively. The descriptive realist might object to expanding the category of just cause for a reason like this: "without the rule of non-intervention, strong states will invade weaker ones with a humanitarian pretext, to pursue their own aggressive aims." The classic example is Hitler's justification for "humanitarian intervention" in the Sudetenland to "liberate ethnic Germans there."[62] I have three responses to this line of reasoning. First, as Grotius observed, just because a maxim is abused, does not mean it isn't true.[63]

Second, if descriptive realism is true, states will act in their own interests whether there is a non-intervention rule or not. If states act regardless of international norms, a blanket norm against intervention does not restrain them effectively. I am not proposing that the non-intervention rule be jettisoned entirely; it would still be in force in the case of capable and responsible states.

My third response is that although a just cause may be present, this does not automatically assert that AHI is sanctioned. Of course I do not mean to say that the liberation of ethnic Germans in the Sudetenland was a just cause. I mean merely to re-emphasize that a just cause is not sufficient to justify the resort to war. The example highlights the importance of right intention as a category of restraint. Even if ethnic Germans were being persecuted in the Sudetenland and there was a just cause for their rescue, Hitler's aggressive aims beyond rescue of the persecuted fail to satisfy the right intention restraint.

The objections from prescriptive realism

The prescriptive or normative realist is not sure that states always do act in their interests, but she believes that states should. The objection from prescriptive realism says that states ought to act in their own interests, and if the United States, for example, has no interests in some foreign country, it is right that the United States should not to risk its own blood and treasure in an intervention to protect the citizens of a foreign land. Altruism has no place in foreign relations, a realist might say.

I think this claim has some merit, insofar as the rights to raise an army and levy taxes arise from the need to defend the legitimate interests of the country's citizens. The army may not be used to pursue the private interests of members of the government or ruling class. It seems illegitimate to ask a country's soldiers to fight for a cause that is of no interest to themselves, their family, or the *patria*.[64]

One response to this line of argument has begun to be developed by the human rights community, which re-casts domestic human rights issues in other countries as economic and security issues for countries in the developed world. For example, William F. Schulz[65] has written a book, *In Our Own Best Interests*, which makes pragmatic arguments that both security and economic prosperity in the developed world are interlinked with the furtherance of human rights (both political and material rights) around the world. Schulz shows that public health threats including HIV in Africa and drug-resistant tuberculosis in Russia (made worse by poor prison conditions in Russia) pose a threat to public health and human security in the United States, and he argues compellingly that human rights are in fact good for business. Abuses of human rights, Schulz maintains, create a spillover of cost and instability that threatens the prosperity and security of individual citizens in the United States and elsewhere in the developed west.

Michael Lund also argues that there are several practical reasons that the United States and other major western powers ought to be very concerned with the internal affairs of other countries. First, he argues that non-intervention is not a sustainable position for democratic countries. Lund claims that public opinion creates significant enough pressure on the government of the United States that despite domestic debate, the fact is that "the United States is prone to get involved eventually in most emerging crises." Second, he points out that the costs of non-intervention are high, both in economic opportunity costs and eventual loss of security. Third, non-intervention "brings a loss of status and influence." If other peer-level powers or the international community consistently take the lead in addressing crises, and the United States does not take a major role, the United States may be "left out when its peers or rivals acquire ever more influence."[66]

Another response to this objection might be that it does not address the question of just cause so much as it addresses the problem of whether anyone has a duty to intervene, and if so, who. If we imagine a situation where states do not contribute troops, but the Security Council has authorized the use of force, we can see that the objection is not really about just cause. For example, if NGOs, or even the United Nations, raised money to pay for a private military firm to protect the refugee camps in Darfur, the objection from prescriptive realism would not apply – it is not really about just cause. I will return to the arguments of the prescriptive realist in Chapter 5 in the section on legitimate authority.

Objection from international law

The objector might say,

> Intervention violates the prohibition on the use of force enshrined in Article 2 of the United Nations Charter. The use of force, or threat of the use of force, for humanitarian objectives, is hostile to the international rule of law.

This view stresses that allowing such a right would be destabilizing to the international legal order.[67] My answer to that objection is in two parts.

First, some legal scholars argue that it is not clear that the charter prohibits intervention, where the aim of the intervention is consistent with other principles and purposes of the charter (such as "promoting and encouraging respect for human rights and for fundamental freedoms and enforcing respect for the 'self-determination' of peoples.")[68] Because legal scholars disagree on these issues, this rebuttal does not really settle the question. Kofi Annan has interpreted the tension to be a false one, however:

> The United Nations Charter, after all, was issued in the name of "peoples," not [of] governments.... Its aim is not only to preserve international peace – vitally important though that is – but also to "reaffirm faith in fundamental human rights and, in the dignity and worth of the human person...." It was never meant as a license for governments to trample on human rights and human dignity.[69]

Even if we accept the critic's characterization of the law as restricting intervention for the purpose of protecting human rights, we can still reply by noting that when legal institutions yield morally intolerable outcomes, the legal institutions are commonly thought of as revisable. Law changes over time, as the concepts of "right" and "wrong" evolve over time, although they do not always evolve perfectly in tandem. Of course international law does not rule out all use of force; the occasions when it is legal are matters of contest among international lawyers.

Might makes right?

This thesis is vulnerable to the objection that if non-intervention may be unilaterally set aside, militarily powerful countries will be justified in forcing human rights onto militarily weak states. This objection is true. My only response is that all the other criteria of *jus ad bellum* would also have to be satisfied. Last resort, likelihood of success, and proportionality, are very high hurdles. I will have more to say about this in Chapter 5.

The objection from anti-paternalism

The concern of those who criticize a human-rights approach to cross-cultural politics is often stated something like this: "You are criticizing a way of life for people who have their own notion of what is the good. What gives you the right to mandate how someone else ought to live?" We can respond to this objection in two ways: first, we will say that people are frequently wrong about the good. This is why we must all be minimalists in our constructions. We do not know what the good life is for another person, nor do we wish to impose our view of the good on others. Therefore, we should stick to the foundational elements of human needs and capabilities that we believe to be true for all people, and about which all people, no matter what their particular religious or ideological beliefs, can reach an overlapping consensus. Upon that consensus, we can build fair institutions – recognition practices that take into account whether internal practices are politically legitimate, and theories of justified intervention into states that do not meet minimum standards of capability and responsibility.[70]

The question will naturally arise, "How can you justify your specification of this particular set of rights for all people across cultures?" Sumner B. Twiss responds to worries that a theory of minimal rights could be accused of being culturally insensitive or distinctively western, or insensitive to communitarian traditions and distinctively liberal, or that one might worry that a sweeping affirmation of human rights is necessarily grounded in problematic metaphysical-moral assumptions about human nature.[71] Twiss' response to those worries is that the evidence shows that these are not distinctively western nor are they distinctively liberal values. Twiss notes several international agreements as evidence of an explicit affirmation of overlapping consensus on human rights. Twiss gives evidence from within many traditions, including the most communitarian of all, Confucianism, for individuals' rights claims against communities. David Little sums up the universal appreciation of human rights in this way, and suggests that opposition to human rights usually comes from those who wish to deny the rights of others:

> As a matter of fact, victims of oppression and discrimination, no matter what "civilization" they belong to, usually have no difficulty appreciating the relevance of human rights protections, and they typically become fervent advocates of those protections. That is as true of Tibetan Buddhists and Uighur Muslims in China as it is of Hindu Tamils in Sri Lanka, or liberal Sunni Muslims in Sudan or Algeria, or Shi'a Muslims in Saudi Arabia, or Ahmadi Muslims in Pakistan, or Baha'is in Iran. Indeed, the denunciation of "Western interpretations" of human rights by the governments of these and other countries usually has more to do with protecting political and economic power than with a sincere concern for traditional values.[72]

We can add additional evidence of an expanding, explicitly stated, and internationally affirmed actual consensus on these issues. The rights I am stipulating were affirmed unanimously by the leaders of all states participating in the 2005 World Summit in the *Outcome Document of the United Nations High-level Plenary Meeting (the 2005 World Summit)*:

> Section 143. Human Security:
> We stress the right of people to live in freedom and dignity, free from poverty and despair. We recognize that all individuals, in particular vulnerable people, are entitled to freedom from fear and freedom from want, with an *equal opportunity to enjoy all their rights and fully develop their human potential*. To this end, we commit ourselves to discussing and defining the notion of human security in the General Assembly.
>
> Human Rights, Democracy, and Rule of Law:
> … Commitment to eliminate pervasive gender discrimination, such as inequalities in education and ownership of property, violence against women and girls and to end impunity for such violence.

The consensus has been ratified unanimously by those who most jealously guard the rights of states, their leaders. Its meaning in practice may of course be little, and its signatories may even be hypocrites. I present evidence of the agreement on non-discrimination and human rights here as a rebuttal against the claim that equal rights for all human beings is a distinctively liberal or Western value, or that the rights I am stipulating constitute a comprehensive view of the good. This document was adopted unanimously by the leaders of all the United Nations Member States. The document also affirms the responsibility to protect and the responsibility to prevent, which is seen as a major development in the adoption of the norm of "sovereignty as responsibility."[73]

The basic human capacities/the overlapping consensus

The Atrocity Standard threshold is consistent with the view that the state, if it is to serve the proper functions of a state, must not deny some citizens the exercise of basic capabilities. Denying rights leads to denying capabilities: capabilities are only manifested when citizens possess rights and the resources needed to fulfill their basic capacities. Capability is shorthand for rights plus resources.

I draw my understanding of rights from evidence that all human beings have similar raw and basic capacities in common. Once we recognize the basic capacities, we have moral intuitions that lead us to an understanding of interference with those capacities as requiring justification. Whether the right precedes the good is a normative issue that I am not exploring here; I am following Nussbaum on this issue and deriving my specification of rights from basic capacities. Capacities plus resources and formal rights yield capabilities.[74] Nominal rights are not the same as capabilities. Women have nominal rights in Afghanistan, for example, to work and to vote, but their capability to exercise these formal rights is often blocked. It cannot be said that they have the capability to work and to vote. Nussbaum explains:

> In some areas, I would argue that the best way of thinking about what rights are is to see them as combined capabilities. The right to political participa-

tion, the right to religious free exercise, the right of free speech – these and others are all best thought of as capacities to function. In other words, to secure a right to a citizen in these areas is to put them in a position of combined capability to function in that area. (Of course there is another sense of "right" that is more like my "basic capabilities": people have a right to religious freedom just in virtue of being human, even if the state they live in has not guaranteed them this freedom.) By defining rights in terms of combined capabilities, we make it clear that a people in country C don't really have the right to political participation just because this language exists on paper: they really have this right only if there are effective measures to make people truly capable of political exercise. Women in many nations have a nominal right of political participation without having this right in the sense of capability: for example, they may be threatened with violence should they leave the home. In short, thinking in terms of capability gives us a benchmark as we think about what it is really to secure a right to someone.[75]

The theorist who would suggest an overlapping consensus and claim unanimous agreement on a core set of values must be careful and conservative, realizing that she has been informed by her own culture and that her views on most things are not universally shared. The overlapping consensus is limited to the commonalities among all human beings. Many people may choose for religious or cultural reasons not to exercise their capabilities. The capabilities approach is sensitive to, and avoids, the pitfalls of ignoring cultural difference and local desires. It does not wish to be another expression of *la mission civilatrice* or the "white man's burden." This diversity is why it is the *possibility* to exercise capabilities and not the actual choosing to exercise the capabilities (Nussbaum calls this functioning) that is so important. Some people may choose to fast or to practice celibacy for religious reasons.

We can discern a very small overlapping area that all human creatures share in common, their capabilities. Choosing celibacy (not exercising sexual capability) is importantly different from having one's sexual choices destroyed by being genitally mutilated as a child, or forced into an unwanted marriage, or being widowed and forbidden to remarry. A woman might likewise choose to stay in the home to raise and educate children and care for the family. She might choose never to leave her house without her husband or without being veiled, for religious reasons. That is importantly different from staying in the house because the state coerces her, or the state refuses to punish local perpetrators of harmful cultural practices.[76]

There is a difference between deciding what is right for oneself and deciding about another's good. The standards Nussbaum enumerates, and human rights approaches in general, are supported by international agreements and by the actual cultural and religious beliefs of most peoples.[77] This project does not aim to put beliefs that are not widely shared onto peoples who have no interest in them. It does claim that most people do recognize and affirm the capabilities as aims for themselves. These capabilities, therefore, are goals states should affirm and that they should take steps to promote (because the state exists to serve the ends of the people, not vice versa). In *Inequality Re-examined*, Amartya Sen writes: "A person's capability to achieve functionings that he or she has reason to value provides a general approach to the evaluation of social arrangements, and this yields a particular way of viewing the assessment of equality and inequality." Capabilities are "the alternative combinations of functionings that are feasible for [a person] to achieve." Put differently, they are "the substantive freedoms he or she enjoys to lead the kind of life he or she has reason to value."[78]

Capabilities are the choices a person has. They represent what she is able to do or to be.[79] Functioning is what the person actually does, is, possesses, or achieves as a result of exercising capabilities (an educated mind, a healthy nourished body, a rewarding career are functionings, not capabilities). Functioning is what a person actually does with her capabilities; capabilities are the positive (and negative) freedoms a person has to do, be, or achieve what she values.

States must not block citizens from exercising the basic human capabilities. Nussbaum argues, following the Rawlsian insight of the overlapping consensus, that we can expect that all persons, from their own points of view and for their own reasons, would affirm the basic human capabilities for themselves. Nussbaum notes that this list is very general, tentative, and open-ended, but here is how it stood at the time of publication of her book, *Frontiers of Justice: Disability, Nationality, and Species Membership*, in 2006:

1 life;
2 bodily health;
3 bodily integrity;
4 senses, imagination, and thought;
5 emotions;
6 practical reason;
7 affiliation;
8 other species;
9 play;
10 control over one's environment (political and material).[80]

This list is more expansive than the Atrocity Standard for just cause, but we can say that states that obstruct the basic human capabilities do not provide the benefits of a capable and responsible state and, therefore, do not possess the right to non-intervention. Some infringements of capabilities will rise to the level of atrocity crimes and constitute just cause for AHI, but it is not the case that any infringement of capabilities or rights is just cause for war.

There are legitimate concerns about a person from one culture articulating a set of criteria that are meant to apply to other peoples' and cultures' very different ways of living. The motivations behind these concerns share the same foundation as the human rights approach: respect for human beings as human beings, with a right to determine their own course in life.

Within certain limits, it is appropriate and desirable that different states should work out the limitation on the exercise of basic capabilities differently, according to their history, culture, and tradition.[81] Justifications for interference with the exercise of basic capabilities can be legitimately criticized from across cultures. Such justifications must be argued for, and arguments can be evaluated according to their factuality, rationality, and consistency. India, for example, has banned speech that glorifies or eulogizes *sati* or "widow burning."[82] This restriction on speech is justified based on the state's aim of eliminating a harmful practice that deprives victims of their lives; the restriction serves to enhance the basic capabilities rather than restrict them in an irrational way. The restrictions on free speech are consistent with the affirmation of the capabilities, in the context of India's particular history, culture, and customs. Nussbaum gives the following additional example of a reasonable restriction on free speech:

> Germany's interpretation of the free speech right, according to which there can be a good deal of legal regulation of anti-Semitic speech and political organizing, is rather different from the U.S. interpretation, which protects such speech unless there is an imminent threat of public disorder. Both interpretations seem right, given the different histories of the two nations.[83]

This restriction is based on the state's aim of preventing new anti-Semitic movements and political organizing in the longer term rather than preventing only imminent public disorder; the ban on anti-Semitic movements seems like a justified exception to the general permission of free speech, given Germany's history with Nazism.

The United States has no such legal regulation against political organizing of anti-Semitic groups. Nussbaum stresses that this approach is compatible with pluralism; It "leave[s] room for the activities of specifying and deliberating by citizens" as in the German, Indian, and American cases mentioned above.[84]

The list represents "a freestanding 'partial moral conception,' to use John Rawls' phrase, that is explicitly introduced for political purposes only, and without any grounding in metaphysical ideas of the sort that divide people along the lines of culture and religion.[85] Nussbaum is careful to insist it is not functioning she is concerned with, but capabilities. The idea is not to force functioning on people who would feel violated by it.

When peoples agree to engage in politics and when they are participating members of international society, expecting to receive rights and benefits, such as the right to non-intervention, parties tacitly consent to the ground rules for the discussion: their reasons are subject to scrutiny according to reason and truthfulness. Cultural practices are not worth saving merely because they are old.[86] If traditional practices present coercive obstacles to achieving basic capabilities for some members of society, the harmful practices must be justified; and if they cannot be justified in accordance with reason and truthfulness, the state must be willing that the coercive, harmful practices should go. The state should do what it can to eliminate such practices and certainly should not officially discriminate or condone such discrimination. Laws restricting work, education, and ownership of property are very discriminatory in many countries, and these practices result in widespread lessening of life chances. Even where laws are changing, local practices lag behind. But where the law changes, it opens up space for the practices to change over time. Delegitimation of slavery is a good example of this process.

Of course, willingness on the part of the state to legislate against a harmful discriminatory practice by no means guarantees that the practice will disappear. The Indian government has officially criminalized the practices of *sati* and bride burning, but the practices persist. The situation concerning gender violence is comparable in many countries. Honor killing is illegal in Pakistan and Jordan, for example, and female genital mutilation is illegal in most of the world, but enforcement is up to local authorities who in many cases support or at least tolerate the practices. The practices have not diminished appreciably as a result of the legislation, prosecutions are infrequent, and punishments are light. In the case of harmful, discriminatory social practices, successful remediation is most often accomplished through the work of local (indigenous) NGOs. I will say more about this in Chapter 5 in the section on likelihood of success.

Where a state is unable to provide conditions where citizens can exercise the basic human capabilities, the state should ask for outside assistance, or at least be willing to accept outside assistance if it is offered, in the form of influence, interference, or even military assistance. Inviting such assistance from the outside preserves a state's right to non-intervention, because it is acting responsibly. It remediates its incapacity by accepting the help of others. If a state is unwilling or unable to deter harmful traditional practices, and it is unwilling to accept outside help, then the state is not serving the ends of its people and cannot claim the right to non-intervention. The test for non-intervention should not be whether a people is governed in accordance with its own customs, but whether human security is provided for by the state. If harmful traditional practices entail severe deprivations of fundamental rights and rise to the level of persecution, there is a just cause for AHI. It may very well be impossible to create respect for human rights or to stop harmful practices in a state by force of arms; but that only means that the proportionality and likelihood of success hurdles would be too high to surmount. It is for those reasons a war should not be fought. It does not mean that outsiders can take no view and have no standing to influence or interfere where they can do so proportionately, with right intention, in the least intrusive available manner.

5 Other *jus ad bellum* categories

Exhortations not to engage in a War rashly, tho' for just Reasons.
Tho' it be somewhat foreign to the Matter in Hand, which is designed only to treat and discourse of the Right of War, to explain what other Virtues, distinct from Justice, require or direct with respect to War; yet by the way we must obviate a certain Mistake, lest any one should imagine, that whenever he has a just Cause given him, he is thereupon immediately obliged to declare War, or that it is warrantable at any Time for him so to do. On the contrary, it happens that it is commonly a greater Piece of Goodness and much more commendable to abate somewhat of our Right, than rigorously to pursue it ... [and to] bring upon others all those inconveniences and Mischiefs which War is attended with.[1]

I have argued that many sovereign states are not owed the duty of non-intervention and that Walzer's conception of just cause is too narrow. If not for the restraining effect of the other *jus ad bellum* categories, my expansion of the just cause criterion to the Atrocity Standard could be argued to yield an excessive expansion of permissible occasions for military intervention. In this chapter, I emphasize the other restraints that act as a brake on the resort to war, although a just cause may be present. We do not need to rely on an ambiguous non-intervention norm as a brake on the resort to force.

Walzer's formulation does not require substantial emphasis on the other *jus ad bellum* categories because Walzer focuses so much on defensive war. He generally treats the just cause of self-defense as a sufficient condition to warrant recourse to defensive war.[2] However, his presentation of the aggressor–defender paradigm, in which the unjust aggressor and the just defender are always identifiable, is an oversimplification. Wars may seem to be just on both sides – especially subjectively; one's own position very often seems to be justified. For the parties involved, as well as for outsiders, it can be very difficult to tell exactly on which side justice is to be found. Often, there is a measure of justice and injustice on both sides. (Wars may be unjust on both sides as well, as Walzer acknowledges.) It may also be impossible to discern what or who started the downward spiral that eventually led to the first use of force. In circumstances where the outbreak of war is preceded by mutual escalation over time, it is often impossible to say who started the chain reaction. Even the first use of force is not

90 *Other* jus ad bellum *categories*

always a clear indication of who exactly is the aggressor. When both sides share responsibility for mutual escalation and eventual outbreak of hostilities, in the kind of security dilemma that John Herz and Herbert Butterfield both called "tragic," it is difficult to extract how much responsibility lies with each side.[3] Susan Woodword observes:

> Without a common authority and accepted procedures to resolve conflict, leaders in independent states can perceive themselves to be acting defensively against an external threat but can be perceived by others as acting aggressively, thereby setting in motion a process of competitive, defensive reactions with no limit.[4]

I emphasize the other *jus ad bellum* categories because just cause alone does not provide a sufficient framework of the whole set of considerations we ought to think about in determining whether recourse to war is, on balance, justified. In the comprehensive view, all resort to war, no matter what the purported just cause (even self-defense), is subject to the constraints of last resort, right intention, proportionality, likelihood of success, and legitimate authority.[5] The other *jus ad bellum* criteria take on a great deal more importance in my formulation of just war theory than in Walzer's.

In my view, sometimes offensive war is justified, but any resort to war, even defensive wars, can only be called just if all of the other *jus ad bellum* restraints – last resort, proportionality, likelihood of success, right intention, and legitimate authority – are satisfied as well. Just as importantly, all of these categories provide a framework for public discussion, debate, and judgment about the wisdom and morality of resorting to war. Truncating the categories in the case of defensive wars truncates the language of the debate. Each of the categories refers to a subject that requires exploration. Structuring the discussion through the traditional *jus ad bellum* lenses promotes a more comprehensive, holistic, and precise analysis than can be achieved if we fold all of the considerations of justice into the category of just cause. Just cause in my formulation is a necessary but insufficient condition for the resort to military force. To precisely express the reasons why a particular war should not be fought, even though there might be a just cause, it is necessary to have access to the language and the frameworks provided by the other categories of restraint.

In *Just and Unjust Wars*, Walzer does not extensively develop the other *jus ad bellum* categories, nor does he insist that they all must be met for a war to be justified. He insists that there must be a just cause (overt aggression). Once overt aggression has occurred, Walzer's main concern becomes *jus in bello*. Walzer assumes that except for in supreme emergencies, the rules of war must be observed. This view remains consistent in Walzer's later writings. He continues to use a similar framework, emphasizing just cause and *jus in bello*; and he does not generally or explicitly use the proportionality, right intention, legitimate authority, or likelihood of success categories. Walzer does use the category of last resort, in particular with reference to pre-emptive war, but in other cases of overt aggression, last resort is assumed to be satisfied. Where there is overt aggression, there is a presumption in favor of military action to resist it.[6] In all other cases, war is not allowed.[7] Walzer's threshold for just cause is higher than mine, and his brakes on the resort to war are mainly (though not entirely, as I will explain below) folded into the category of just cause. My just cause category is broader, but there are other brakes on the restraint to war in the form of the other *jus ad bellum* hurdles.

Last resort

Walzer's views on last resort

Regarding wars of anticipation, or pre-emptive self-defense, Walzer writes: "One always wants to see diplomacy tried before the resort to war, so that we are sure that war is the last resort."[8] However, Walzer makes clear that the phrase "last resort" is not to be taken literally. He thinks it is impossible to arrive at the last resort – "we can never reach lastness, or we can never know that we reached it. There is always something more to do: Another diplomatic note, another UN resolution, another meeting."[9] Walzer says, therefore, last resort is of limited usefulness as a constraint, even in theory. However, his view is more complex than that. He expresses two general views on last resort in *Just and Unjust Wars*. In the weaker view, last resort is of limited usefulness and is not a guide to actual practice. In the stronger view, parties should be certain that no other alternative is available, and that grave harm is underway or imminent, before resorting to force.

For Walzer, in the weaker formulation, last resort is a cautionary reminder that other options ought to be considered before the resort to force, but that is all.

Last resort is not a practical, but a conceptual guide. "It is a metaphysical condition." It does not mean that alternatives must have actually been tried, but rather it means that alternatives must have been considered – a thought experiment, not an actual experiment, is required:

> We say of war that it is the "last resort" because of the unpredictable, unexpected, unintended, and unavoidable horrors that it regularly brings. In fact, war isn't the last resort, for "lastness" is a metaphysical condition, which is never actually reached in real life: it is always possible to do something else, or to do it again, before doing whatever it is that comes last. The notion of lastness is cautionary – but this is a necessary caution: look hard for alternatives before you "let loose the dogs of war."[10]

Walzer finds that in certain contexts, last resort "doesn't seem to play an important role" at all.[11] In defensive wars, the aggressor has no right against being warred upon. Because force is already being used, or imminently will be, the requirement of last resort seems not to be relevant at all in a defensive war. Walzer also finds that last resort plays no important role in reprisals. He writes that in some cases, such as in a long string of terrorist attacks, forceful tit-for-tat reprisals might be the only option, and, therefore, the first, not the last resort. In such cases, Walzer writes, it is not necessary that other methods be tried before the resort to force, because the reprisals are always in direct response to previous raids. Reprisals, although forceful, are not full-scale invasions, so they are measures short of war; therefore, Walzer argues that reprisals are not subject to the last resort constraint.[12] Nevertheless, Walzer writes, "If the notion of last resort were taken seriously, it would limit reprisals in a radical way."[13]

Walzer says if we take last resort seriously, it means that all reasonable alternatives to the use of force must have been tried. Sometimes, at least, he thinks we should take last resort seriously. In 1988 and 2001, Walzer articulated this stronger view on last resort as follows, with particular reference to the resort to terrorism:

> It is not so easy to reach the last resort. To get there, one must indeed try everything (which is a lot of things) – and not just once, as if a political party or movement might organize a single demonstration, fail to win immediate victory, and claim that it is now justified in moving on to murder. Politics is an art of repetition. Activists learn by doing the same thing over and over again. It is by no means clear when they run out of options.... 'Last resort' has only a notional finality. The resort to terror is not last in an actual series of actions; it is last only for the sake of the excuse. Actually, most terrorists recommend terror as a first resort; they are for it from the beginning.[14]

Walzer also advocates a high threshold for last resort in the case of humanitarian intervention. Outsiders are not permitted to use force against an abusive regime until massacres, enslavement, ethnic cleansing, or genocidal killings are actually underway; foreigners must wait at the border, giving diplomacy and domestic politics every chance to work before bringing force to bear. Here last resort is folded into just cause: until genocide is underway, there is no just cause; once genocide is underway, last resort is already satisfied.

The requirement of reaching last resort is not meant to tie the hands of a victim of aggression from self-defense, nor to force the victim to wait to respond and allow its enemy time to gather more strength to attack. Walzer ties the difference between a preventive attack and a pre-emptive attack to the imminence of the threat. On the one hand, a preventive attack is "an attack that responds to a distant danger, a matter of foresight and free choice."[15] It is not a last resort. On the other hand, in a pre-emptive war of self-defense, there is nothing left to be done that has a reasonable hope of successfully averting war; the last resort, before war, has been tried.

In the case of the Six-Day War, Walzer's example of a justified pre-emptive war, "day by day, diplomatic efforts seemed only to intensify Israel's isolation."[16] The failure of diplomacy, and the increasing isolation, indicates that the last resort hurdle was cleared.[17] If diplomacy might still reasonably be hoped to avert war, the first use of force cannot be justified, because it is not the last resort. Therefore, Walzer argues, the 2003 resort to force against Iraq was unjust; "a war fought before its time is not a just war."[18] Walzer argues that the sanctions and inspections should have been given more time to work.

Historical views on last resort

Grotius affirmed that force should be a last resort. Gentili, however, argued that preventive war might sometimes be just: "one can sometimes anticipate that the trend of events will lead to a situation of extreme necessity; in such cases one is fully justified in taking preventive action."[19] Gentili was not only writing about pre-emption of imminent attack; he meant that force was sometimes justifiable to prevent the formation and consolidation of "probable and possible" threats as well:

> One ought not to delay, or wait to avenge at one's peril an injury which one has received, if one may at once strike at the root of the growing plant and check the attempts of an adversary who is meditating evil. ... A defense is just which anticipates dangers that are already meditated and prepared, and also those which are not meditated, but are probable and possible.[20]

Grotius explicitly and vigorously disagreed with Gentili, and devoted several pages to arbitration as a means to avoiding the rash resort to war:[21]

> It is then only our Interest to run to Arms, when we cannot otherwise have Justice done us by our Enemies. The way to prevent War between those, who, not belonging to the same Jurisdiction, have no common Judge to appeal to, is to put the Matter to Arbitration.[22]

Whenever war may be avoided by appeal to a common judge or by arbitration, it should be; Grotius is very clear that war ought to be prevented by making use of diplomacy and arbitration wherever possible. For Grotius, the last resort hurdle is cleared only if diplomacy, courts, and arbitration cannot solve a dispute that rises to the level of just cause for war: "where the power of law ceases, there war begins. Injury, or the prevention of injury, is the only just cause for war."[23] By this Grotius means to disallow war as a means of settling disputes that might be otherwise settled, for example, through arbitration, but he allows that wars may be justly undertaken to "prevent wrongs not yet committed."[24] Grotius' endorsement of prevention is not an endorsement of the early kind of preventive war allowed in Gentili's construction: by "wrongs not yet committed," Grotius explicitly means that the danger must be immediate, not merely a "supposed intention,"[25] seems to be referring to Gentili's argument: "The danger must be immediate, which is one necessary point. But they are themselves mistaken, and mislead others, who maintain that any degree of fear ought to be a ground for killing another, to prevent his supposed intention."[26] Grotius says leaders should take heed of Cicero's council that many wrongs are done through fear. In that discussion, he approvingly quotes Livy, who writes, "Great infamy redounds to those, who by anticipation perpetrate the criminal act which they fear."[27] In the event of a conspiracy and a planned attack, Grotius insists that there is no right of preventive self-defense until the attack is otherwise unavoidable (that is to say, unless it is the last resort). This reaching of last resort is the difference between an unjust and a just cause, so in this sense just cause and last resort are inextricable. The intended victim's knowledge of the attack or enhanced preventive military measures might be enough to prevent the attack, or arbitration may still be effective. Pre-emptive force in Grotius is only permissible as a last resort against immediate danger.[28]

My view on last resort

I endorse Walzer's maxim that "a war fought before its time is not a just war" and I expand it with some additional requirements that I hold to be entailed by last resort. I extend Walzer's Maxim by adding "a war that might have been prevented by earlier action is not a just war." On this view, it is impermissible to ignore an intensifying conflict, and when war becomes necessary, to then claim that it is the last resort.

First, I agree with the principle that last resort is the only brake that separates the just cause of pre-emption from the unjust cause of prevention. Last resort is linked to just cause in this way: once the last resort, short of war, has failed to ward off the threat, a war that would have been preventive, becomes a pre-emptive war. Getting to last resort is the obstacle that blocks preventive war. Even if the cause is otherwise just, preventive war is one that does not (by definition) satisfy the last resort criterion. In Walzer's words, it is "a war fought before its time."[29]

Second, I would add: "a war that could have been prevented is not a just war." Because political communities, in their relations with one another, have signed on to the idea that war shall be fought only as a last resort, this agreement has an operative quality about it that generates an obligation on the part of states to do proactive things to avoid wars before they become imminent. If states see a situation brewing that they can reasonably predict might need to be addressed with force of arms in the future, states are obligated, because they have promised only to fight wars as a last resort, to address the problem early with non-violent means. Attempting to prevent the necessity of war by using appropriate preventive or deterrent diplomatic, economic, political, and military measures is an obligation that is entailed by signing onto the constraint of last resort. As David Welch observes: "If national leaders were more attentive to the normative claims of others, and more circumspect about their own, they could better anticipate and manage conflicts, and in some cases, avoid them altogether."[30] While major means of attempting to avert war may be diplomatic, economic, and political, appropriate military deterrence or defensive military measures may also help prevent the outbreak of war so long as they are not provocative and do not reinforce the spiral of escalation. A show of force might be sufficient to deter governments from committing acts which might trigger full-scale war by signaling the political will to use force if necessary.

Third, last resort is not just an agreement we make with other countries. Signing on to the promise of last resort is also a promise to the people who might be called into military service in legitimate states: we will not send you (or your children) to war, unless it is (really) the last resort. In other words, "we will do what we can to avoid sending you (or your children) to war." A fiduciary or prescriptive realist might make a similar argument: states are bound by their obligation to protect their own citizens' well-being to try and resolve conflicts early, by less costly (in both blood and treasure) means than war. This promise to states' own citizens entails an obligation to pursue preventive diplomatic, political, economic, social, or military action to prevent the necessity of violent conflict.

If decision-makers fail to explore and exhaust the preventive possibilities, war may eventually become necessary, when it could have been prevented. In cases like this, decision-makers can claim that the war has become necessary, but they cannot claim that it is the last resort. A necessary war that might have been prevented fails the test of last resort, and it cannot be said to be a just war. In cases like this, the resort to force should still be taken, but we should acknowledge that it might not have been necessary to do so if earlier preventive action had been taken. A necessary war is a war that should be fought; but it is a misuse of the language to say that any necessary was is, by virtue of its having become necessary, a just war.

One strand of just war thinking holds that there is a "presumption against war." On this view, the presumption against war must be overridden by the necessity of fighting against something even worse than war. This school of thought is associated with the arguments of James Childress. Another school of thought, associated with the arguments of James Turner Johnson, holds that there is not a presumption against war, but a presumption against injustice. The injustice that constitutes the just cause for war is condemnable, but if force is required to correct the injustice, there is no presumption against resorting to force. On this view, when war satisfies the *jus ad bellum* criteria, we need not feel guilty about making the decision to resort to force.

I will not defend either of those views here, but I would like to add that fighting from necessity is not always the same as fighting as a last resort; so in my view, even necessary wars can be unjust. When deciding to fight a war that might have been prevented, decision-makers should do so "with a long face and as though [they] were ashamed of it."[31] The injustice is not in fighting a (really) necessary war; the injustice is in failing to have fully explored preventive possibilities, which might have resolved the conflict and prevented war from becoming necessary. To sum up, it is not the same thing to fight a war as a last resort as it is to fight a war that, although it has become necessary, perhaps could have been avoided if preventive diplomatic, political, economic or military tactics had been pursued.

One clarification is in order at this time. The agents in just war theory are both state-level actors as corporate bodies and individual-level actors as decision-makers. It should be noted that in the case of a war that could have been prevented, blame falls on the decision-makers who should have acted, but failed to act, to prevent escalation of conflict. If a President ignores a conflict and allows it to escalate, failing to take appropriate preventive action, and then a new President comes into power and prevention is no longer possible, that new decision-maker is not to be blamed for resorting to war now that it has become necessary; his predecessor is to be blamed for not taking action that might have prevented a foreseeable war. Nevertheless, the ultimate resort to war by the state should not be called "just," because preventive options were not attempted and exhausted.

The requirement that states effectively utilize early warning and engage in appropriate preventive diplomatic, economic, political, and military measures is also generated by the proportionality criterion. It is less costly by far to prevent than to fight a war. Early action is also entailed if we take the likelihood of success criterion seriously. Conflicts are much more likely to be successfully solved if pre-violent conflict resolution is attempted.[32] I have included preventive action here under last resort as well, because I think it is important to insist that the promise "we will not wage war unless it is the last resort" entails engaging in a comprehensive policy of early action toward prevention of violent conflict.

It is also true that there is an international consensus on this obligation. The "Responsibility to Protect," which was affirmed by all member states of the United Nations, incorporates the responsibility to prevent violent conflict. The 2005 United Nations "World Summit Outcome Document," unanimously affirmed by all United Nations Member States, sets out the international consensus affirming the duty to prevent violent conflict in this way:

> 74. We stress the importance of prevention of armed conflict in accordance with the purposes and principles of the Charter and solemnly renew our commitment to promote a culture of prevention of armed conflict as a means of effectively addressing the interconnected security and development challenges faced by peoples throughout the world, as well as to strengthen the capacity of the United Nations for the prevention of armed conflict.

> 75. We further stress the importance of a coherent and integrated approach to the prevention of armed conflicts and the settlement of disputes and the need for the Security Council, the General Assembly, the Economic and Social Council and the Secretary-General to coordinate their activities within their respective Charter mandates....

> 138. Each individual State has the responsibility to protect its populations from genocide, war crimes, ethnic cleansing and crimes against humanity. This responsibility entails the prevention of such crimes, including their

incitement, through appropriate and necessary means. We accept that responsibility and will act in accordance with it. The international community should, as appropriate, encourage and help States to exercise this responsibility and support the United Nations in establishing an early warning capability.

Decision-makers have access to multiple conflict early-warning indicators, but there is an apparently difficult-to-bridge gap between the existence of early warning indicators, analysis of such data, and the coordination of effective early responses, particularly complex multilateral responses.[33] This was very tragically illustrated in the Rwandan genocide, and it continues clearly to be a vexing problem for presently existing international institutions. To engage successfully in a comprehensive policy of early action and preventive diplomacy, states should improve their capacities to respond quickly to early warnings of developing conflict.

This view is slightly counter to Walzer's strong view on last resort in the case of humanitarian intervention. Although my view holds with Walzer's that force should be a last resort, it departs from Walzer's practical stance that foreigners must wait outside the borders until the killing has begun. My threshold is lower, at the Atrocity Standard (including persecution); but some scholars who accept Walzer's higher threshold of massive human rights abuses reject the idea that preventive intervention is unacceptable. Keohane and Buchanan put the argument for preventive intervention clearly:

> We begin with the assumption that it can be morally permissible to use force to stop presently occurring massive violations of basic human rights. We then argue from this assumption that there is at least *a prima facie* case for the moral permissibility of using force to prevent massive violations of basic human rights. The core justification for using force to stop rights violations as they are occurring – the need to protect basic human rights – can also justify the use of force to prevent rights violations.[34]

In the ICISS report, "the responsibility to prevent" is invoked in the case of genocide "actual or apprehended."[35] By "apprehended," the commission meant to convey that "you don't wait until it's happening, you see that it is on the way, and you go in with force."[36] Pre-emptive force to challenge the perpetrators on the ground may be justified; and if diplomacy is failing, it may satisfy last resort.

One possible objection to this line of argument is that pre-emptive force or preventive interference cannot be a last resort, because it is equivalent to righting a wrong that has not yet occurred.[37] I responded to this objection in Chapter 3 on just cause, but I re-state the objection here as it applies to last resort, and I would also add two more points. First, if it is permissible to wage war to stop massive human rights abuses, it is permissible to wage war to pre-empt them, as suggested by Keohane and Buchanan, above. Second, early warnings that a population is under threat of genocide generally entail persecution or rights deprivations that in themselves constitute just cause in my new formulation. If the stage is being set for massive human rights abuses such as genocide or ethnic cleansing, the state will likely commit other crimes against humanity in the process.

When a population is in danger of ethnic cleansing, the regime will likely be engaged in persecution, such as rounding up and arresting members of the group, denying some groups equal rights before the law, or denying other fundamental rights on prohibited grounds. It should be noted that in states like this, basic political and legal protections for free speech (particularly countervailing speech to the hate propaganda) are lacking; freedom of expression and assembly are denied.[38]

If a state is committing rights violations but not planning genocide, the state's repressive practices may still be a harbinger of violent rebellion and civil war. Government repression is a "very strong leading indicator" of rebellion, as are "increased political restrictions."[39] So we have reason to believe that influence, interference, or perhaps even a military strike (subject to all the other *jus ad bellum* restraints) to rectify these lesser offenses might prevent more destructive violence from breaking out.

Dehumanizing propaganda is highly correlated with violence. It is often present in advance of the outbreak of genocidal violence.[40] Certainly in the case of official dehumanization, such as the Hutu Power government-sponsored anti-Tutsi propaganda including the "Hutu Ten Commandments" and the violence-inciting hate broadcasts of Radio Mille Collines, outsiders would have been justified in attempting first to influence the Hutu-led government to change its behavior and thereby possibly to derail the processes of dehumanization and polarization that were precursors to the genocide.[41]

In my view, it is not true that because genocide is not yet in the execution stage, the government has not done anything that merits a military response. The international community is no longer required to wait at the borders for the killing to begin. If the international community is to fulfill its avowed responsibility to prevent, this re-conceptualization is required.

For example, in the case of the Rwandan genocide, it was clear to the UNAMIR Force Commander that genocide was imminent before the slaughter was underway. An informant had provided the location of a cache of machetes, and UNAMIR Force Commander, Gen. Romeo Dallaire, proposed a strike against the cache.[42] This would have been a use of force on a small scale that perhaps could have been sufficient to signal the international community's political will to prevent the *Interhamwe* attacks on civilians. I do not think that in a traditional state-against-state war, that we can say that preventive strikes avert war; they merely start the war. However, in the case of a civil war or genocide where intervention is contemplated to protect non-combatants, military measures that signal the intention of the intervening force to act may deter acts of genocide. On the other hand, such military measures may signal to committed *genocidaires* that they must accelerate their operations, so any show of force must be backed up by the capability, availability of resources, and political will to use that force.

Diplomacy backed by threat

The deterrent possibilities of "diplomacy backed by threat" in an environment where military intervention is permissible in the affairs of sovereign states should not be underestimated. Once the bar to non-intervention has been removed from genocidal killing to atrocity crimes including the widespread or systematic denial of fundamental rights on discriminatory grounds, it is possible for outsiders to challenge regimes with diplomacy backed by the threat of force over persecution (or even use force, as a last resort). The credible threat of force may act as a deterrent where lesser material interference such as sanctions fails. Persecution may be the groundwork for greater crimes like genocide, but with the new just cause framework these lesser crimes are grounds for influence, interference, and intervention. Preventive diplomacy may be more likely to succeed, and just resolutions may be achieved more easily, when the parties believe that the international community will otherwise intervene with force to stop atrocity crimes.

A possible objection to whether this is a good thing is that "victims" might manipulate the circumstances to appear in need of "rescue," when they are really seeking a different goal. I have mentioned this in Chapter 3, with reference to Kuperman's and Crawford's moral hazard objection. The point I wish to make here is that bringing mediation to bear early in a situation that might otherwise escalate into violent conflict is better, even if the international community is manipulated into providing mediation, than being manipulated into a military intervention later.

I disagree with Walzer on the exception he makes to the requirement of last resort in the case of reprisals. I treat what Walzer calls reprisals under the just cause category of defensive interventions into sovereign states that either cannot or will not control the activities within their borders that threaten other states. The last resort criterion applies to defensive interventions just as to any other resort to force. Last resort would act as a lever to inspire negotiations between the two parties if it were, as Walzer says, "taken seriously."

Last resort does not require decision-makers to postpone military action to the benefit of a party that will not negotiate in good faith. Negotiation is not meant to allow one party to forestall war while he makes increased preparations for war; it is meant to prevent war from becoming necessary. For example, "many have argued Britain's policy of appeasement in the 1930s did more to undermine than it did to secure peace. ... By risking a little war, a great war may have been avoided."[43]

To summarize, in my view, signing on to the idea of last resort requires that when early warning indicators show that violent conflict is likely on the horizon, early action should be taken to prevent the resort to war from becoming necessary. For a war to be properly called a last resort, preventive possibilities must have been actually exhausted or set aside as unlikely to succeed, disproportionate, or indiscriminate. Getting to last resort is not easy, as Walzer says in his stronger version of last resort. It requires that decision-makers evaluate and respond to early warning signals, when this is possible, in order to prevent war from becoming necessary. If war becomes necessary in spite of reasonable efforts at early action and prevention, then (and only then) decision-makers can claim that war is the last resort.

Post-9/11 arguments

Some scholars argue that last resort is an unduly restrictive, even a dangerous restraint, and that because of changes that they see in the world, particularly since the attacks of September 11, 2001, preventive war is now permissible. For example, Henry Alan Stephenson argues in defense of the 2002 *National Security Strategy of the United States* that in the current threat environment, last resort should be jettisoned as a category of restraint. Preventive war is necessary, and it should not be ruled out by last resort. Weapons of mass destruction, rogue states, and terrorist threats have rendered the last resort rule out-of-date. Stephenson thinks that just war theory should be updated to reflect the current threat environment, and last resort should be done away with as irrelevant to our times, and dangerous.[44] Stephenson is not talking about reprisals; he is advocating preventive war as a just cause, made necessary by a fundamental change in the nature of the threat faced by the United States.

In response to the idea that last resort ought to be cast aside by virtue of the new threat environment,[45] and preventive war thereby allowed as a just cause for war, Jeff McMahan writes:

> justifications for preventive war as they are actually asserted tend to be overly permissive in their implications ... when the Bush administration sought to justify the second Iraq war ... it appealed primarily to three claims: that Iraq possessed weapons of mass destruction, that it had a recent history of aggressive war, and that it had indulged in bellicose rhetoric directed against the USA. But ... all of these claims were also true, *mutatis mutandis*, of the USA itself, with the Bush administration particularly noisy in issuing threats against Iraq, Iran, and North Korea. But no one in the administration would have conceded that any of these countries had a right to attack the USA in preventive self-defense.[46]

Jus in bello *implications of last resort*

Peter S. Temes argues that we should do away with the criterion of last resort because:

> What nations do instead of war – blockades, propaganda campaigns, and restrictions on trade – often accrue terrible harm for the weakest among an enemy nation's civilians while leaving the military and political leadership intact. Thus they enact precisely the reverse of the discrimination principle.[47]

Temes is right insofar as sanctions that target civilians as a means to a political end are immoral because they violate the principle of non-combatant immunity. However, much progress has been made on designing "smart" sanctions, which target only the relevant military and political apparatus.[48] We should scrutinize our attempts to influence and interfere through the same *jus ad bellum* and *jus in bello* lenses; decision-makers should ask whether a particular preventive strategy of material interference is proportionate, likely to succeed, and whether it is indiscriminate. If sanctions aim at harming civilians, in the hope that civilian suffering will bring government capitulation, these violate the principle of non-combatant immunity; they are indiscriminate. Temes' argument then, should remind us that we should apply the *jus ad bellum* and *jus in bello* constraints to material interference short of military intervention. There is no need, however, to eliminate the category of last resort as Temes suggests.

Although sanctions that use civilian suffering as a means to a political end violate the principle of non-combatant immunity, sanctions that aim to target military capability or the political leadership of the target state, but cause civilian suffering as a side-effect, might be rescued by the doctrine of double effect. If the sanctions are intended to restrict economic, social, and military opportunities for the leadership of the state, and the sanctions do not use civilian suffering as a means to compel the leadership to submit, it seems to me that the doctrine of double effect might credibly be invoked. Furthermore, the non-combatants may support the sanctions, in spite of the hardship caused. Nevertheless, care should be taken to minimize civilian suffering, and civilian suffering may not be used as a means to achieve the political goal.

Sanctions in South Africa, including an arms/oil embargo and social sanctions (such as barring South Africa from international sporting events), diminished foreign investor confidence and national self-esteem; and the financial impact on blacks and coloreds was not as significant as opponents of the sanctions thought it might be.[49] Temes' criticism points to the necessity of targeting sanctions, but his conclusion that last resort should be abandoned is not convincing. Sanctions can work, and when they are targeted at the ruling segment of the society and supported by the persecuted population as was the case in South Africa, it is hard to call them immoral.

Likelihood of success

Walzer's view

Walzer does not specifically discuss likelihood of success in *Just and Unjust Wars* as a category of restraint. He does imply that likelihood of success is not an important consideration in wars of self-defense:

> The wrong the aggressor commits is to force men and women to risk their lives for the sake of their rights.... Groups of citizens respond in different ways to that choice, sometimes surrendering, sometimes fighting, depending

on the moral and material conditions of their state and army. But they are always justified in fighting; and in most cases, given that harsh choice, fighting is the preferred moral outcome.[50]

Walzer mentions likelihood of success in *jus in bello*, briefly, when he talks about the responsibility of commanders in particular battles: lives may not be wasted. Generally, however, owing to his focus on defensive wars (and the justice he ascribes to all defensive wars); likelihood of success is not an important element of Walzer's arguments in *Just and Unjust Wars*.

Historical views on likelihood of success

"Suarez and Grotius both required that a reasonable hope of success precede the launching of an offensive war. For Suarez, a fifty-fifty chance of victory was sufficient.... [He] specifically denied that reasonable hope applied to defensive wars."[51] Grotius maintained that if a defensive war is likely to be lost, surrender is preferable to fighting. The likelihood of success rule held for Grotius in wars of national self-defense as well as for all other just causes. Grotius expressed the rule on national self-defense this way:

> It is often a duty which we owe to our country and ourselves to forbear having recourse to arms. After the college of heralds had pronounced a war to be just, we are informed by Plutarch in the life of Numa, that the senate further deliberated whether it was expedient to undertake it. According to our savior's beautiful and instructive parable, a king, when he is obligated to go to war with another king, should first sit down (an expression implying an act of deliberation) and consider, within himself, whether with 10,000 men he is able to encounter one who is coming with twenty times that number; and if he finds himself unequal to the contest, before the enemy has entered his territories he will send an embassy to him offering terms of peace.[52]

On the question of whether the justice of the cause has a bearing on likelihood of success, Grotius (but not Suarez or Gentili) thought so:

> In so far as concerns the actual outcome in a majority of cases, it is permissible to assert that God customarily interposes His judgment in the fortunes of war in such a way that success falls not infrequently on the side where right also lies.[53]

Vitoria thought that it was unlikely that wars to spread Christianity would be successful, because "war, with its massacres and pillage, could obstruct the conversion of the barbarians rather than encourage it."[54] Wars to spread values and practices held to be universally desirable might actually obstruct the spread of those values and practices.

Likelihood of success is expressed in terms very close to proportionality. Success is defined as creating a net gain in justice. To lose a war waged for a just cause is to create a net loss in justice, because the just end sought is not achieved, and loss of life and other destruction is caused in the effort. Therefore, if a war is not likely to be won, it ought not to be waged, even for a just cause. An outcome with greater evil than good effects would not satisfy proportionality, so if it was not likely to succeed, commencing such a war would be disproportionate.[55] In this way, likelihood of success and proportionality are inextricable. A war that is not likely to succeed cannot be proportionate (because it will not achieve its objective, and it will cause damage along the way.)

Comprehensive view on likelihood of success

Likelihood of success means that the actor must be able to reasonably hope to prevail and to end the war with a just peace, while still observing the rules of war (complying with *jus in bello*). This rule has meaning and restraining effect similar to the restraining effect of proportionality and right intention, insofar as those rules also require that a war that cannot likely be won by fighting justly ought not to be commenced. Prior to commencing hostilities, the actor should have reason to believe that the outcome he seeks, the institution of a just peace and the remediation of the just cause, is reasonably likely. This is a well-accepted understanding of the category's meaning. I endorse that view; and following Grotius, but departing from Walzer, I insist that likelihood of success, like all the *jus ad bellum* criteria, applies to both defensive and offensive wars. In the case of a war of national self-defense, the likelihood of success criterion is less forceful when the proportionality considerations are very high – that is when the consequences of loss would be catastrophic; the likelihood of success hurdle is lower. When the consequences of loss would not be catastrophic, the likelihood of success hurdle is higher. When facing a genocidal aggressor, a state (or a rebel movement) does not need to meet the criterion of likelihood of success to justify resisting. Conversely, suicidal rebellions are ruled out by the likelihood of success criterion, except in the case of rebellion against a genocidal regime.

Suicidal self-defense, as in the case of Melos, presents a just cause, but this does not mean that a defensive war is clearly justified according to the comprehensive framework (as opposed to the Walzer's view, which finds all wars of self-defense to be just). The Melians' decision to fight the Athenians was unlikely to succeed, at least. We do not have to say that the Melians' decision to fight rather than to surrender was completely and clearly just or unjust, but we can say, more helpfully, that a just cause was present, but the other restraints were not clearly satisfied. The richer version of just war theory gives us more tools for our inquiry, and more to talk about. We can certainly say that likelihood of success was not met. Last resort was not necessarily met; the Melians tried to negotiate a peace, but did not try to negotiate a surrender that might have been preferable to being slaughtered. The comprehensive framework accords more closely than Walzer's view with our intuitions that sometimes a defensive war ought not to be fought. My point here is to illustrate that both the content of the debate and also the conclusions are significantly changed by requiring likelihood of success in defensive wars.

I would add one innovation to the view summarized above. Taking likelihood of success seriously means that decision-makers are required to carefully evaluate the likelihood of success that different tactics might have in rectifying the just cause. Actors should tailor their tactics to best meet the ends sought. By best, I mean "effectively and with the least possible damaging effects"; the imperative is to find the appropriate tool for the job. We do not want to "use a sledgehammer to kill a fly on someone's head when a flyswatter is handy,"[56] but putting flypaper in the next room is unlikely to be efficient, too. In other words, before commencing influence, interference, or intervention, actors should discern what tactics are most likely to be successful at rectifying the just cause and should plan to fight (or use another tactic) in line with that guidance. Simply having the greater force capacity on one's side does not make one likely to succeed; one must have a plan of action that is likely to achieve remediation of the just cause.

To calculate likelihood of success, actors must have an idea of how the tactics they plan to use will achieve the ends they seek. Force is not always the best choice. Some just causes, like genocide and ethnic cleansing, can only be countered successfully by challenging the perpetrators on the ground with force.[57]

Other just causes, such as persecution of women in the form of genital mutilation, honor killing, and widow immolation, can best be addressed with material interference other than military force, e.g. supporting local NGOs financially. As I just noted in the previous section, Vitoria thought that it was unlikely that wars to spread Christianity would be successful, because "war, with its massacres and pillage, could obstruct the conversion of the barbarians rather than encourage it."[58] Wars to spread respect for human rights and to discourage harmful traditional social practices might also tend to obstruct rather than assist a campaign for human rights. Just causes like these, unlike genocide and ethnic cleansing, can be addressed with international persuasion and providing incentives for governments to increase their populations' compliance – the prize being admission to the "club of civilized nations," or sometimes more material rewards such as trade, aid, or removal of sanctions.

Whatever the tactic identified, it is more likely to succeed the earlier it is begun. Conflicts are more likely to be successfully resolved with minimum cost when preventive diplomacy is undertaken early, because generally:

> The issues in dispute are fewer and less complex; the conflicting parties are not highly mobilized, polarized, and armed; significant bloodshed has not occurred, and thus a sense of victimization and a desire for vengeance are not intense; the parties have not begun to dehumanize and stereotype each other; moderate leaders still maintain control over extremist tendencies, and the parties are not so committed that compromise involves massive loss of face. This and emerging case study research provide strong prima facie evi-

dence that pre-violent conflict conditions may be more fundamentally tractable.[59]

Preventive diplomacy is more likely to succeed at lower cost if it is commenced early, if possible before dehumanizing propaganda begins to circulate, as Lund suggests, but no later. We can have an idea of what type of interference is best suited to rectifying particular just causes by looking back at what has worked and what has not worked in previous similar cases.[60] The crucial point I wish to make is that before resorting to war, decision-makers must be able to say that the tactics they intend to employ are likely to rectify the just cause. In most expressions of just war theory, likelihood of success is not specified quite in this way; success is often defined as victory in war or as overpowering the target state, after which time presumably a settlement will be made on the just cause. My view is that we must only define "success" in terms of rectifying the just cause. A determination of likelihood of success involves a careful consideration of the tactics to be used in order to remedy the just cause. We cannot simply aim to overpower the adversary by whatever means available, then hope to rectify the just cause as part of the post-war settlement. A good illustration of the difference is NATO's "Operation Allied Force" (the 1999 NATO air-war to prevent ethnic cleansing in Kosovo), about which I will say more in the next chapter.

Strong states imposing liberalism by force?

I argued in Chapter 3 that there is just cause for military intervention in a case where some part of a state's population is denied basic human rights or the exercise of some basic capabilities. In a case like this, the degree of local affirmation of the values for which an intervener would fight has a great deal of force in calculations about likelihood of success. If a tyrannical regime is denying basic human rights to some persons against the wishes of the majority of the population, deposing the regime by force and then holding elections may be likely to succeed in rectifying the just cause – the denial of basic human rights, in this case, would be renounced by the majority of the population. However, if the majority of the local population accepts the practices of the regime as legitimate, the tactic of deposing the regime by force and then holding elections will be unlikely to succeed in securing a just peace (and protecting human rights). Alternatively, maybe a majority group is oppressed by a tiny minority, and an intervention would give control back to the people who have been oppressed, perhaps leaving the former ruling group vulnerable to revenge. In both types of cases, deposing a dictator and holding elections is fraught with peril because the majority of people might support official oppression of some other set of persons.

Holding elections too early can crystallize and give the appearance of legitimacy to the status quo. Holding elections where conditions on the ground will not permit them to be held fairly, where election rigging is likely, may also lead to worsening, rather than improvement, in stability and legitimacy for the new government.

A different tactic for encouraging respect for human rights must be found, if deposing the regime and holding elections is unlikely to succeed. We do not have to assume a bogus right of a community to oppress some of its members, or of the sovereign state to be the final arbiter of its internal affairs; the reason not to try and institute human rights reforms by force (where the majority will *not* support the reforms) is because the tactic is unlikely to succeed. If the majority of people will support reforms and will create a constitution that equally respects the human rights of all its members, the tactic of deposing a despotic regime might be likely to succeed in restoring justice. Likelihood of success requires consideration of these issues. Perhaps the tactics will have to include addressing issues normally understood as *jus post bellum* questions; the institution of a just peace might require post-conflict international trusteeship, oversight, and occupation for many years, as is the case in Bosnia and Herzegovina, Kosovo, Afghanistan, and Iraq. Although the scope of cases in which Walzer would find intervention permissible is narrow, he has begun to argue that "standing occupations" may be necessary in the case of failed states.[61,62]

The criterion of likelihood of success, like the proportionality restraint, has generally meant that it is more permissible (subject to all the other *jus ad bellum* restraints) to wage war against weak states than against strong states. Therefore, it is not surprising that small states have so jealously guarded the non-intervention norm. No matter how just the cause, an offensive war against Russia, China, the United States, or a similarly strong power would very likely be ruled out as disproportionate and unlikely to succeed. This has not necessarily been so in the case of wars against smaller, less well-armed states. Recent history, however, puts this generally accepted maxim into some question. Given the potential ferocity of insurgent forces, even small and "weak" states present a high hurdle for likelihood of success.

Proportionality

Walzer's view

Proportionality is the accommodation for prudence within the argument for justice, and Walzer thinks it is a rather blunt tool.[63] Aside from the obvious cases, for example, "it was appropriate that the United States did not threaten atomic war in 1956 when the Soviet Union 'intervened in Hungary' the second time," Walzer doubts the usefulness of *jus ad bellum* proportionality calculations. In some cases, however, we cannot tell in advance whether a particular resort to war will actually work out to be proportionate, and we cannot tell afterward whether it was, either. Walzer is not explicitly discussing proportionality, but he writes:

> If some powerful state or regional alliance had rushed troops into Rwanda when the massacres first began or as soon as their scope was apparent, the massacre, the exodus, and the cholera plague might have been avoided. But

the troops would still be there, probably, and no one would know what hadn't happened.[64]

Although he does not spend much time on proportionality as a *jus ad bellum* category, Walzer does say a few things about it. He conceptualizes proportionality as a sliding scale. If the gravity of the just cause is extreme, the justifiable cost can be very high. If the harm being caused by the injustice is slight, then it would be unjust to wage war when the foreseeable costs of the war would be high, except in the case of national self-defense, which Walzer thinks can never be forbidden by proportionality concerns. Walzer finds that this criterion is so difficult to use that it is nearly useless in *jus ad bellum*. In practice, Walzer thinks that it is hard to violate the principle of proportionality in ways that are clearly evident, because "the values against which suffering and destruction are measured are so readily inflated."[65]

Walzer is referring to the *jus in bello* understanding of proportionality when he writes: "Proportionality is a matter of adjusting means to ends."[66] Walzer gives an example of a clear violation of proportionality with this quotation from an American officer, referring to the town of Ben Tre in Vietnam: "We had to destroy the town in order to save it."[67] This of course refers to micro-proportionality, a particular war crime rather than the war itself; but it can be extrapolated to refer to the macro-question. If a country will be destroyed in the process of being "saved," Walzer would likely say that this can hardly be called proportionate.

Historical view on proportionality

Aquinas' just war doctrine allows for humanitarian intervention to rescue a people suffering under a tyrant, but not "if it produces such disorder that the society under the tyrant suffers greater harm from the resulting disturbance than from the tyrant's rule."[68]

For Grotius, the just cause must be *of sufficient importance* to warrant its defense by armed force. There are causes which are just, but which are not of sufficient importance to warrant their defense by armed force. The question of importance is a question of proportionality and prudence rather than whether the cause is just. It is possible to have many just causes and few occasions of just recourse to war. The benefit to justice gained by the defense of the just cause must be outweighed by the foreseeable harm caused by fighting the war. Whether a cause is weighty enough to merit defense is a judgment we make based on "an imaginative, anticipatory comparison of the harm caused by unchecked evil with the damage resulting from the effort to check or punish that evil."[69] Such comparisons are much easier to make in retrospect; despite the difficulty of making anticipatory judgments, Grotius insists we engage in this type of exercise and thereby avoid imprudently or rashly resorting to war. Proportionality, even when the cause is just, is a strong brake on the resort to war. In cases where the just cause to be addressed cannot be rectified without inviting disproportionate harm to either side or to innocent third parties, war must be foregone. It is better in these cases, Grotius writes, to "yield our right rather than enforce it."[70] Grotius goes on to say that when facing enslavement but having no prospects of success, it is better to surrender and be enslaved than to fight and to be destroyed. Likelihood of success and proportionality are inextricable: an outcome with greater evil than good effects would not be proportionate, so if we can foresee that it is not likely to succeed, commencing war would be disproportionate as well.[71]

Comprehensive view on proportionality

Although Walzer is right that proportionality is difficult to determine in advance and even in retrospect, we are still obligated to use our best efforts to engage in the anticipatory reflections required by Grotius. I endorse Grotius' view and extend it by adding an emphasis on prevention.

As Walzer noted (above) regarding a hypothetical Rwandan intervention, success of preventive measures is difficult to determine; we cannot be sure precisely how much these efforts would have really helped, because that would require measuring things that did not occur. Taking proportionality seriously suggests that decision-makers should take the most cost effective route to remedying the just cause. We know that prevention, where it works, is always less costly than fighting, so taking proportionality seriously requires that we take preventive measures where possible. Because the just cause criterion has been expanded in my view, outsiders have a right of interference in matters that were (under Walzer's understanding of just cause) thought to be strictly internal affairs. The impact of this re-statement of the non-intervention rule, in practical terms, is that outsiders are permitted under the new rule to interfere (and if necessary, intervene) earlier. "Earlier" often translates to "more proportionately," with a lower cost/benefit ratio, especially if armed conflict may be averted altogether by root cause or immediate prevention.[72]

However:

> Very often, those with the means to act prefer to play the odds, sometimes betting that the situation will somehow resolve itself, or that it will simmer without reaching a boil, or that the resulting conflict will prove less dire than predicted, or that conflict if it does break out can be quickly contained. The result, according to the Carnegie Commission on Preventing Violent Conflict, was that the international community spent approximately $200 billion on conflict management in seven major interventions in the 1990s (Bosnia and Herzegovina, Somalia, Rwanda, Haiti, the Persian Gulf, Cambodia, and El Salvador) but could have saved $130 billion through a more preventive approach.[73]

The number of excess deaths is not indicated in the report, but one could hypothesize using counter-factual reasoning in a similar way that Brown and Rosecrance calculated the amount of money that could have been saved by the international community (excess costs to states involved in the conflict were not calculated).[74] As I argued regarding last resort, signing on to the constraints, including proportionality, generates positive obligations on the part of states to participate in developing an international system of rules, norms, and institutions where preventive action can become automatic, rather than ad hoc. Proportionality then, as well as last resort, requires an effort to be made early at resolving conflicts. As Thomas Hurka observes:

> Imagine that a war will achieve certain goods at not too great a cost, but that the same goods could be achieved by diplomacy. Here the war may not be disproportionate in itself, but it is disproportionate compared to the alternative, since it causes additional destruction for no additional benefit.[75]

I would add to Hurka's point that if preventive diplomacy were still possible, the resort to force contemplated in the quotation above would also not meet the criterion of last resort.

When prevention fails, decision-makers must make counter-factual calculations using past conflicts as a guide. We can look to past conflicts to help us estimate harms likely to occur as a result of intervention, and compare that analysis to our best estimates of harm likely to occur if force is forgone.[76] Proportionality is difficult to calculate in advance, but once we have signed on to accepting the guidance of just war principles, we are obliged to try. Decision-makers can use counter-factual analysis to estimate costs. Using past conflicts as a guide, decision-makers can construct an educated range of estimates. The difficulty of this process should give decision-makers pause; there are many unknowable variables, and a wide margin of error is inherent in counter-factual analysis. When the consequences of not fighting are minor, there is no right to make war (even where there is a just cause, like self-defense.) The unknown consequences of a resort to war are always a weighty obstacle. When the consequences of not fighting, or of fighting and losing, are likely to be catastrophic, the weight of those consequences may overcome the gravity of the knowable and the unknowable (but possibly imaginable) dangers of war. Analysis may sometimes lead to relatively clear-cut answers, while sometimes information may not be available as easily. The most crucial point here is that decision-makers are obligated to seek and utilize information, and attempt to calculate the likely harm to be caused by material interference or armed conflict vs. the good of rectifying the just cause.

Benefits expected, or positive outcomes to be included in proportionality calculations, may only include the immediate benefits of rectifying the just cause. Side benefits such as access to oil, or anything at all other than what is directly linked to remedying the just cause of the war, may not be permissibly included in the proportionality calculation. As Jefferson McMahan explains:

> If just cause indicates the range of goods that may permissibly be pursued by war, then no goods that fail to come within the scope of the just cause, or

are instrumental to achieving it, can count in the proportionality calculation. If they did, that would imply that a war is justified, at least in part, by the fact that it would achieve certain goods that cannot permissibly be achieved by means of war.[77]

Calculable costs include proximate and long-term costs in lives saved or lost, environmental damage, financial cost of fighting, and damage to property. A comparison is required between the expected costs of resorting to war and the foreseeable harms that will develop if resort to war is foregone. These questions include the same calculations mentioned above, and we should also include opportunity costs (insofar as they are associated only with failing to rectify the just cause).[78] The costs of non-intervention can be very significant, as discussed above; in fact, the costs of non-intervention must be more significant than the costs of intervention for the proportionality criterion to be satisfied.

It is not only the harm that would be caused by entering a war that must be considered when we think of proportionality. We must compare that estimate with the estimate of the harm that will likely occur if military force is not brought to bear. For example, in the case of a civil war "aiding an insurgency that would win a civil war without outside assistance seems somewhat redundant, unless outside intervention will end the war quickly and thus reduce overall suffering."[79] Decision-makers have access to information from which they can extrapolate. Organizations such as the Carnegie Commission, OSCE, the Fund for Peace, Amnesty International, Human Rights Watch, Genocide Watch, and many others are engaged in monitoring, early warning, and analysis, gathering data that decision-makers are obligated to weigh. Sometimes analysis will lead to more compelling answers than other times.

So, we "aim to compare the war and its effects to what the world would have been like had the war not occurred, i.e. to a counterfactual situation."[80] How can this be done? This is a difficult tool to employ with precision. But, as Tetlock and Belkin argue about social scientists who warn against the "methodological rat hole" of counter-factual analysis, Walzer is wrong to imagine that just war theorists can abandon our attempts to specify proportionality at an acceptable cost.[81] Some situations are more easily understood than others. There are many methods of forecasting possible futures, and a review of all the methods by which analysts might forecast various scenarios is beyond the scope of this book.[82] I only wish to say that such forecasting is morally required, even though doing so is sometimes very difficult. In some cases the results may provide clear-cut guidance, and in other cases they may not, but the analysis would at least have been helpful in the first instance.

Jefferson McMahan and Robert McKim argue that proportionality considerations do not require counter-factual analysis. They offer the following thought experiment in support of their claim:

> [A] child is in the path of a speeding truck. A passerby snatches the child out of the way. It is not necessary to know what would have happened had

the passerby not acted in order to know that she saved the child. Indeed, suppose that someone else would have snatched the child out of the way if the passerby had not. It remains true that the passerby saved the child – that her act prevented the death – even though it is not true that the child would have been killed if she had not acted, since in that case another cause would have operated to produce the same effect.[83]

David Mellow (correctly, in my view) points out that the example given by McMahan and McKim does not sufficiently account for the complexities, difficulties, and unknowns that are likely in war. It is very unlikely that any war, even the quickest and clearest-cut, could be fought in a way that is analogous to the example above. Mellow gives a counter-example in which the passerby can save the child, but in so doing will injure an innocent bystander. This example is more closely analogous to what is likely in a military confrontation. Mellow argues that in this case the passerby must look to see whether someone else might be able to save the child without harming the innocent bystander.[84] I would add that usually passersby do not just suddenly happen upon a situation analogous to the one above. More often, the bystanders wait, seeing the child in the road and hoping she will move, or the truck will stop, and perhaps do something themselves prior to the truck's imminent collision with the child. I would argue that the best thing to do, if possible, would be to stop or detour the truck while it is still far away from the child, or move the child out of the way early, thereby preventing the dangerous last minute maneuvering. If the bystanders suddenly came upon the situation, they might have to take emergency action, but emergency ethics do not make good general principles. In any case a counter-factual comparison between taking action and not taking action must take place, and McMahan and McKim's dismissal of the need for counter-factuals is not convincing.

We also will want to think about long-term as well as proximate or near-term proportionality.[85] *Jus post bellum* is an important consideration in determining whether to get into a war; can it be gotten out of, once in?

Another question to consider regarding long-term proportionality is whether widespread acceptance of the threshold for AHI I have proposed might be likely to promote self-interested interventions[86] behind false claims of humanitarianism, or whether the existence of such a norm would deter governments from committing atrocity crimes.

Let us assume for the moment that the effect of widespread acceptance of AHI to stop atrocity crimes would deter future would-be dictators (and would also signal contemporary dictators to "shape up") by signaling that impunity for atrocity crimes no longer can be assumed. In a post-AHI just peace, perpetrators would face justice for their crimes, and they would not be able to keep their ill-gotten gains.[87] I cannot prove that this would provide a deterrent effect, but for the purpose of the argument, let us assume that it would provide a strong deterrent effect. The next question to consider is whether it might be appropriate to include this long-term benefit of deterrence against human rights abuse in proportionality calculations for particular cases.

If the AHIs are in themselves proportionate without using this extra bit of weight in the proportionality category, the prospective benefit of future deterrence is pleasing. However, it would certainly not be acceptable to say that deterrence is a sufficient element that can permissibly be counted in the determination of whether a contemplated AHI meets the proportionality standard. We cannot count the hoped-for benefit to others in our proportionality calculations. The act of resorting to AHI must be a moral act on its own merits, and the proportionality calculations may only include harm and benefit to the parties in the conflict. Otherwise, it would be possible to justify an AHI that could cause more harm to than good to the people the AHI was supposed to help. We cannot resort to a war that would otherwise be unjust in order to prevent some possible future immoral act in another country from occurring. Ramsey teaches us "it is never right to do wrong that good may come of it."[88] If it is wrong to resort to this particular war on its own merits, we may not resort to it for the sake of its possible deterrent effect later. Therefore, the hoped-for deterrent effect of the AHI should not be calculated under proportionality benefits, of goods to be expected from the war. We cannot really be sure of this effect, first of all; but even if we could, we can only count the direct benefits of rectifying the just cause. This is because the costs and benefits calculated can only rightly be those accrued to the parties in the conflict. The benefits of deterring future tyrants would accrue to other people insofar as they might not be oppressed by future tyrants.

I argued in Chapter 4 that acceptance of the Atrocity Standard would not increase the number of self-interested interventions. However, even if I am wrong and the objection from descriptive realism is true, that wider, future effect would not count against a particular instance of justified AHI under the proportionality rubric (for the same reasons that the value of the deterrent effect would not be counted.)

Proportionality calculations are only as good as the intelligence informing them. In other words, if one affirms that decisions about resorting to war ought to be guided by considerations of proportionality and likelihood of success, it should follow that one also affirms that accurate intelligence must be gathered and used to inform those calculations. Transparency of modern communications, NGOs on the ground, and international monitors, as well as old-fashioned spies, are all sources of information. There is a moral imperative to collect, evaluate, analyze, and respond to information (within the bounds of respect for the fundamental rights of persons.)

Proportionality also requires responding to early warnings; addressing conflicts early is less costly than waiting. And then, even though it is difficult, decision-makers must have the best possible knowledge of actually existing conditions as a baseline from which to extrapolate what might be expected in alternative possible futures.

In the best possible case, proportionality and likelihood of success are still estimates. Prudence and morality dictate that they must be the best-informed estimates we can manage. If we do not gather sufficient intelligence and then simultaneously claim that we have calculated proportionality and likelihood of success, we are making a false claim. If we fail to collect intelligence, and then refuse to become involved because we have no information, that is not compatible with our assertion that we affirm just war principles. We would be acting as though we affirmed principles of isolationism. We know that we have the obligation to be aware of what is happening on the ground, because we have signed on to proportionality and likelihood of success (and last resort). We cannot fulfill our responsibilities without early and adequate information, collected and analyzed in a systematic and proactive way, and then acted upon by decision-makers. If intelligence estimates or analysis suggest that the resort to war will result in more harm than good, the resort to war fails the proportionality test. If decision-makers ignore this analysis or intelligence and decide to commence a war in spite of this failure, the decision cannot be called just in my formulation of the theory, even in cases of self-defense.

Jus in bello *concerns in proportionality*

If a war cannot be won by fighting within the rules, it weighs so heavily on the negative side of proportionality that it might be true that such a war ought never to be fought. Walzer argues that in the face of a sufficiently weighty just cause, the rules of war may be legitimately cast aside. Walzer calls this the supreme emergency exemption. This exemption is contested in the literature. If we can do anything when threatened with annihilation, and the rules of war can be set aside, Daniel Bell argues that Walzer ends up with another version "of the realism he seeks to avoid."[89]

The question of whether the rules of war can be set aside for the sake of a sufficiently weighty just cause is beyond the scope of this book. For the purposes of this project, I assume that *jus in bello* requires adherence to international humanitarian law and in particular, my view insists that the Atrocity Standard may not be breached. Whether a sufficiently weighty just cause might sometimes be rightly considered a supreme emergency, during which non-combatants may be targeted and terrorism and torture might be justified, is a complex question. The scope of this book will not permit a thorough and satisfying exploration of the many complicated arguments on both sides. International humanitarian law is clear that none of these practices are permitted, and I will not argue against that here. The question of supreme emergency constitutes an extreme and rare case, in contrast to the more frequent cases of possible AHI. I am not dismissing the question of supreme emergency by not addressing it here; however, the question is so deeply complex and difficult that a sufficient treatment of it would require a substantially broader project.

Right intention

Walzer's view on right intention

Walzer writes of intention as though it is synonymous with motive; I will argue below that they are not synonymous. Walzer has little to say on right intention as a *jus ad bellum* category. However, he emphasizes that the frequent criticism of right intention – that it is impossible to know what a state's real intentions (motives) are – is overblown. It is possible to discern some indication of a state's real intentions with careful analysis, although not perfectly, for these are "matters of evidence." It is a different thing to say that outsiders might not know the complete truth about intentions than it is to say that we cannot know anything at all. Motives are going to be mixed.[90] As Johnson observes: "A pure good will is a political illusion," but "we can expose the hypocrisy of soldiers and statesmen who publicly acknowledge these commitments [to justice] while seeking in fact only their own advantage."[91] It is easier to discern post hoc, although there may be some value in historians rendering judgment and as a guide to future action.

Historical view on right intention

For Aquinas, the only right intention in war is to seek a just peace, especially with the current enemy. Holding with Augustine, who wrote that the evils in war were of the spirit – the spirit of vengefulness, the implacable cruelty, and lust for power – "The canonist Raymond of Penafort (*c*.1175–1275), an older contemporary of Thomas Aquinas, wrote 'the intention must include no hatred, vengefulness, nor cupidity and must be to obtain justice.' "[92] However, later theorists, Suarez and Grotius among them, both held that an impure motive does not detract from the justice of war. A just war could spring from hatred; a leader may legitimately respond to a just cause with self-serving motives. His motives, however, are distinct from the just cause.[93] The hateful roots need not detract from the justice of the war, as long as the war is conducted in accordance with the rules of war so as not to diminish the chances for a just peace later, and so that actions taken during the war contribute to restoring justice.

Grotius writes:

> Note that this often happens: a just cause for war indeed exists, but a vice arises in the action because of the spirit (*animo*) of the agent. This can occur in two ways: (1) something else, not illicit in itself, moves the spirit to a greater degree and more efficiently than right (*jus*) itself, for example, the desire for honor or some utility, or (2) there may be present a manifestly illicit spirit, like the delight of one who gains satisfaction from another's ill without respect to what is good. ... But these, where a just cause is not lacking, do indeed make clear the existence of sin. Nevertheless they do not render the war itself, properly speaking, unjust.[94]

I should emphasize here that the grounds for continuing the war must be just, along with the grounds for having started the war; once the just cause has been rectified, the war must cease, in order to satisfy the right intention criterion. In other words, the right intention is to reach a just peace, and to rectify the just cause. Once the just cause has been met, the permissible intention of the fighting is exhausted, and fighting should cease, to make way for just peace. At this point that it will become clear whether the just cause was proclaimed with the right intention, or as a cover for a self-interested intention that diverges from justice.

Samuel Pufendorf (d. 1694) is in agreement with Grotius, Vitoria, and Vattel as to the permissibility of humanitarian intervention in limited circumstances. However, hoping to overcome the theoretical difficulty posed by the likelihood of rulers to undertake wars for self-interested purposes, Pufendorf and Vattel (unlike Vitoria and Grotius) restrictively insist that the victims of the oppression must invite the assistance: "Otherwise any man might make war upon any man upon such a pretense."[95] The motive for the intervener might be self-interested, but if the actions of the intervener are in line with just cause, right intention is satisfied.

The comprehensive view on right intention

I will make three points in this section. First, intention is different than motive.[96] Motive is generally some good that the agent seeks for itself. Second, motive is not necessarily relevant to right intention; that is, an actor may have a bad motive, but if the actor's intention is only to do actions consistent with restoring a just peace, the criterion of right intention is met. In other words, the intention of the intervener must be limited to restoring justice; but his motive may be self-interested.[97] If the actor will gain side benefits by restoring justice, and those side benefits motivate the actor, this is permissible, as long as the actions taken are limited to remedying the just cause and instituting a just peace. Third, mixed motives are not necessarily harmful and very often can even be beneficial, because with some self-interested motive, states are most likely to follow through and really establish a stable peace.[98] I will expand on these three points in turn, below.

Motive is why an actor does something, and intention is what the actor actually intends to do. John Stuart Mill explains the difference in this way:

> The morality of the action depends entirely upon the *intention* – that is, upon what the agent *wills to do*. But the *motive*, that is, the feeling which makes him will so to do, when it makes no difference in the act, makes none in the morality: though it makes a great difference in our moral estimation of the agent, especially if it indicates a good or a bad habitual *disposition* – a bent of character from which useful, or from which hurtful actions are likely to arise.[99]

We judge intentions by their fruits, which are actions; we do not judge actions by motives. An actor may be motivated by the hope of having good trade relations or better national security. Motives are generally expressed in terms of self-regarding interests. Intentions can be expressed in terms of actions taken. Intentions must be limited to acting within the laws of war, and only taking actions that are likely to remedy the just cause. If the actor's intentions are otherwise, or his actions after the war commences show that he is pursuing an intention different from remedying the just cause, the right intention criterion is not met. If a war is begun with right intention, but later expanded or escalated with the intention of pursuing of an interest that is incompatible with or reaches beyond the just cause of the war, the right intention criterion is no longer satisfied.

Second, although the intention of the intervener must be limited to restoring justice, his motive may be self-interested. If the actor will gain side benefits by restoring justice, and those side benefits motivate the actor, this is permissible, as long as the actions taken are limited to remedying the just cause and instituting a just peace. For example: imagine that the motive behind the Iraq War (2003) was really to secure Western access to Iraqi oil, but the intention of the intervening actors was to institute a just peace and secure a humanitarian outcome for the Iraqi people, and the access to oil was merely an expected side effect, and an animating motive. The presence of this animating motive would not (on its own) mean that the resort to war was unjust. However, if during the invasion troops protected oilfields instead of civilians, and acted with the intention of securing oil fields rather than the intention of securing a humanitarian outcome, the war would not meet the standard of right intention.

Third, mixed motives are not only acceptable, but may be beneficial, as long as the actor *acts* with right intention. It is beneficial if an intervening state has a self-interested, animating motive when undertaking humanitarian military intervention, because it is from this sort of motive that "political will" derives:

> Humanitarian intervention is most likely to succeed when the political interests of the intervening states are strongly engaged, because only then will other important factors be present, such as adequate resources and commitment to persevere in the face of adversity.[100]

Where interests on the part of the intervening state are not impacted, for example in the cases of Somalia, Rwanda, and the Sudan, we often see a lack of political will for states to become and remain effectively involved. If the actor's intention is limited to restoring justice, his/its motivation is irrelevant to the question of right intent. If an actor mounts a humanitarian intervention because the actor anticipates a new regime that is respectful of human rights will be a good trading partner and offer new markets or resources, but the actor is using humanitarianism as a cover, this in itself does not violate right intent. As long as the intended actions are limited to rectifying the just cause, the actor's motives may remain "hidden from all but God." One's actions, not one's motives, are the only visible (therefore, judge-able) evidence of one's intention in the eyes of human observers.

We can see in retrospect what an actor's intentions were by the actions that he took; we do not judge actions by motives. Motivation does not enter into the picture at all, unless that motive spills over into the action taken, and the actions become inconsistent with or goes beyond the restoration of justice: if a war is motivated by ethnic hatred, we will likely see massacres or ethnic cleansing, and these actions cannot be said to be consistent with the intention of restoring a just peace with one's current enemy. If the just cause is merely an excuse for motives like these, the intention of the actor is really not to restore a just peace, but to commit ethnic cleansing, and obviously the right intention criterion will not be satisfied.

To sum up, if selfish motives are compatible with a humanitarian outcome, motives remain irrelevant. What matters is that all action taken is intended toward rectifying the just cause and instituting a just peace and that no other actions taken detract from those goals. Right intent can be judged during wartime by evaluating whether actions taken are in line with the pursuit of a just peace, whether fighting is in accordance with the *jus in bello*, and whether when the just cause is rectified, the fighting ends. Motivations and reasons for seeking a just peace with the current enemy are not required to be pure, and in any case, motivations are even less discoverable than intentions. On whether waging war for selfish motives but with a beneficial effect is a sin, I will follow Gentili to say I am not qualified to answer; "this is a question for theologians."[101] But it is better, and here we move toward the *jus ad bellum* category likelihood of success, that the intervening state has some motive (some national interest) that serves its own purposes, for seeing to the restoration of a just peace. Such a motive is necessary for a state actor to maintain the political will required to follow through with establishing justice. This of course begs the question of whether corporate bodies such as states can have motives, but it is accepted that states do have interests, at least as perceived and articulated by their leaders.

To judge retrospectively whether an intervention was objectively a humanitarian intervention or a pretender, we can adopt the following criteria, suggested by Ramsbotham and Woodhouse:

> (i) was there a humanitarian cause? (ii) was there a declared humanitarian end in view? (iii) was there an appropriate humanitarian approach – in other words, was the action carried out impartially, and were the interests of the interveners at any rate not incompatible with the humanitarian purpose? (iv) were humanitarian means employed? (v) was there a humanitarian outcome?[102]

The criterion of a humanitarian outcome requires counter-factual analysis of what would have happened if the intervention had not occurred, so Ramsbotham and Woodhouse believe that the question of whether there was a humanitarian outcome is exceptionally difficult to answer.[103] This is not to suggest that our judgment of whether an intervention was actually "just" can always be determined by the outcome. We can verify by its outcome that an intervention was rightly intended, but it is also true that a well-intended and well-executed intervention could ultimately fail, and there could be a non-humanitarian outcome. That does not mean the original decision to intervene was unjust. However, if a state clearly had non-humanitarian intentions, we might be able to judge that as outsiders only after the end of hostilities, when its intentions have become apparent.

Jus in bello *implications of right intention*

Right intention is closely connected to *jus in bello*, and right intention requires the *jus in bello* be observed. Grotius noted that state of mind was related to intent to conduct the war justly. For example, the uprooting of vines, burning of fruit trees, and other spiteful destruction would not be consistent with waging the war with right intention. Kant affirmed the view of St. Thomas Aquinas that the only right intention in war is to reach a just peace with the current enemy: "no nation at war with another shall permit such acts of war as shall make mutual trust impossible during some future time of peace." Fighting must, therefore, be conducted in such a way as to preserve some trust in the way of thinking of parties on both sides, "even during the midst of war, for otherwise no peace can be concluded and the hostilities would become a war of extermination."[104]

Possessing right intention means that the party intends to rectify the just cause, and only by just means (to follow the laws of war, or *jus in bello*). If an agent cannot intend to fight according to the laws of war and still have a reasonable likelihood of success, it cannot satisfy right intention (this begs the question of supreme emergency, which I am setting aside). In other words, a perverse motive becomes a problem if it spills over into the prosecution of a war. If the conduct of a war gives evidence that the war is being fought out of line with right intention, with spite instead of with an eye toward a future peace or to realize personal gain rather than to establish justice, the right intention criterion is no longer met. Right intention requires that the war be fought justly and that when the just cause is remedied, the intention is met and the war is to be ended with a just peace.

Legitimate authority

Walzer's view on legitimate authority

Walzer does not explicitly address the *jus ad bellum* criterion of legitimate authority nor does he mention the related criterion of public declaration. However, he does make statements about unilateralism and multilateralism in both *Just and Unjust Wars* and *Arguing About War*, from which we can infer some indicators of his likely view on this subject. In both books, as well as in numerous public speeches, Walzer approves of India's unilateral intervention in East Pakistan (now Bangladesh), Vietnam's unilateral intervention against the Khmer Rouge and Pol Pot in Cambodia, and the Tanzanian unilateral intervention to oust Idi Amin in Uganda. Walzer explains that official governments of single state actors are legitimate authorities, and in fact they are the only actors we actually have. "It wasn't the U.N. that overthrew Pol Pot and stopped the Khmer Rouge massacres," Walzer writes. "And so long as we can't be sure of its ability and readiness to do that, we will have to look for and live with unilateral interventions."[105] Walzer writes that these three cases were matters of universal interest, to be sure; but only these local actors interested themselves in the cases and (for their own political reasons) could have undertaken these operations.[106]

Walzer writes, "no one really wants the United States to become the world's policeman, even of-last-resort, as we would quickly see were we to undertake the role." Nevertheless, "multilateralism is no guarantee of anything."[107] Walzer does not require multilateralism or the seal of approval of any international organization or body, such as the United Nations, for any resort to war, including humanitarian intervention, and he does not believe that such authorizations yield greater legitimacy by virtue of a purer intention. If single countries have mixed motives, so will coalitions: "The collective will to act is sure to be as impure as the individual will to act."[108] On balance, for Walzer, there is not necessarily more justice in a multilateral than a unilateral resort to war. I disagree with Walzer on this, and I will say why in the section on my view, below.

Although Walzer never writes that domestic legitimacy is required for states to raise an army, in *Just and Unjust Wars*, he does write that states that initiate massacres are criminal states, and they no longer have the right not to be warred against; their defensive wars are no longer just (except possibly in the case of self-defense against an even worse genocidal regime).

Historical view on legitimate authority

For St. Thomas Aquinas, the authority of the prince to raise an army is only for the defense of the people and in their interest. The prince's authority is given to him to be used in the interests of his people. It is similar to a parent's authority over a child, or a policeman's authority in his community. It is not ownership, but something more like stewardship or caretaking. Thomas describes legitimate authority this way:

> It is not the business of a private individual to declare war, because he can seek for redress of his rights from the tribunal of his superior. Moreover it is not the business of a private individual to summon together the people, which has to be done in wartime. And as the care of the common weal is committed to those who are in authority, it is their business to watch over the common weal of the city, kingdom or province subject to them. And just as it is lawful for them to have recourse to the sword in defending that common weal against internal disturbances, when they punish evil-doers, according to the words of the Apostle (Romans 13:4) "He beareth not the sword in vain: for he is God's minister, an avenger to execute wrath upon him that doth evil;" so too, it is their business to have recourse to the sword of war in defending the common weal against external enemies. Hence it is said to those who are in authority (Psalms 81:4): "Rescue the poor: and deliver the needy out of the hand of the sinner."[109]

120 *Other* jus ad bellum *categories*

By legitimate authority, he meant official, or public, authority. Force is only to be used by public authorities, for public purposes. The authority to "bear the sword" comes from the duty of the public authority to watch over and protect the commonwealth. The authority to "summon together the people" or raise an army, is for public service. According to John Kelsay (interpreting Thomas Aquinas):

> Power is a kind of "trust." It is not an occasion for personal gain. Rulers are to protect the weak, not to exploit them. They are supposed to administer the state in ways that benefit the many, rather than the few. Indeed, rulers who use their power for personal gain are not really legitimate. They are tyrants, and in some cases they must be removed from power. In some cases, that is, a legitimate ruler or group of rulers may consider that the impact of a neighboring tyrant requires that they band together to remove him.[110]

Vitoria notes that defensive war may justly be declared and waged by anyone, including private persons; offensive war, however, may only be declared and waged by a commonwealth. Vitoria's use of the word commonwealth, rather than prince or other name denoting a figurehead, is important. For Vitoria, the right of war rests with the commonwealth; the prince may speak for the commonwealth, but if the commonwealth determines he is not acting in its interest, it may declare war against its prince and depose him. Althusius and Bodin also argued that the sovereignty rests with the people, not one ruler.

Comprehensive view on legitimate authority

Like all the just war criteria, legitimate authority is more adequately judged, explained, and analyzed in terms of degrees, rather than in terms of binary opposites. Actors can be understood as more or less legitimate. There are many different types of actors, including, among others: single-state actors, both legitimate and illegitimate; multi-lateral ad hoc coalitions of legitimate states; institutionalized organizations of states like the United Nations, NATO, and ECOWAS; and sub-state actors such as insurgent groups, non-violent resistance movements, and terrorists.

Only capable and responsible states possess the legitimate authority to raise armies and to wage war. I endorse the view ascribed by John Kelsay to Aquinas, that the power of the state is a kind of trust. Legitimate authority derives from the responsibility to serve and protect the public interest. War cannot be legitimately waged in the private interest, or by a tyrant. Incapable or irresponsible states do not possess legitimate authority to raise an army. Their defensive wars are not just, both because they lack a legitimate authority to wage war and also because they lack a just cause (except possibly in the case of self-defense against an even worse genocidal regime).

Sub-state actors, whether individuals or rebel movements, if they are resisting an incapable or irresponsible state, may have a just cause for resort to force, and they always have a right to ask for outside influence or interference. They cannot be said to possess legitimate authority to wage international war. If their actions must rise to the level of violent resistance, they should be guided by the *jus ad bellum* and the *jus in bello*. Rebels must limit their attacks to military targets; techniques that target civilians are never permissible.

Single state actors are formally legitimate authorities for making war, and capable and responsible states possess all the legitimacy that is required for satisfaction of the criteria "legitimate authority" in my understanding of the just war tradition. Yet, multilateral actors seem to be *more* legitimate than legitimate single state actors. Multilateral actors deserve this clout because multilateral actors are less prone to adventuring, and more inclined to act in line with right intention rather than in line with narrow individual self-interest.[111] When more than one or two state actors are involved in resorting to war, it is more likely that sufficient arguments have been marshaled to convince multiple actors that the contemplated use of force is justified. Deliberation is required, and a coalition must be formed prior to initiating war.

As we distinguished between objective and subjective bilateral justice, one being "real" and one being "apparent," we can also distinguish between formal and substantive multilateralism. Formal multilateralism creates the impression of legitimacy, but substantive multilateralism gives the qualitative effects, or the substance, of greater legitimacy.[112] A great power leading a coalition of the willing may create the impression of legitimacy, but if the coalition merely accepts the will of the great power, this is apparent, not real, multilateralism. Substantive, or real, multilateralism means that actors deliberate and come to negotiated agreements on plans and actions.

A multilateral force or at least a multilateral authorization (at least more than one or two states ought to agree that the other constraints against the resort to war have been met) is more likely to make decisions in accordance with public interest than a single state actor; therefore, multilateral forces possess greater substantive legitimacy than single actors. Walzer disagrees with this, because he thinks the interests of each state will merely be "super-added,"[113] but I think the consensus-building process would tend to cancel out single-state interests reasonably effectively. The legitimacy accorded multilateralism has increased as the capacity and experience of United Nations peace operations have grown.

David Little observes: "The broader the coalition, the less likely intervention will be seen to serve the interests of a single state."[114] Multilateral action, or at least multilateral agreement on the decision to resort to force, certainly does create international legitimacy which matters a great deal in making a war easier to prosecute and conclude quickly, thereby reducing needless suffering.

Multilateral response is ideal, but if the circumstances are so urgent that preparing a multilateral response is seriously delayed or impossible, states may act individually. Real multilateralism has the advantage of creating international legitimacy, but it has the disadvantage of sometimes requiring difficult and unwieldy cooperation and coordination. Disagreements over targets, tactics, and burden-sharing have also presented obstacles. "Napoleon reputedly said, 'Let me always fight against alliances.'"[115] Until the international community has created an institution that can reliably respond to threats to international peace and security, unilateral action may sometimes be the best course of action. For example, in the case of Rwanda, although a multilateral force was authorized, it was apparently impossible for officials to coordinate logistics in a timely enough manner to effect a meaningful response. In such a case, where the gravity of the just cause is overwhelming and time does not permit coordination of efforts, unilateral action is more likely to succeed. As Robert Kennedy has observed:

> In traditional just war theory, in cases of negligence or failure on the part of the superior authority, the inferior community's right to declare and wage war was revived. The evident failure of the United Nations to provide security and to vindicate rights is often not taken in the modern discussion to be an abdication of its authority with regard to war.[116]

Multilateral efforts are more legitimate, but any capable and responsible state meets the minimal criterion of legitimate authority. Single state efforts are preferable when the alternative is that no action will be taken, or in the case of emergency, or when multilateral action might be so hampered by coordination problems that it will be untimely.

General Wesley K. Clark, who commanded the NATO intervention in Kosovo, has also demonstrated that NATO could have more quickly brought an end to the ethnic cleansing in Kosovo, thus saving lives, if he had been allowed to bomb the electric power grid in Belgrade sooner. Clark argues convincingly that multilateral bargaining over target lists posed an obstacle to speedy, effective prosecution of the war.[117]

George Moose, US Assistant Secretary of State for African Affairs, described the bureaucratic hurdles to participating in a multilateral response to the Rwandan genocide, once an intervention force had been authorized, in this way:

> And then the [50 armored personnel carriers] thing ... we spent so much time wrangling about who was going to pay for them, who was going to pay for refurbishing them, who was going to transport them, who was going to pay for the transport, [and] who was going to pay for the training of the Ghanaians so that they could use them. Again, it's sort of bureaucracy at its very worst, and at our level, we couldn't break through that. Somebody else would have had to intervene to say, "This is nonsense. Get on with it. Do it." But the point is that it's the kind of bureaucratic gridlock that often happens. But in this situation, [it] shouldn't have been allowed to happen.... When I think back upon it, there are three things that come to mind [as shameful.] It was the decision on whether to call it genocide. It was the Mille Collines radio[118] decision, which [was] truly atrocious that we weren't able to do something because of some legal nicety about international radio conventions. Then, the APC thing [was] sort of emblematic, symptomatic of the difficulties we were having in doing what we said we wanted to do –

namely, be supportive of those countries that were prepared to commit to this operation.[119]

Allen Buchanan argues that experience has shown the existing international institutions are not able to prevent massive human rights abuses effectively and consistently. Alongside this fact, Buchanan argues that the principle of respect requires that persons do not stand idly by while human rights abuses take place. These two facts taken together generate an obligation to create a new institution, or to fix the existing institutions, such that the international community can fulfill its responsibility to prevent. This is, in my view, a very sensible and clear moral argument.[120]

Jus in bello *considerations*

Legitimate authority to raise armies and wage war is only possessed by legitimate regimes acting in the interests of their citizens. When a legitimate state is at war with an illegitimate state, the soldiers fighting for the illegitimate state are generally conscripts, not fighting in their own interests, but because they have been coerced to fight. Walzer does not distinguish between armies of volunteers and armies of conscripts,[121] but in *Law of Peoples*, John Rawls has suggested that armies of conscripts must be treated with special consideration, because it is not by any legitimate authority that those conscripted soldiers are fighting. In Rawls' view, extra care must be taken not to kill these soldiers, who are conscripts, when killing them might be avoidable. Actors fighting with legitimate authority who are at war with an illegitimate state should target the leadership instead of the conscripted army, where doing so might be possible. I think this is a generally reasonable argument, and it captures a special problem of legitimate authority. Illegitimate leaders have no right to raise an army, but they do so routinely. The soldiers in their army may only be fighting as a result of coercion, including threats of torture and death to themselves and their families. Perhaps then, such conscripted soldiers are in some way victims of their state, deserving of rescue themselves.[122] One ought not to kill them if one can avoid it by killing or arresting the illegitimate leadership instead (consistent with the principles of self-defense and proportionality). Of course civilians in any type of state may never be the direct target of attacks, even in a well-ordered state where the war is being fought in their interests and with their support.

As mentioned above, *jus in bello* proportionality can be adversely affected if multilateral alliances cannot agree on the most efficient means of fighting. I will say much more about this in the Kosovo chapter.

Conclusion

Walzer's theory belongs to the aggressor–defender paradigm, in which all wars fought for a just cause (against an unjust aggressor) are justifiable. In such formulations, there is little need of the other *jus ad bellum* categories. In these theories, just war thinking is mostly folded into the categories "just cause" and "conduct of war." In Chapter 4, I expanded the category of just cause to include some offensive wars, and in the first part of this chapter, I argued that the aggressor–defender paradigm is insufficient. As Grotius wrote,

> we must obviate a certain mistake, lest any one should imagine, that whenever he has a just cause given him, he is thereupon immediately obliged to declare war, or that it is warranted at any time for him to do so.

On the contrary, although there may be a just cause, this is an insufficient condition to permit a justified decision to resort to war. I have argued that the restraints of last resort, likelihood of success, proportionality, right intention, and legitimate authority must all be satisfied; that offensive wars are sometimes just; and that defensive wars are sometimes unjust. In my formulation, the other *jus ad bellum* categories take on more significance than they have in Walzer's presentation.

I have strengthened some of these restraints with a few innovations. I will not define the full meaning of each category of restraint in this conclusion; I will merely highlight what I have added that is new. Under the category of last resort, I argued that states are bound not to ignore conflicts that appear reasonably likely to escalate into crises requiring a military response. Attempting to prevent the necessity of war by using appropriate preventive or deterrent diplomatic, economic, political, and military measures is an obligation that is entailed by "signing on" to the constraint of last resort. Affirming the principle of last resort is a promise to other states, and to a state's own citizens, that decision-makers will try to prevent war from becoming necessary. If states fail to take reasonable preventive action, and war becomes necessary, states cannot claim truthfully that war, having now become necessary, is the last resort. It is the only resort, but it has become the only resort as a result of missed opportunities and failures to prevent.

I further argued that we should apply the *jus ad bellum* and *jus in bello* constraints to material interference short of military intervention, and in particular I argued that we should use these theoretical lenses to evaluate the justice of economic, political, and social sanctions.

Under the categories of likelihood of success and proportionality, I argued that states are obligated to engage in the best possible analysis and to use these calculations before making a decision about the resort to war. Even wars of self-defense are subject to the proportionality and likelihood of success constraints in my view, unlike in Walzer's.

Under the category of right intention, I argued that motive and intention are different from each other, following Mill. As long as an intervening state's actions are in line with the just cause for the war and the institution of a just peace *post bellum*, we can say that right intention is satisfied. If a state has mixed motives that are in conflict with the pursuit of a just peace, and the states actions are no longer in line with just cause, it becomes evident that right intention is no longer met. Right intention, and right action, must be maintained throughout the prosecution of the war.

I argued that multilateral authorization for war, particularly AHI, is generally more legitimating than a unilateral decision. The more broadly-based the multilateral coalition is, the stronger its claim to legitimacy might be. The result of my emphasis on the other *jus ad bellum* categories of restraint, beyond just cause, is that wars that are imprudent, unnecessary, or wrongly intended cannot be considered to be just, no matter what the putative strength of the just cause might be. My expansion of the just cause category in Chapter 3 does not lead to an excessive justification of the actual use of military force, because just cause is only one of several (now more robust) categories of restraint. Whether this will lead to more or less frequent interference or intervention, therefore, is an empirical rather than an ethical question.

Finally, I argued that the purpose of just war theory is not only to judge whether resort to war is just, but to structure the discussion. It is useful to have access to the language of all the categories, so citizens and decision-makers can discuss resort to war holistically and comprehensively, rather than focusing mainly on just cause.

6 Intervention in Kosovo

In the first part of this chapter, I will set out the historical background to NATO's 1999 intervention in the Federal Republic of Yugoslavia (FRY), describing the competing claims of national self-determination, history, and abuse on both the Serbian and Kosovo Albanian sides of the conflict over Kosovo. In the second part of this chapter, I will set out Walzer's analysis of NATO's resort to force as written in his essay, "Kosovo." Then I will consider whether the war met the *jus ad bellum* criteria as specified in my framework as developed in Chapters 3 and 4. I find that the intervention met the criterion of just cause, despite simultaneous subjective justice and competing claims of victimhood by the Serbs and Albanians. The criterion of legitimate authority was also met robustly. However, a determination that last resort, proportionality, likelihood of success, and right intention were satisfied is more problematic. I argue that there are good reasons to find the satisfaction of these criteria wanting and, therefore, that it would be difficult to call the 1999 intervention a just war. Finally, in the conclusion to the chapter, I will explain how my theoretical framework leads to a different understanding of the justice and injustice of NATO's intervention than Michael Walzer's framework as developed in *Just and Unjust Wars*.

Historical background

Contemporary discussions between Kosovo Albanians and Serbian officials about the status of Kosovo are characterized by nearly opposite claims about the region's history and by competing self-conceptions of victimhood. Serbs and Kosovo Albanians have independent traditions claiming a historic, national right to occupy the Kosovo region. The history of the region is marked by violence against non-combatants on both sides, and a feeling of persecution and victimhood exists among both Serbs and Kosovo Albanians. Because the patriarchate of the Serbian Orthodox Church is in Kosovo, Serbs make an argument that the region is holy to them; it is like a "Serbian Jerusalem."[1] Kosovo is considered the "cradle of Serbia's identity and the mainspring of its ancient culture."[2] The Serbs also have a national mythology of Serb martyrdom, even genocide, at the hands of the Ottomans and then the Kosovo Albanians. In this version of history, the Ottomans and then the Albanians have repeatedly waged violent campaigns against the Serbs, who have always been victims of aggression. The Kosovo Albanians also claim to have ancient title to the land, being descendents of the ancient Illyrians who settled in the region in 1000 B.C. The Serbian claim on Kosovo is entirely illegitimate in this version of history. The Kosovo Albanians also include in their claims a credible history of atrocities and ethnic cleansing perpetrated against them by Serb authorities when Serbs have governed the territory.

There is evidence for the claims of both the Serbs and the Kosovo Albanians. The minority Serb population in Kosovo has suffered revenge attacks at the hands of the Albanians in the wake of World War I, during the Italian occupation of Kosovo during World War II, and presently, in the wake of the NATO intervention. However, the Serbian mythology of thoroughgoing genocidal victimization and martyrdom at the hands of the Albanians does not seem borne out by the facts. Part of the problem is that Albanians adopted Islam during the Ottoman occupation, and Serbs often (mis)identify all Balkan Muslims as "Ottoman Turks," the hated occupier. As evidence in their argument that it is the Serbs, not the Kosovo Albanians, who are victims of genocide, Serbian commentators point to the fact that the Kosovo Serb population has declined sharply over time in comparison to the population of Kosovo Albanians. It is quite true that non-combatant Serbs were driven out by revenge attacks on them after Operation Allied Force, and these attacks on non-combatants are appalling.

However, the decline in the number of Serbs residing in Kosovo, relative to the number of Albanians, has been underway since 1961. Other factors have contributed significantly to the demographic changes.[3] First, Kosovo has always been economically very poor. Economic opportunity for Serbs is better further to the northeast, mainly in Belgrade; so many Serbs have simply decided to leave Kosovo for economic reasons. It has not been an economically attractive proposition for Serbs to move into Kosovo, or to stay in Kosovo, even with the promise of free land and houses from the government in Belgrade, because the region is so impoverished. Second, the Kosovo Albanians have the highest birthrate in Europe, and the Serbs have the lowest birthrate in Europe.[4] The tradition of having large families among Kosovo Albanians has been asserted by some Serbs to be evidence of genocide against the Serbs by "aggressive breeding" on the part of the Albanians. It is more likely that the high birthrate among Albanians is correlated to rural living, lower education levels, and poor access to medical care and information about birth control. All of these variables are generally correlated with higher birthrates. While it is true that the difference in birth rates has contributed to the increase in the ratio of Albanian to Serb population in Kosovo, Noel Malcolm argues that the relative decline in Serb population is a result of the low Serb birthrate and high abortion rate.[5]

The Jasenovic system of concentration camps was an example of violence against Serbs that has become a symbol of Serbian victimhood or martyrdom.[6] The Jasenovic concentration camps, run by the fascist Croat Ustaše forces during World War II, killed between 56,000 and 97,000 Serbs, Jews, Roma, Muslims, and other non-Catholic minorities, as well as Croatian political and religious opponents of the regime.[7] Serb nationalist leaders have often used the memory of Jasenovic to generate support for Serbian nationalist causes and to stir up feelings of victimization.[8] Although Jasenovic was in the fascist-controlled Independent Republic of Croatia, not in Kosovo, memories of the death camps would also generate hostile feelings against Kosovo Albanians, who are seen as having been collaborators during World War II.

The Kosovo Albanian claims of repression at the hands of the Serbs date back to at least the first Balkan war. The Balkan allies (Serbia, Bulgaria, Greece, and Montenegro) defeated Turkey (the Ottomans), in 1912. The Great Powers (Britain, Germany, Russia, Austria-Hungary, France, and Italy) convened in London in December 1912 to settle the issues left at the end of the conflict. Among those issues was the status of the territory that now makes up Albania and Kosovo. Austria-Hungary and Italy supported the creation of an independent Albanian state including the territory of what is now Kosovo because the region was populated mainly by ethnic Albanian Muslims. Nevertheless, the great powers ceded Kosovo to Serbia, instead of including it within the borders of the new Albanian state.

When Kosovo was ceded to Serbia, the Serbs attacked the population of Kosovo in a campaign of widespread massacres and forced deportations during 1912 and 1913. Leon Trotsky reported on the massacres for a Ukrainian newspaper. "Shocked by the evidence of atrocities he encountered," he wrote: "The Serbs in Old Serbia, in their national endeavor to correct ethnographic statistics that are not quite favorable to them, are engaged quite simply in the systematic extermination of the Muslim population."[9]

During 1912 and 1913, it is estimated that 25,000 Kosovo Albanians were killed. Other accounts were kept by the Catholic Church, and by a Carnegie Endowment commission sent to investigate in 1914. The commission reported:

> Houses and whole villages reduced to ashes, unarmed and innocent populations massacred, such were the means which were employed and are still being employed by the Serb–Montenegrin soldiery with a view to the entire transformation of the ethnic character of regions exclusively inhabited by Albanians.[10]

After World War I, the tables were turned as Serb soldiers were forced to retreat through Kosovo during the winter. Retreating Serb soldiers found no quarter with the Kosovo Albanians, and many of those attempting to make the retreat froze to death. It is also said that Kosovo Albanians killed many Serb soldiers who did try to seek shelter among them, beheading the soldiers and donning their uniforms in order to lure other Serb soldiers into ambushes.

In 1918, the Kingdom of Serbs, Croats, and Slovenes was formed. Kosovo and Vojvodina were integrated as territory of the Kingdom. The Muslim population in Kosovo was subject to widespread repression including arbitrary arrest and extra-judicial killings, and many thousands were forcibly deported to Turkey.[11]

During World War II, fortunes reversed again. Kosovo was overrun by the Axis powers, and it was placed under control of the Italians as part of "greater Albania." During this time, the Serbs residing in Kosovo suffered under the occupation, but Julie Mertus notes that the Kosovo Albanian population "experienced the occupiers as liberators." The fascists established Albanian-language schools and gave the Albanians the right to bear arms, which some Albanians used to "take revenge on Slavs, harassing and driving out Slavic families."[12] After the defeat of the Axis powers, the Yugoslav government sent in forces to take over Kosovo; at least 36,000 Kosovo Albanians are estimated to have been killed in the process. The re-absorption of Kosovo into Yugoslavia was a bitter disappointment to the Kosovo Albanians, who thought Kosovo would remain a part of Albania after the war.[13]

In 1946, both Kosovo and Vojvodina became autonomous provinces within the Republic of Serbia. In 1974, a new Yugoslav constitution was engineered by Marshal Tito aimed at curtailing Serbian dominance in the federal system. This constitution gave Kosovo and Vojvodina a high degree of autonomy and the formal status of constitutional equality with six other federal units: Serbia, Montenegro, Croatia, Bosnia and Herzegovina, Macedonia, and Slovenia. Once the 1974 Yugoslav constitution was adopted, Kosovo and Vojvodina possessed "full autonomy, equivalent to republican powers."[14] The autonomous provinces, sometimes called federal units, possessed votes at the federal level that were equal to the votes of Serbia and the other republics; they were republics "in all but name."[15]

The new Yugoslav Constitution of 1974 – which would remain in force until the final breakup of Yugoslavia – gave the autonomous provinces of Kosovo and Vojvodina a status equivalent in most ways to that of the six republics themselves, with their own direct representation on the main federal Yugoslav bodies. Incorporated in this constitution were some important changes already made by another batch of amendments issued in 1971: these had given the autonomous provinces equal status with the republics in most forms of economic decision-making, and even in some areas of foreign policy. Amendment XXXVI had stipulated that the Presidency of Yugoslavia would be a collective body with two representatives from each Republic and one from each autonomous province. The 1974 Constitution added another important right, which was that the autonomous provinces could issue their own constitutions. (Up till then their constitutions or "statutes" had been handed down to them by the Serbian assembly.) So, although the 1974 Constitution continued to exert that Kosovo and Vojvodina were parts of Serbia, but most criteria of constitutional law they were at the same time fully-fledged federal bodies.[16]

This arrangement left Belgrade (in its view) without sufficient authority over its provinces:

> It [Belgrade] also lacked the economic, legislative, and judicial authority necessary (in its leaders' view) to govern effectively. The governments of Vojvodina and Kosovo could veto any policy from Belgrade that applied to

the entire territory, while Serbia proper had no equivalent power over decisions within the two provinces.[17]

The 1974 constitution created major changes in Kosovar and Vojvodinan self-rule. First, all schoolchildren were granted the right to an education in their "mother languages." Economic independence was strengthened as provincial banks were established.[18] Foreign aid flowed directly to the republics rather than to the federal government, a phenomenon that Susan Woodward argues promoted the breakup of Yugoslavia and encouraged the separatists to take up arms. This economic independence weakened the federal system's ability to coordinate implementation of austerity measures called for by the IMF and the World Bank in the mid-1980s. The political autonomy of Kosovo and Vojvodina also made it nearly impossible for the federal government to implement the reform program; this, Woodward argues, was the basis for the revocation of Kosovo's autonomy, about which I will say more below.[19]

During this period (1974–1989) in Kosovo, most political, administrative, and police power was held by Albanian communists, and the position of the minority Serb population in Kosovo was regarded by many as perilous:[20] "In 1986, 60,000 Serbs petitioned for protection, perhaps with some cause."[21] Serbia's government faced mounting pressure from the public and from parliament to reign in Kosovo Albanians, in an atmosphere of increasing nationalism coupled with promotion of a theme of victimization among Serbs, including accusations of genocide against Serbs in Kosovo:[22]

While events in Kosovo at that time were not covered widely by the Western press, the *New York Times* reported in 1987 that

> ethnic Albanians in the government have manipulated public funds and regulations to take over land belonging to Serbs ... Slavic Orthodox churches have been attacked, flags have been torn down. Wells have been poisoned and crops burned. Slavic boys have been knifed, and some young ethnic Albanians have been told by their elders to rape Serbian girls. ... In one incident, Fadil Hoxha, once the leading politician of ethnic Albanian origin in Yugoslavia, joked at an official dinner in Prizren last year that Serbian men should be used to satisfy potential ethnic Albanian rapists. After his quip was reported this October, Serbian women in Kosovo protested, and Mr. Hoxha was dismissed from the Communist Party.[23]

In 1986, Ivan Stambolic was elected President of Serbia, and he made his protégé, Slobodan Milošević, leader of the Serbian Communist Party.[24] Stambolic was frustrated by his inability to do anything about the situation of the Serbian minority in Kosovo. In particular, he was critical of the 1974 constitution and the federal presidency:

> Kosovo and Vojvodina had a say in the running of Serbia as a whole, but Serbia was unable to interfere in the internal affairs of the provinces. So,

while Kosovo frequently voted against Serbia on the federal presidency, the collective body which had replaced Tito, Serbia itself was constitutionally unable to do anything about what was increasingly perceived as the perilous condition of the Kosovo Serbs. Stambolic did understand, however, that Serbia needed to proceed with caution, since fanning the flames of Serbian nationalism would be a disaster. Until now Milošević was regarded as his sidekick, and although in a powerful position, he had never expressed any particular interest in the national question.[25]

During Tito's rule, expressions of nationalism had been discouraged. On April 24, 1987, however, the "good communist, Milošević, was transformed into a good nationalist."[26] Milošević traveled to Kosovo Polje, site of the mythical battle where the Ottoman Turks had battled the Serbs 600 years earlier, to listen to the concerns of an assembled group of Serbs residing in Kosovo. Some violence broke out between the Serbs and the (ethnic Albanian) police; Milošević famously roared "No one should dare to beat you!" Milošević became very popular, and he continued to exploit nationalist sentiments. Woodward argues that the decline in Yugoslav prosperity after the end of the Cold War – made worse by strategies of economic and political reform put forward by the international financial institutions – contributed to the environment that made nationalism so popular and made the rise of Milošević possible.[27] By "playing the Kosovo card,"[28] within six months of his speech at Kosovo Polje, Milošević outmaneuvered his less nationalist mentor, Ivan Stambolic, and assumed the Presidency of the Serbian League of Communists.[29]

In March 1989, Slobodan Milošević unilaterally removed the heads of the Vojvodina, Kosovo, and Montenegro Communist Parties and replaced them with Serbian nationalists. Shortly thereafter, these operatives used the votes they possessed in the federal system (votes granted by the 1974 constitution) to nullify the 1974 constitution. They adopted a new constitution, and all political power was handed over to Belgrade. Susan Woodward argues that it was not merely an ethno-nationalist agenda that motivated Milošević's revocation of Kosovo and Vojvodina's autonomy: "Pressure from the IMF and the banking consortium organized by the U.S. State Department" was "a primary reason for the Serbian constitutional revision reducing its provinces' autonomy."[30] Without control over Kosovo and Vojvodina's internal affairs, Belgrade could not oversee implementation of the structural adjustment program.

The Albanians argued that the revision was illegal under the 1974 Constitution, and the members of the Kosovo Assembly roundly rejected it, after which the Assembly was declared dissolved by the authorities in Belgrade:[31]

> On July 2, 1990, three days before the Kosovo Assembly was dissolved, 114 of the 123 Albanian delegates in the Kosovo Assembly met on the steps of the Assembly building, which had been locked. There were enough of them to constitute a quorum, and they issued a declaration giving the Albanians the status of a nation entitled to their own republic. After the Slovene and

Croatian declarations of independence in June 1991, the demand for a republic was changed to a demand for independence.[32]

Commentators compare the institutions set up by the Serbs under the new 1990 constitution to the institutions of apartheid in South Africa, where a small minority elite exercised complete control of all the organs of state power and restricted the provision of services based on group membership.[33] Post offices were closed in rural areas. The government in Belgrade stopped providing essential services such as water, healthcare, and sanitation in many regions, and international aid organizations (Oxfam, Save the Children, and the Soros Foundation) stepped in with humanitarian relief.[34]

Ethnic discrimination was institutionalized through a process of legislative and practical Serbianization. This legislation aimed at increasing the ratio of the Serb to Albanian population in Kosovo, and aimed to fortify Serbian culture and language in Kosovo by mandating that schools were to teach only a Serbian curriculum in the Serbian language. Eighteen thousand Albanian schoolteachers were fired *en masse*, along with 115,000 out of a total of 170,000 other public employees.[35] Land grants and loans were provided as an incentive to Serbs who might be willing to move to Kosovo from elsewhere, and it was illegal for any Kosovo Serb to sell or lease land to a Kosovo Albanian.[36]

The Albanians, constituting 90 percent of the population, lived under police rule in an apartheid-like system. Arbitrary arrests, harassment, detention and mistreatment of Kosovo Albanians by Serbian police authorities were widespread. "It is said that at least one member of every Albanian family had been called to a police station, was waiting for a trial, or had spent some time in jail."[37]

It is alleged that the Serbian authorities mass-poisoned Albanian schoolchildren in March and April of 1990, although that has not been proven. It is known, however, that 7,000 schoolchildren did become ill, perhaps through poisoning. A 1995 UN toxicology report indicated the presence of components used by the Yugoslav National Army to make Sarin.[38] The Yugoslav government attributed the illnesses to "mass hysteria" owing to the tense political climate.[39] These circumstances were strong indicators that greater violence might break out.

The Organization for Security and Cooperation in Europe established a "Mission of Long Duration" in 1992 to monitor events, provide and collect information, and promote dialog. The presence of the Mission seemed to decrease overt, official Serbian harassment of ethnic Albanians. In an effort to further deter Milošević' from acting against the Kosovo Albanians, President George H.W. Bush issued what became known as the Christmas Ultimatum or Christmas Warning, on December 24, 1992. The message was that "the USA was prepared to use force against Serbian troops in the event of any conflict [in Kosovo] caused by Serbian action, and President Clinton repeated the warning in 1993."[40]

In Kosovo, the unofficial President in the parallel system, Ibrahim Rugova, argued that Kosovars could not resist Serbia's domination successfully by military means. Rugova put it this way: "The Serbs only wait for a pretext to attack the Albanian population and wipe it out. We believe it is better to do nothing and stay alive than be massacred."[41] The League for a Democratic Kosovo (LDK), comprising 700,000 members under the leadership of Rugova, instituted a program of non-violent resistance and non-cooperation with the Belgrade government. LDK set up a parallel government, which held elections, provided services, and collected voluntary taxes from Kosovo Albanians in the mother country, in Kosovo, and in the diaspora.[42] This strategy was aimed toward providing services needed by the Kosovo Albanians and also toward impressing the international community with the legitimacy of the Kosovo Albanians' claim to the right of self-government. LDK leaders took inspiration from the intellectual-led independence movements of Eastern Europe. The LDK hoped that if it could build credibility as the de facto government, providing services and holding elections, while pursuing a policy of disengagement with Serbia, the international community would eventually accept Kosovo as an independent state.

One unfortunate effect of the LDK/Rugova's policy of non-engagement with the Belgrade government was that over a million Kosovar Albanians boycotted the Presidential election of 1992. In large part because of this boycott, Slobodan Milošević was able to remain in power when challenged by Milan Panić. As a young man, Panić had defected from communist Yugoslavia to the United States during a cycling competition. He became wealthy in the pharmaceuticals business, and returned to Yugoslavia at the invitation of President Milošević, who hoped that the Serbian–American, Panić, would be able to help convince the United Nations Security Council to lift sanctions against Yugoslavia. According to Tim Judah, Panić was a democrat who "believed that business, money, and economics could solve the problems of the Balkans. He was uninterested in ethnic conflict and genuinely wanted peace."[43] Panić was appointed Prime Minister in July 1992, by the Yugoslav Parliament, and announced in early December that he would run against Milošević for the Serbian Presidency.

In June 1992, the CSCE suspended Yugoslavia's voting privileges on matters concerning Yugoslavia, and in July 1992, the CSCE suspended Yugoslavia's privileges to participate in meetings altogether, citing "clear, gross and uncorrected violations of human dimension commitments."[44] Milošević favored refusing to renew the mandate for the CSCE mission in retaliation. Panić favored the presence of CSCE monitors in Kosovo, and his opposition was an important obstacle that prevented Milošević from effectively forcing the monitors out for several months.[45] Since the presence of international monitors benefited the Kosovo Albanians by ameliorating human rights abuses, it should have been in the Kosovo Albanians' interest to see the moderate Milan Panić elected as President of Serbia instead of the arch-nationalist Slobodan Milošević. However, the LDK strategy embraced "the Leninist principle of 'the worse, the better' – that is to say, that Milošević was good for them." On this assumption, "the worst thing that could happen was that he might be replaced by a Western-minded democrat."[46] A case for secession could be built with Milošević in power. If he lost, and a moderate was elected, it would be more difficult for the Albanians to demand full independence.

Panić did not offer support for Kosovo independence, so the LDK leadership calculated that their goals would not be served by supporting him.[47] The modus operandi of the parallel system was total disengagement from the federal government. This meant not participating in the census, boycotting all Serbian elections, and refusing to participate in anything that might give the Kosovo imprimatur of legitimacy to the Serbian claim to sovereignty over Kosovo. By creating a break from Serbian institutions, and relying on the parallel institutions run by Kosovo Albanians, the LDK hoped to achieve their long-term goal of achieving total independence from Serbia. The Kosovo Albanians boycotted the elections of December 20, 1992, and:

> As a result, Kosovo's seats in the Serbian legislature (42 out of 250) [were] filled by the small number of Serbian voters, and the incumbents include[d] some of the worst Bosnian war criminals, such as Arkan (Zelijko Raznjatovic). Had the Albanians participated in these elections, they could have won all of the seats, and that would have been enough to deprive President Milošević of his majority. Yugoslav policy might then have developed very differently.[48]

In the near term, the decision to boycott this particular election had terrible immediate consequences for the Kosovo Albanians. Milošević won the Presidency, and shortly afterward he was able to oust Milan Panić. On July 2, the Belgrade government refused to extend the mandate of the CSCE missions in Kosovo, Vojvodina, and Sandjak.[49] As a result, the CSCE was forced to withdraw. With the monitors gone, and with the election outcome such as it was, Serb repression of Kosovo Albanians increased.[50]

Rugova and the LDK continued to believe that by pursuing a strategy of nonviolent resistance and by maintaining a parallel state, Kosovo Albanians would eventually receive the support of the international community in their bid for independence.[51] However, Belgrade argued that Kosovo (along with Vojvodina) was no longer a federal unit, and so it was not entitled to the same status as the republics. Rugova, citing Kosovo's status as a voting federal unit (just like the other seven units) under the 1974 Constitution, requested international mediation. However, on the basis of Belgrade's claim that Kosovo's status was a Serbian internal matter, the Kosovo question was kept off the table in the international peace process designed to prevent conflict in the disintegrating Yugoslavia.

Alex Bellamy argues that this was a legal blunder with malevolent consequences. Prior to Milošević's constitutional maneuvering, which Bellamy argues was illegal, Kosovo had a legal personality in the Yugoslav constitution, which meant that the international community was obligated to respond to Kosovo's requests for mediation at the London Conference. Because Kosovo had a formal status that was in many ways similar to the status of a republic, although the status was somewhat ambiguous, Bellamy argues that the London Conference should have treated Kosovo and Vojvodina as it treated Croatia. Bellamy argues that its refusal to do so amounted to assisting Milošević and his cause.

Premature recognition of Croatia by Germany is widely believed to have led to the bloodshed there, and Kosovo, like Croatia, did not meet the EU's Badinter criteria (for security of minorities residing there if Kosovo became independent). Furthermore, recognition of Kosovo would have set a precedent for recognizing smaller regional statehoods below the level of the main republics. It is easy to see why the western countries would not have wanted to repeat the tragic consequences of premature recognition of Croatia, and it is also easy to see why they would not want to start what they feared might be a dangerous precedent of recognizing ever smaller seceding units.

Although the London Conference did not address the Kosovo question, Rugova still believed that if the Kosovars showed the international community that they were self-governing, they would eventually be able to internationalize the conflict. However, the LDK's strategy was unable to inspire sufficient international interest in their case to bring about a resolution. The cumulative effect of the failure of Rugova's "government" to achieve progress on the Kosovo question, especially after Dayton, left many Kosovar Albanians disillusioned with Rugova's shadow government and the non-violent resistance movement. The lesson many Kosovars took from Dayton was that violence brings international interest to bear, but non-violent resistance is of no use, or is counterproductive. Miranda Vickers sums it up this way:

> Rugova's policies, while relying on the international community to appreciate the justice of the Albanian cause in Kosovo, had failed to change the situation. As long as there appeared to be relative peace in Kosovo, the international community would avoid suggesting substantive changes. Thus by opting for nonviolent resistance, the Kosovar leadership had reaped no benefits whatsoever. Instead they suffered humiliation and their people became even more desperate.[52]

There are several reasons the Kosovo question was not included in the EC Conference on Yugoslavia (later called the International Conference on Yugoslavia), despite Kosovo's former status as a federal unit of Yugoslavia, and despite calls from the European Parliament (and the Kosovo Albanians) to allow Kosovo and Vojvodina to participate in the peace talks. Although the Serbian repression in Kosovo was well-known, and there had been real foreboding about the possibility that the situation would deteriorate (as evidenced by the Christmas Ultimatum), violence did not actually reach the level of massacres until early 1998, when Serb forces launched attacks in Likoshan, Cirez, Prekaz, and Racak, killing many noncombatants along with KLA fighters. Because there had been no massacres, the international community was hopeful that preventive diplomacy had been successful in the Kosovo case. The stern warning given by the Bush administration against Serb violence in Kosovo, the Christmas Ultimatum of 1992 (reaffirmed in 1993) was thought to have been a successful deterrent.[53] Given the relative calm in Kosovo and the violence in Bosnia, it was far more urgent to reach an agreement on Bosnia than on Kosovo. The Dayton conference was about Bosnia, after all, not Kosovo.

Kosovo was not "added on" at the London Conference or at Dayton because attaching Kosovo to other settlements might have been a deal-breaker. The Kosovo question was put on the back burner in order to avoid inflaming Milošević and spoiling opportunities for resolution of other crises at the London and Dayton conferences. It could also be said that in retrospect, it appears Kosovar Albanian concerns were set aside in the interest of achieving other settlements.

Kosovo Albanians were disappointed in the Dayton Accords, and in light of the continuing repressive practices of the Serbs in Kosovo, the policy of non-violence began to seem more and more irrelevant to some Kosovo Albanians. In the eyes of some, violent resistance was overdue. On February 6, 1996 – ten weeks after Dayton and exactly three years before Rambouilliet – the Kosovo Liberation Army (KLA) claimed responsibility for an attack on six civilian houses in a Serbian refugee settlement. The KLA faxed a communiqué to media outlets urging Serbs to take the attack as a warning that they should leave the province. In April 1996, the KLA perpetrated separate but simultaneous attacks on four police patrols, killing five Serb policemen. KLA attacks continued, along with follow-up communiqués, throughout the spring and summer of 1996. In the early days of KLA attacks, the rebels did not enjoy much popular support. Rugova, along with many others, felt that whoever was carrying out these attacks was tempting the Serb forces to launch indiscriminate and disproportionate attacks against the Kosovo Albanians.

In the Spring of 1997, when the government of Sali Barisha in Albania collapsed, the floodgates opened for hundreds of thousands of automatic weapons to be taken out of Albania, and the KLA imported a significant portion of these weapons into Kosovo.[54] However, according to Tim Judah, few Kosovo Albanians were willing to join the now much better-armed uprising. Everywhere, "the refrain was the same: look what happened in Bosnia."[55]

Serbian military responses to KLA attacks appeared disproportionate and somewhat indiscriminate. Ironically, the KLA began to garner more popular support, and more membership, as the grim cycle of retributive violence, provoked by its attacks, became more and more vicious. When the Serb military attacked villages it suspected to be sheltering KLA guerrillas, the KLA's provocation was overshadowed in the minds of most observers by the willingness of the Serbian government to respond disproportionately and indiscriminately. The KLA's standing was helped in particular by the well-publicized images of murdered non-combatants including children, young women, pregnant women, and the elderly.[56]

Despite the reports of violence coming out of Kosovo after Dayton, the United States did not immediately respond. When the United States and NATO did become involved, it was not to address the question of Kosovo's autonomy, as the non-violent resistance movement had hoped it would, but to address massive human rights abuses rising to the level of massacre. It is sometimes argued that Albanian separatists provoked the massacres, or even perpetrated them, in order to bring international intervention to bear in their quest for national self-determination and an independent state of Kosovo. The Christmas Ultimatum, combined with the "lessons of Dayton" mentioned above, gave the KLA reason to believe that violent conflict within Kosovo might be the only route to independence.[57]

Franz Josef Hutsch allegedly spent several months from September 1998 to December 1999 with the KLA. He testified as a witness for the defense in Slobodan Milošević's war crimes trial in the Hague that ethnic-Albanian separatists in Kosovo mounted attacks on Serb police patrols with the intention of provoking disproportionate, indiscriminate attacks on civilians. This tactic was meant to "force them [Serbs] into a trap"[58] in order to create documentary evidence of massacres and hasten foreign intervention. It was not clear from the testimony how the Serbs would be "forced" to respond with indiscriminate and disproportionate attacks on civilians. Hutsch also testified that the KLA tried to lure the Serbs into attacking civilians in early 1999, specifically for the purpose of creating images that would be shown during the Rambouillet negotiations.[59] Alan J. Kuperman also quotes a KLA negotiator as saying, "The more civilians were killed, the chances of international intervention became bigger, and of course the KLA knew that."[60] It should be noted that this quotation only implies that the KLA could anticipate the prospect of a benefit from higher civilian casualties. If this tactic was employed by the KLA, it was unjust and condemnable. Willfully using non-combatant suffering as a means to a political end is a violation of *jus in bello*. If this was the case, the just cause for intervention would exist to rescue the Kosovar noncombatants both from the KLA and from the Serbs. The KLA were only able to provoke massacres because of the nature of the Serb regime and its willingness to abuse non-combatants. Had the regime been responsible, it would not have responded with indiscriminate and disproportionate attacks on civilians. This does not excuse the KLA. The KLA were not "good guys" to the Serb "bad guys;" there were bad guys on both sides, with civilian noncombatants caught in the middle.

Some KLA leaders knowingly caused civilian suffering and death to further their political aims, and they should be prosecuted. In fact, at least seven KLA members have been prosecuted for crimes against humanity (including murders, rape, and other inhumane acts) in the International Criminal Tribunal for Yugoslavia. One of those indicted is Ramush Haradinaj, who was Prime Minister of Kosovo from March 2004 until his indictment was announced in March, 2005. It is possible that some KLA leaders will not be held accountable for atrocities committed during the war and will assume government positions, perhaps leadership positions, in an independent Kosovo.

Reciprocity among combatants, the existence of crimes against humanity and war crimes on both sides of a conflict, does not mitigate the just cause for intervention. It shows that the civilians in need of protection are in danger from both parties. The fact that NATO was a de facto ally of the KLA is a testament to the element of truth in Walzer's argument in *Just and Unjust Wars* that outsiders may not know enough about the loyalties, resentments, and alliances within societies to make good judgments about whether to intervene. I would not say that foreigners ought then never to intervene; but we should understand that outsiders may be easily manipulated, and this should give prospective interveners pause, even in cases of massive human rights abuse.

Prekaz

On March 6, 1998, forces under direction of the Serbian authorities massacred more than 50 members of the Jashari family in the village of Prekaz i Ulët/Donji Prekaz (Prekaz). Adem Jashari, a KLA leader; was killed in the attack, along with an estimated 57 others, mostly members of his family, including 18 women and ten children under the age of 16.[61] The Jashari compound was a well-fortified KLA base. Serb troops had previously attempted to raid the compound, but they were beaten back by weapons fire. However, the fact that the Jashari compound was indeed a KLA base was overshadowed in the public mind by the presence of women, children, and the elderly victims among the dead. Stacey Sullivan observes: "To all but the men who provoked it, it looked like a slaughter of innocents."[62] After the killings at Prekaz, the KLA's influence and popularity increased dramatically:

At this point, village militias sprung up all over Kosovo to defend their villages. Many of them were linked to the parallel structures, but they called themselves the KLA, even though a number still considered Rugova to be their President. This was the beginning of the war.[63]

Cease-fire

In an effort to address the violence in Kosovo, on June 23, 1998, the United States dispatched Ambassador Richard Holbrooke, who had mediated the Dayton Accords with President Milošević present the entire time. The meetings yielded a cease-fire agreement between the Belgrade government and the KLA. The agreement was to be monitored from the air by NATO and on the ground by the Organization for Security and Cooperation in Europe (OSCE).

The OSCE's mandate to establish the Kosovo Verification Mission (KVM) was established by agreement between the OSCE and the FRY on October 16, 1998. The KVM's mandate was to verify compliance with the cease fire, and to monitor, document, and investigate the internationally acknowledged human rights crisis.[64] The presence of the monitors had beneficial effects on the human rights situation in Kosovo. According to the OSCE's analysis of the human rights findings of the KVM, when human rights division monitors were present on buses, in courtrooms, or in police stations, there was noticeable improvement – the frequency of beatings and harassment by authorities was reduced. When the KVM opened a field office in one small town, "within days several hundred villagers returned to their homes. They had been afraid to live in the village, but the mere presence of the OSCE–KVM gave them confidence."[65] The monitors were successful, but they could not be left on the ground when the conflict escalated; and their role was local, so they could not mediate the problem at the strategic level between Serbs in Belgrade and the KLA leadership inside and outside of Kosovo.

The success of the KVM in reducing violence seems to have convinced US policy-makers "that the situation was being brought under control." However, it became clear in retrospect that

> although the mission was able to accomplish a great deal to promote peaceful resolution of differences at the local level, it was unable to cope with the much larger strategic actions taken by the Serbs and Albanians to escalate the conflict.[66]

Recak/Racak

Serbia maintained at every juncture that the Kosovo situation was an internal matter. On January 16, 1999, however, when the bodies of more than 40 ethnic Albanians were found at Racak (and the images of the bodies were posted immediately on the internet and published on the front page of the *New York Times*), the United States responded strongly.

The following excerpt is from the report of the OSCE–Kosovo Verification Mission, some members of which witnessed the aftermath (bodies) of the killings at Racak:

> At Racak on 15 January, 45 Kosovo Albanians were killed. Events at Racak and facts as verified by the OSCE–KVM indicated evidence of arbitrary detentions, extra-judicial killings and the mutilation of unarmed civilians by the security forces of the FRY. The OSCE–KVM team, upon investigation on 16 January, found 40 bodies in different locations (five others had already been removed for burial by relatives). All had been shot. Some of the dead showed signs of having been killed arbitrarily at close range, including 20 men who were reportedly arrested the day before; others appeared to have been shot whilst running away. Some of the bodies had been decapitated. Among the dead were a woman and a 12-year-old child. Accounts of surviving residents said they recognized some of the policemen who took part in the actions as being from Stimlje/Shtime town. They also claimed that they recognized some of the assailants as being Serb civilians from Stimlje dressed in police uniforms. At a meeting in February the OSCE–KVM noted that a police commander in Urosevac/Ferizaj attributed the Racak killings on 15 January 1999 to the abduction of a Serb policeman from Stimlje in early December 1998. He maintained that the tension in Racak had built up and that the colleagues of this policeman had reacted in such a furious way because of the abduction.[67]

In the immediate aftermath of Racak, the day the bodies were discovered by villagers, there were outside witnesses, and press photographers, and OSCE Monitors present. Immediately upon seeing the bodies, OSCE Ambassador William Walker, a senior American diplomat, publicly accused Belgrade's government forces of perpetrating the massacre. Ambassador Walker phoned Secretary of State Madeleine Albright and National Security Adviser Samuel "Sandy" Berger, awakening them in the middle of the night, and attributed blame entirely on the Serb forces. The Serbian government responded with denials, suggesting that the KLA had attacked the peasants itself, in order to frame the Serbs for the massacre. The Serbian government demanded the removal of Ambassador Walker, and made accusations that the OSCE had helped the KLA redress the bodies of dead KLA fighters as non-combatant peasants, to make the innocent Serbs look guilty of targeting civilians.

Secretary Albright was overwhelmed with the conviction that she must do whatever she could to ensure that the United States would use force to stop further massacres if necessary. Albright's primary motivation for pushing military force in Kosovo was moral, although she also thought it would be strategically better for Balkan stability if Milošević was actually removed from power.[68] Albright lobbied so tirelessly for intervention that the war was called, in some circles, "Madeleine's War."

The images of the bodies at Racak powerfully influenced the decision-makers in Washington and Europe, as did the strange and incredible-sounding tenor of the Serbian denials, particularly the accusation that the OSCE had re-dressed the bodies. As President Clinton put it, "Whatever threshold they had to cross, I think they've crossed it."[69] As Dayton and Prekaz were turning points for the Kosovo Albanians, Racak was the turning point for the Americans.

After the incident at Racak, Ambassador Richard Holbrooke went again to see Slobodan Milošević, to try and prevent further escalations in the violence in Kosovo. Ambassador Holbrooke recounts the conversation this way: "His reaction was, 'Kosovo's an internal matter.' We said, 'We accept the fact that Kosovo is inside the Yugoslav national boundary, but that does not give you the right to squash its people.'"[70]

The United States and its allies summoned representatives from both sides of the conflict to Rambouillet, France, for what was billed as a final attempt at negotiating a settlement. The "Rambouillet Accords" document was unacceptable to both the Serbs and the Albanians. The Serbs "dismissed the Ramboulliet text as a 'non-agreement' and a western diktat."[71] First, the agreement proposed by the contact group called for the withdrawal of most of the Serbian military and police forces and the insertion of a NATO-led peacekeeping force. Second, the question of Kosovo's status would have been determined by a referendum to be held in three years, which might have resulted in full independence for Kosovo. Milošević was unwilling to accept either of these terms, and it has been argued that these terms would have been impossible for any Yugoslav leader to have accepted. Serbia regarded Kosovo as the cradle of the Serb civilization, and independence or secession was completely unacceptable. Furthermore, to accept the NATO security force provision would have effectively meant that NATO forces would be free to base and to travel all over the FRY, including in Belgrade.

Appendix B, section 8, of the document reads in part:

> NATO personnel shall enjoy, together with their vehicles, vessels, aircraft, and equipment, free and unrestricted passage and unimpeded access throughout the FRY including associated airspace and territorial waters. This shall include, but not be limited to, the right of bivouac, maneuver, billet, and utilization of any areas or facilities as required for support, training, and operations.[72]

The Rambouillet agreement did not satisfy the Kosovar Albanians either; they were interested in independence rather than autonomy. Wording was added to the document calling for a referendum to be held on independence after three years, which the Serbs would surely have rejected; the Kosovars signed the agreement on March 18 in Paris. In large part, they signed because the United States had made it very clear that if the Kosovar Albanians signed but the Serbs did not, NATO bombing would commence forthwith.[73] Richard Holbrooke recalls:

> Madeleine [Albright] and [her public affairs aid] Jamie [Rubin] announced that if the Albanians accepted our deal and the Serbs didn't, that would be a *casus belli* for military action against Milošević and the Serbs. This was completely unorthodox, and I asked Sandy [Berger] afterwards if he knew it was going to be said, and he didn't, and it just caught him off balance. By doing it, they left the US government in a dilemma: either we didn't mean what we said out there would be a war, because there was no chance that Milošević was going to accept.[74]

Despite the threat of immediate NATO bombing, the Serbian government refused to sign. Milošević seems to have doubted NATO would be able to maintain consensus required to continue bombing for long. Stephen Hosmer argues that Milošević: "assumed that he could promote the erosion of NATO resolve by (1) engaging in ethnic cleansing, (2) undermining support for the war by NATO and other foreign publics, and (3) exploiting Russia's support for the FRY."[75] Hosmer argues Milošević calculated that by aggressively pursuing ethnic cleansing in Kosovo, thereby causing a humanitarian crisis, Milošević could make the bombing appear to be counterproductive. By destabilizing Macedonia and Albania with refugee flows, ethnic cleansing would work to stop the bombing. In this way, Milošević would also have been able to both get the bombing to stop and reduce the size of the Albanian majority in Kosovo.[76]

The 1,500 unarmed monitors from the OSCE Kosovo Verification Mission were pulled out of Kosovo on March 20, 1999, just after the collapse of the Paris negotiations and just before bombing commenced. By this time, ethnic cleansing was already underway in Kosovo:

by March 20, the UNHCR estimated, 20,000 Kosovar Albanians had been driven out of their homes since the beginning of the Paris meeting there were also the first indications that a well-organized campaign had begun masked Serbs from special MUP units were reportedly systematically forcing people from their homes, indicating that the infamous "Operation Horseshoe" was being implemented.[77]

Serb patrols went through entire villages, turning on the gas in houses, then tossing grenades into the houses to ignite the gas and cause the buildings to explode. Serbia massed 40,000 troops in and around Kosovo. Large-scale military operations were underway. According the report of the Independent International Commission on Kosovo, it is not clear whether the documents allegedly detailing "Operation Horseshoe" were fake or real; what is clear in retrospect, however, is that "there was a deliberate effort to expel a huge part of the Kosovar Albanian population and such a massive operation cannot be implemented without planning and preparation."[78] The pattern of logistical arrangements made for deportations and the coordination of efforts by the Yugoslav National Army, the paramilitary groups, and the police, shows that this huge expulsion of Kosovo Albanians was systematic and deliberately organized.[79]

On March 22, the NATO allies dispatched Ambassador Holbrooke, alone, on one last diplomatic mission to Belgrade to try and impress upon President Milošević the seriousness of NATO's determination. Holbrooke made clear that if Milošević would not pull his troops back from Kosovo, there would be "swift, severe, and sustained" bombing.[80] However, it was already too late. President Milošević appears to have been committed to the plan of ethnic cleansing, and his troops were already dug in on the ground in Kosovo. Milošević apparently was undeterred for several reasons. First, for reasons previously mentioned, he did not believe that NATO could maintain enough cohesion to sustain bombing for long. He expected some dissent within NATO from Greece, and expected considerable support from Russia as well. Milošević was in part correct; he did receive some such support, and as a result, the early targets hit, especially targets in Belgrade, were largely "soft kills." It was only possible to achieve consensus in NATO on these kinds of targets early in the campaign.[81]

Other reasons that Milošević might have thought he could prevail were the widely publicized belief of NATO that bombing would only be required for three or four days, and President Clinton's public statement ruling out the use of ground troops. This presumably gave Milošević confidence that the JNA and Serbian Ministry of Internal Affairs (MUP) would face only KLA resistance on the ground.[82] The JNA and MUP were much better equipped and better organized than the KLA; this may have further encouraged Milošević in the belief that he could accomplish his goal of reducing the ratio of ethnic Ablanians to Serbs in Kosovo in spite of bombing. In fact, Milošević was correct; the bombing in Kosovo was ineffective against ethnic cleansing, and in fact it "created an environment that made it feasible" for ethnic cleansing to take place.[83]

On March 24, 1999, NATO launched its first bombers. When the bombing began, the Serbian forces on the ground in Kosovo accelerated their ethnic cleansing campaign. The question is often raised whether the Kosovo Albanians fled Kosovo because of the NATO bombing, or because of Serb attacks. Although we cannot take this to be conclusive, it is interesting to note that at least one study has concluded that while NATO bombing in Kosovo did not stop the ethnic cleansing, it did not cause the flight of refugees either:

> By comparing the estimated numbers of people who left each municipality over time to the times when NATO airstrikes occurred, the AAAS study concludes that only a small fraction of Kosovar Albanians fled Kosova/Kosovo as a direct result of NATO bombing raids. It also concludes that the mass exodus of refugees from Kosova/Kosovo occurred in patterns so regular that they must have been coordinated. In the context of descriptive accounts given by refugees, the most likely explanation for the migration is the implementation of a centrally-organized campaign to clear at least certain regions of ethnic Albanians.[84]

Walzer's view and my view on NATO's "Operation Allied Force"

There are two kinds of permissiveness to worry about in just war theory. The permissiveness in my framework is a result of expanding the just cause category; this permissiveness is addressed by tightening the other restraints. The permissiveness to worry about in Walzer's framework is that in the face of a just cause like genocide or self-defense, the other *jus ad bellum* categories of restraint take on less importance. In the first part of this section, I will summarize what Walzer has written on this case, then I will show how my framework leads to a different analysis.

Walzer finds NATO's Operation Allied Force to have been justified, even obligatory, to stop massive human rights abuses. Walzer explains his judgment:

> In some parts of Kosovo the harsh realities of ethnic cleansing were already visible before the decision to hit the Serbs with missiles and smart bombs was made. And given the Serbian record in Bosnia, and the mobilization of soldiers on the border of Kosovo, and the refugees already on the move, military intervention seems to me entirely justified, even obligatory.[85]

Given Walzer's understanding of the just cause, and his belief that ethnic cleansing was already underway before a decision was made to bomb Serbia, his judgment on the Kosovo conflict is consistent with the argument in *Just and Unjust Wars*. Walzer's insistence that outsiders stay out of civil wars does not apply once genocide, massacres, or ethnic cleansing is underway.

Famously, Walzer is skeptical of outside involvement in civil wars because, *inter alia*, outsiders do not have sufficient knowledge of the local loyalties and resentments. On the "ordinary brutality" side of the wide gulf between "nastiness on one side and genocide on the other," outsiders are required to stay out, because they cannot know the situation well enough to make a judgment about intervention. But once the threshold to massive human rights abuse is crossed, we aren't required to know any more than that. A just cause of genocide or ethnic cleansing is sufficient for us to know; our putative ignorance as outsiders does not matter much once massive human rights abuses are underway. Walzer explains, in an article published in Dissent in May, 1999, by way of analogy:

> [The fires are] deliberately set, the work of arsonists, aimed to kill, terribly dangerous. Of course every fire has a complicated social, economic, and political background. It would be nice to understand it all. But once the burning begins something less than full understanding is necessary – a will to put out the fire: to find firefighters, close by if possible, and give them the support they need.

His judgment that NATO's resort to war in Kosovo was justified does not rely on whether the other *jus ad bellum* restraints were satisfied; this is consistent with the argument in *Just and Unjust Wars*. In Walzer's paradigm, all defensive wars and wars to stop massive human rights abuses are just. In fact, in the face of aggression, there is a presumption in favor of fighting.[86] In Walzer's view, last resort is met, by definition, in these wars. Attacks are already underway or imminent. *Ad bellum* proportionality and right intention are not matters of importance in making a judgment about the justice of fighting these wars. Walzer has much to say about the way the war was fought, but he does not attach these *jus in bello* considerations to his determination of whether the *resort to war* was justified.

My view is distinct from Walzer's in several ways. Most importantly, even if we assume for the sake of consistency with Walzer's argument that ethnic cleansing was underway before the decision was made to bomb Serbia, which I do not think we can say with certainty, my view would still insist that the other *jus ad bellum* categories of restraint retain their importance. Just cause alone is an insufficient framework for organizing the debate and for analyzing whether and why resort to force is wise and morally appealing, or at least the less awful choice *on balance*.

I would like to clarify a couple of points regarding the case. It might be objected that the details of the case are unimportant for distinguishing theoretical views, but my view insists on a comprehensive and clear-cut framework for discussion, debate, and judgment. I suggest that using all the *jus ad bellum* categories to organize the debate brings us to a more satisfying and comprehensive understanding of the degree and type of justice and injustice in each case. Just as importantly, the comprehensive view gives us a framework for pinpointing in just which ways the proposed resort to force is more or less justified, prudent, and necessary (or not). We can say the resort to force was more or less just in this way and in that way, rather than calling the resort to force very clearly or entirely "just" or "unjust." In the following section, I present my view on

NATO's intervention in contrast to Walzer's. The discussion is organized in the just war framework.

Just cause

I disagree with Walzer that it was clear that ethnic cleansing was underway in Kosovo before the decision was made to bomb Serbia. First, I do not think we have complete information about when the decision was made to initiate the bombing. It is also not clear whether the killings at Racak and, especially, Prekaz, were actually direct attacks on civilians (the non-combatants being the intended object of the attacks) or whether civilians were killed in the crossfire of KLA-JNA firefights. This matters in making a determination of whether Walzer's threshold for just cause was met. If civilians are caught in the crossfire, this is more like civil war and less like ethnic cleansing.

The stated just cause for Operation Allied Force was to prevent further ethnic cleansing in Kosovo. When the operation failed to meet this objective, the goal became the expulsion of the Serb forces and the return of the refugees. Both of these satisfy the just war criterion of just cause, even in Walzer's high-threshold formula. There are other possible *casus belli* that would have met the requirement of just cause as specified in Chapter 3, although these were not NATO's stated just cause.

On the part of NATO, the intervention could have been formulated as a humanitarian intervention to stop crimes against humanity. The Serbian government did not fit the description of "a capable and responsible state," governing Kosovo in the interest of its population. I argued in Chapter 3 that persecution constitutes just cause for foreigners to assist the beleaguered population by means of influence, interference, and military intervention (subject to the other restraints of last resort, proportionality, likelihood of success, right intention, and legitimate authority).

In my view Serbia lost its right to non-intervention, and a just cause for intervention arose, when Serbia "revoked Kosovo's autonomy [and took measures] aimed at changing the ethnic composition of Kosovo and creating an apartheid-like society."[87] Under the more restrictive understanding of the non-intervention norm that I laid out in Chapter 3, the Belgrade government would not have had the option of declaring Kosovo to be an internal matter. Persecution of ethnic Albanians in Kosovo at the hands of officials, especially police, included violation of the right to life, and the right to be free from torture and other forms of ill-treatment. Serbs were also persecuted by KLA forces. There was official and widespread ethnic discrimination in employment, education, and access to health care.[88] All of this together means that the FRY would not have been entitled to exercise the right of non-intervention.

By 1999, according to the Atrocity Standard, it would have been justifiable for the outside community to intervene in the civil war on behalf of the Kosovo Albanians, not because their claim to independence was necessarily just (which, rightly or wrongly, the international community did not affirm it to be). The strongest rationale would rather have been that the tactics used by the Serb forces in response to KLA attacks on Serb police and military targets were so indiscriminate that they constituted persecution, if not massacres. However, this is not a clear-cut case where one side has a monopoly on justice. It is clear that the KLA committed atrocity crimes as well, including killing non-combatant Serbs and ethnic Albanians believed to be Serb collaborators.

If the decision to bomb was made before Ramboulliet, as has been argued, then it's not clear that NATO's stated just cause was met at the time the decision was made. However, in my view a just cause existed for intervention before Ramboulliet. Last resort was not met, but there was a just cause.

We can say that NATO's stated just cause was met at the time the first bombs were dropped (if not when the decision to drop them was made). On March 22, 1999, the security forces reporting to the Belgrade government were already engaged in systematic attacks against civilians. Ambassador William Walker describes conditions on the ground as the OSCE monitors were leaving Kosovo that day:

> We started hearing about this with our last people coming out.... Some of them were saying that right behind us were the tanks and the armored personnel carriers. It was obvious that the Yugoslav forces had a plan to move in right behind us. They wanted us out of the way as soon as possible, so they could start doing what they were going to do, and then did it. And this is my reply to those people who said that the elements of the holocaust began when NATO started bombing. My answer is absolutely not – it started well before the bombing. I was never able to confirm that this "Operation Horseshoe" actually existed. But there was obviously a plan ready to execute, in which troops and equipment would move very quickly into Kosovo.[89]

Certainly by the time air strikes commenced in 1999, ethnic Albanians were being attacked by Serb forces.[90] In my view, however, just cause alone is not sufficient to trigger AHI.

Likelihood of success

The likelihood of success criterion, like proportionality, asks decision-makers to assess the likelihood that the tactics they choose to reach their goals are likely to work. In my statement of this criterion in Chapter 4, I emphasized that other, less coercive and damaging types of interference rather than military intervention might work, and if so, those should be tried first. I will say more about missed opportunities for preventive diplomacy in the section on last resort; here I will mention only that preventive action is much more likely to succeed when it is commenced before violence begins.[91] Between 1990 and 1997–1998, preventive efforts would have been more likely to succeed, because the minimal aims of the relevant actors were not necessarily irreconcilable. Once the spiral of violence escalated, with expatriates returning to strengthen the KLA, the KLA's assassination of Serbian police officers and the Serb military retaliating by killing civilians, the moments where preventive diplomacy might have been most likely to succeed had passed.

Likelihood of success requires that before commencing a war, decision-makers consider how likely they are to be able to remediate the just cause. To make such a judgment, decision-makers must know what tactics are likely to be most effective, within the bounds of the *jus in bello*. I argued in Chapter 4 that tactics should be tailored to the just cause. Merely possessing overwhelming firepower and defeating one's opponent does not automatically mean that success in remedying the just cause is likely.

Tactics in NATO's Kosovo campaign were not effectively tailored to the ends being sought for three reasons. First, the ethnic cleansing was being perpetrated by close action on the ground, moving from village to village. Air power is not capable of distinguishing between the aggressor and the victim while a village is being attacked. Air power cannot stop close quarter massacres.

Second, to maintain the 'no losses' strategy, NATO aircraft had to fly too high to confirm targets visually, thereby increasing the likelihood that the bombing would kill the very people NATO was trying to rescue as well as innocent Serb civilians. Walzer makes a similar argument under *jus in bello*, but he does not include likelihood of success as part of *jus ad bellum*. The decision to resort to war does not include a discussion of tactics. In my view, we have to satisfy ourselves that we can fight (and win) while observing the laws of war, before we can justly resort to force.

Without NATO forces on the ground to call in air strikes, either NATO needed to rely solely on unmanned aerial vehicles and satellite photos, or work closely with the KLA, providing them with radios and capability to call in air strikes, which NATO, not fully trusting the KLA, decided against.[92] Finally, Serbian command-and-control was in Belgrade, not in Kosovo. Therefore, air strikes on Kosovo would not interfere significantly with the day-to-day operations of the decision-makers in Belgrade.

For these reasons, the NATO air campaign would not have been likely to succeed tactically at its stated goal, which was preventing ethnic cleansing in Kosovo. "Boots on the ground" would have been required to prevent ethnic cleansing. However, air power was (due to domestic political considerations) apparently the only possible option for the NATO alliance. NATO's hope for success, therefore, had to be strategic. NATO had to hope that the bombing campaign would discourage the Serbian authorities from carrying out the ethnic cleansing, not that the bombing would actually be tactically effective on the battlefield. Some strategists felt that a few days of "bombing lite" would provide Milošević with a face-saving way out. As it turned out, however, Milošević seemed to be content to let the bombs rain down on Kosovo as long as NATO wanted to drop them. On the other hand, NATO could rain down bombs as long as Milošević wanted to wait them out. So, bombing Kosovo led to a stalemate between the two powers, and meanwhile ethnic cleansing was not successfully countered.

NATO's strategy included losing no aircraft, so member countries would not face domestic pressure to get out of the conflict. The United States, especially, was under the influence of the Somalia syndrome. Military casualties would have created domestic political pressure on the NATO allies, and this pressure would have been a signal to Milošević that the commitment of individual NATO countries was under pressure. If NATO had started losing planes, Milošević would have doubted NATO's ability to maintain cohesion, and he would have been encouraged to wait out the bombing.[93] NATO's decision to fight only from the air was, therefore, likely to succeed in furthering NATO cohesion and its credibility as a unified actor, but it was unlikely to succeed at remediating the just cause.

In the case of ethnic cleansing, directly challenging perpetrators where they stand, with military force, is the most effective means of stopping the perpetrators.[94] In Kosovo, airpower was just not a precise enough tool for the mission at hand, ground forces were ruled out, and NATO allies could not agree to hit important targets in the Serbian capital at the outset of the war. Tactically speaking, it is hard to say that the likelihood of success criterion was met in this case.

The United States initially ruled out sending ground forces, but NATO did create an invasion plan after it became clear that the war might be lost. However, the alliance wanted to avoid sending ground forces, so it had to find a way to persuade Milošević to come to the negotiating table. The only way to put enough pressure on Milošević to get him to change his activities in Kosovo was to bomb targets close to his own heart and close to his own source of power. The air war became more successful when the alliance became willing to bomb targets personally important to Milošević and other high-level decision-makers in Belgrade, including some of their personal possessions (even Milošević's house). In a further effort to get negotiations started, "Milošević was informed of NATO's likely invasion plans by Viktor Chernomyrdin during the latter's first visit to Belgrade on May 27."[95] When the ground troops option was apparently back on the table,[96] and bombing had been taken to Belgrade Milošević and the Yugoslav parliament became willing to accept the agreement brought by Viktor Chernomyrdin and Martti Ahtisaari. Command-and-control targets in downtown Belgrade included the electrical power grid, television station, and bridges used by commuters and ordinary Serbs as well as for command and control purposes. It should be said that if the intention of NATO was to bomb downtown Belgrade and use civilian suffering to force Milošević to capitulate, this would have been an unacceptable use of non-combatants as a means to a political end.

Right intention

I argued in Chapter 4 that Right Intention consists of two parts. First, the intervener must intend only to rectify the just cause of the war, and all actions taken must be in line with rectifying that right intention. Right intention also has a *jus in bello* implication: the intervener must be able to declare truthfully at the beginning of hostilities that he intends to fight according to the laws of war. The only right intention of a war is to restore a just peace with the current enemy, and nothing must be done during the conduct of the war that would make a just peace impossible to reach. In the case of the Kosovo war, it is apparent that NATO's intention was limited to the stated just cause of the war. NATO intended to stop the Serbian forces from expelling or killing the Kosovo Albanians, and it did not have any other intention that conflicted with this goal. Therefore, the first part of the *jus ad bellum* requirement of right intention was met.

It is more difficult to determine that the second part of right intention was met as robustly. Right intention requires that actors intend to observe the *jus in bello*. Although NATO intended to fight the war in line within the bounds of the *jus in bello*, some commentators, including Walzer, have argued that NATO's air-war only strategy is not compatible with the *in bello* principle of discrimination. The air-war strategy entailed flying at a very high altitude, to safeguard aircraft and pilots from Serb ground fire. At such a high altitude, it would be likely that strikes would sometimes hit the wrong targets, and thereby kill non-combatants. It is arguable that the principle of discrimination was impossible to reconcile sufficiently with the intended practice of very high altitude bombing.

According to Human Rights Watch, between 488 and 527 civilians were killed as a result of NATO air strikes in 90 separate incidents.[97] One notorious case of errant bombing killed three Chinese nationals; the Chinese embassy was accidentally attacked when outdated maps were used in target identification. There were several accidental bombings of refugees; some of these events were alleged by NATO to have been orchestrated by Serb forces, who concentrated Albanian refugees under bridges and in factories that NATO was likely to hit. Some attacks were on targets regarded by NATO as legitimate military targets, and the coincident loss of life was unintended but foreseeable. For example, on April 12, a train tressel at Grdelica, 200 miles south of Belgrade, was struck at the time a passenger train was crossing the bridge, killing ten and wounding 14 Serb civilians.[98] In another case, on April 14, a convoy of Albanian peasants fleeing Kosovo on tractors hauling wagons was struck in error in Djakovica. The refugees' convoy was apparently mistaken for a military convoy or an armored column, killing 75 Kosovo Albanians. A retired special forces commander has speculated that a KLA soldier was captured and had the code for the radios KLA soldiers used to radio in air strikes to NATO "beaten out of him"; the code was then used by Serb forces to call in a NATO air strike on the convoy.[99] In any event, after the convoy was hit, the air-war rules of engagement were amended. Targets had to be visually verified immediately before they were struck. This put NATO aircraft and pilots at greater risk of being shot down, but the forces felt it was necessary to minimize civilian casualties. The revision of the rule seems to me to strengthen the argument that NATO intended to comply with the principle of discrimination.

However, to meet right intention, the military actions planned and taken must be in line with remediating the just cause. The right intention in the Kosovo conflict was to stop the ethnic cleansing on the ground. General Clark makes a moral case that to act with right intention, tactics should have aimed to "relieve the direct pressure the Serbs were putting on the Kosovars. How could we morally justify not striking at the Serbs on the ground, if we had the ability to do so?"[100] Whether the NATO forces had the ability to do so, however, is questionable, in terms of political will and domestic political support. It was not likely possible for President Clinton to have raised support from Congress and the American people to have sent ground troops into Kosovo. This problem points to the spectrum along which we judge all these categories. Right intention was met as far as was politically possible.

Legitimate authority

State actors hold legitimate authority to engage in offensive humanitarian war. A multilateral actor has a stronger degree of legitimacy than a single state actor, but we might be concerned that NATO is ideologically fairly homogenous. The intervention was not posed to the security council for authorization because it was expected that China and Russia would veto any authorization to use force. However, there was substantive as opposed to formal multilateralism, and, therefore, it meets the test for legitimate authority in my conception of the criterion. The intervention was not authorized by the United Nations Security Council, and so it was "illegal," but this is independent of the requirements of legitimate authority as I described them in Chapter 4. United Nations Security Council Authorization would have made the intervention more strongly legitimate in the sense of international consensus and approval, but it is not required for the category to be satisfied.

I argued in Chapter 4 that multilateral organizations are generally more legitimate than single state actors, when the decision-making power is substantively shared. NATO had at the time 26 member states, and any one of them at any time could have demanded an end to the bombing campaign. Furthermore, any one of them could, and did, veto particular targets. In the Kosovo case, NATO enjoyed strong international legitimacy because of its consensus decision-making. When the number of countries participating is high, and especially when there is some diversity of ideology or political culture among the actors, a multilateral body is more strongly legitimate than a single-state actor. There is a spectrum from less to more legitimate; NATO decision-making has more legitimate authority than a US–UK only bilateral body would have had, but it is less strongly legitimate than a more diverse body such as the United Nations. Paul Mojzes argues:

> [A] military alliance like NATO cannot claim to be the "international community, and hence is probably not the *"legitimate authority"* which can authorize AHI. If NATO were to be judged as *"legitimate authority,"* what is to prevent any other alliance, one created *e.g.* by Islamic countries, or an alliance that Russia or China may make, from claiming in the future also to be the locus of legitimate authority? The U.N., despite its limitations, is a better locus of decisions about humanitarian intervention."[101]

Intervention in Kosovo 151

As also noted in Chapter 4, multilateral actors are sometimes hindered by challenges in reaching consensus, decision-making, and coordination. There is a trade-off between legitimacy offered by the participation of many actors and the coordination problems such participation can pose. For example, General James P. McCarthy (ret.) notes:

> In Kosovo, because the NATO approval process effectively permitted any nation's leadership to withdraw a target from the list, the target sets were relatively ineffective strategically. If a key target was taken off the list, NATO – continually looking for ways to demonstrate its resolve – had to find other targets to hit instead. Striking these lower priority targets may have been more destructive and less effective than would have been the case had NATO leaders allowed military forces to strike the original targets. Military leaders respect the right and rationale of nations and political leaders to establish the parameters for military operations, but the consequences of politically withholding individual targets can be significant because it reduces operational effectiveness and increases the number of targets required to achieve the desired effect. NATO's compromises on targeting also undercut its political and strategic objective – which was to shorten the war and minimize the damage as just war theory advises.[102]

It is possible to argue that an unintended effect of the consensus system was that the war was longer and more destructive than it might have otherwise been. Multilateral actors are more legitimate than single-state actors, but the greater number of actors brings coordination problems and, in the Kosovo case, challenges for *jus in bello* proportionality.

Last resort

Viewed through the lens of Walzer's just war theory, it would seem that last resort was satisfied in the Kosovo case. There was nothing more to be done at the time of the commencement of bombing. The last negotiation, the last diplomatic mission had been finished, and ethnic cleansing was underway. In my understanding of last resort, however, it is not enough to say that a war has become necessary to call it a last resort. We must also be able to say that everything that could reasonably have been done to try and prevent the conflict, was done. That is not the case in the Kosovo conflict.

Other avenues of negotiation could have been pursued to try and avert this conflict.[103] We cannot say for sure that war would have been averted, but some preventive possibilities for non-violent conflict resolution were ignored, avoided, and refused, by all the parties. The result was that the parties in conflict became more entrenched in their positions, and, therefore, the conflict became much harder to resolve diplomatically. As noted in Chapter 4, Michael Lund suggests this is a general rule; the longer conflicts brew, the more deeply entrenched parties become in their positions, and the more difficult it becomes to avoid violent confrontation.[104] It is possible that had mediation been brought to bear early enough, the parties' positions might have been reconcilable, and the war might have been avoided. A war that could have been avoided is not a just war.

In the Kosovo case, waiting outside the borders for internal politics to resolve themselves in fact simply allowed conditions to deteriorate further, making an eventual settlement more difficult to achieve. The spiral of attacks and counterattacks created resentments and entrenchment of the parties' positions, and diminished the chance for face-saving solutions to be found. Had international mediation been brought to bear earlier, and particularly had the non-violent resistance movement been engaged in the early 1990s after the Kosovo Assembly was dismantled, perhaps violent conflict could have been avoided.[105]

In the case of the London Conference, in retrospect we can discern "a grotesque expression of the sidelining of Kosovo."[106] In October, 1991, just after the referendum on independence, Ibrahim Rugova wrote a letter to the chairman of the European Community Conference on Yugoslavia, Lord Carrington, asking that the chair give "his 'full and immediate consideration' to the recognition of Kosova as a sovereign state" (to which letter Carrington never replied).[107] Rugova followed up with another letter, requesting that his party be allowed to participate in the peace talks at the London conference. The Kosovo "shadow government" was willing, and trying, to participate in preventive diplomacy and negotiation, but they were excluded from any such process in spite of strong indicators that violent conflict might erupt in Kosovo.[108]

Kosovo Albanians boycotted the December 1992 Presidential election, when Milan Panić opposed Milošević. Rugova, for his part, refused to participate in any campaign to encourage Kosovar Albanians to vote, although international mediators attempted to persuade him. According to Bellamy, "the key problem was that these requests were not accompanied by promises of international assistance to Kosovo if Panić were elected."[109] The blame for this shortsightedness must fall mostly on Rugova, but the international community could have done more to inspire the Kosovar Albanians to vote; Bellamy suggests that Rugova could have been offered greater participation in the peace process, for example, which he sorely wanted. A Panić victory could have translated into the continued presence of the OSCE Mission of Long Duration. The Kosovo commission notes that the Mission had a deterring effect on human rights abuse, and the commission concluded that much more effort should have been put on trying to maintain a strong international presence within Kosovo; one way to have done that would have been to offer incentives to Rugova to encourage Kosovo Albanians to vote in the 1992 Presidential election. It might have been worth inflaming Milošević by inviting the Kosovars to the peace talks, if that would have meant Albanians would vote and oust Milošević.

Prior to the 1991 referendum, the Kosovar position was that Kosovo was entitled to the status of an independent republic within Serbia. Until 1998, the Serbs had indicated they would accept Kosovar autonomy, although not independence.[110] During the mid-1990s, many compromise proposals were circulating among the Kosovars, including the partition of Kosovo and the three Republic proposal, under which Kosovo would have been assigned a status similar to that of Montenegro.[111] The International Commission on Kosovo notes that:

> the Kosovar Albanians in this period were being urged by President Berisha in Tirana to be more conciliatory and to open up talks with Belgrade. Had the international community been more attentive in these years, it could've put pressure on Milošević to negotiate seriously with the LDK. If Western powers have treated the LDK with greater respect, they – like Berisha – also could have encouraged this nascent discussion of political options involving autonomy short of independence.[112]

Chances for negotiation on these issues were missed at the London Conference as noted above, and again at Dayton, when the minimal demands of the parties might not have been so far apart as to have been irreconcilable. We cannot know what would have happened, because the topic was not broached in a serious way.

Dayton brought disillusionment to the Kosovo Albanians and renewed confidence to the Serbs. After the Dayton Accords were signed on November 21, 1995, the situation grew increasingly intractable. Waiting outside the borders created conditions for the moral hazard situation in Kosovo.[113] The period of 1995 to 1998 was marked by increasing KLA attacks on Serbian police and military targets, and by increased Serbian police repression and harassment of Kosovar Albanian civilians in an effort to root out the KLA. By 1998, face-saving options were few. Options had narrowed, and once international mediation was finally attempted, the minimal demands of the parties proved irreconcilable.[114]

By not publicly helping Rugova's government to make progress in at least gaining a return to pre-1990 autonomy, the international community did not help to keep that parallel system stable. When the Rugova government could not make progress on the Kosovo status question with the international community, extremist elements inside the country and in the diaspora became increasingly frustrated. When these elements began increasing military provocations, the situation became polarized, and the moderates were sidelined domestically. By helping the moderates achieve some goals short of independence, the international community might have strengthened the moderate position, thus preserving a more flexible set of options for negotiations and averting polarization. As opposed to the more irredentist elements in the diaspora, who had a romantic notion of a Greater Albania, and the KLA extremists who wanted full independence, the moderate Kosovars were influenced by the Eastern European independence movements led by intellectuals. These Kosovars envisioned a velvet revolution of their own and a more progressive, European identity for Kosovo; they may have been willing to settle for meaningful autonomy rather than full independence.[115] Had Rugova and Panić been at the negotiating table in the mid-1990s, instead of the KLA and Milošević in 1999, the war might have been averted.

Some commentators characterize the international community's decision to delay dealing with the Kosovo question as "sacrificing Kosovo" in order to secure the cooperation of Milošević as a negotiating partner. Miall, Ramsbotham, and Woodhouse argue: "During 1995 and 1996 the West courted Milošević in order to gain a settlement to the Bosnia issue, in effect sacrificing conflict prevention in Kosovo in order to achieve a war ending in Bosnia."[116]

Ambassador Holbrooke has referred to Milošević as both the cause of and the solution to many of the problems, often quoting a Yugoslav journalist, who characterized Miloševi as "both arsonist and fireman." The fireman was needed if the arsonist's fire was to be put out. Soon after the Dayton agreement was signed, the EU unconditionally recognized the FRY, increasing the frustration and desperation of the Albanian population. Although the outer wall of sanctions remained in place, its removal conditional on the improvement of conditions in Kosovo, the "outer wall" was insignificant: "it did not impress Milošević, who was not moved to initiate discussions on the future of Kosovo because Yugoslavia could not return to the IMF."[117] The international community's willingness to leave Kosovo aside at Dayton seems in retrospect to have encouraged Milošević in the belief that he could do as he wished in Kosovo.

Signing on to last resort requires states to do what they can to minimize the likelihood that a conflict will progress to violence. However, policy-makers should be careful to ensure meaningful progress is being made to defuse the conflict, rather than allowing outlaw states to stall and avoid combat until it is more convenient for them. The West allowed Milošević to avoid opening an additional front, to his advantage, when it could have used his desire not to open an additional front as leverage to encourage negotiations on Kosovo.

Finally, Rambouillet does not appear to have been a good faith effort at negotiation on the part of the United States and its allies. The document was impossible for Milošević to accept, and it is likely that the United States knew that. Whether the intention was to start from a strong position and then have Appendix B to give away, we cannot say. Nevertheless, Appendix B was not given away, so if that was the intention, it was not followed. Whether there was intention of *bona fide* negotiation is unclear. It is possible that the decision to bomb was made before the Rambouillet conference. In this case, it is possible that Rambouillet was intended rather as a means to legitimate the just cause for bombing and garner domestic and foreign support, in the manner of what Richard Ned Lebow has called a "justification of hostility crisis."[118] We cannot say with confidence that the negotiations at Rambouillet satisfied last resort.

Proportionality

Ad bellum proportionality requires that decision-makers can reasonably expect that the good likely to be achieved by fighting the proposed war is greater than the harm likely to be caused by fighting it. Decision-makers also should be able to expect that the harm that would be caused if the war were forgone is likely to be greater than the harm that would be caused by fighting. Calculations like these require that consideration be given to various possible scenarios or trajectories a war might take, before it is started. Proportionality calculations necessitate imagining possible outcomes, given a baseline of known elements and adjusting predictions about outcomes based on different values for variable unknowns. As noted in Chapter 4, some commentators find this approach to proportionality to be so difficult to employ that it is nearly useless. Nevertheless, decisions about going to war must be based on some anticipatory calculation of plausible consequences of going to war and of avoiding war.

In the case of Kosovo, in March, 1999, the baseline of elements that were thought to be known (by decision-makers in NATO member countries) included the idea that the Serbian regime in Belgrade was intent on pursuing a military plan of ethnic cleansing in Kosovo. The regime had a history in Kosovo of engaging in repression and a recent history of, at best, indiscriminate counter-insurgency attacks, and at worst, massacres of civilians. Given these known elements, the foreseeable consequences of foregoing military intervention would have been that the ethnic cleansing would proceed unopposed from the outside, and/or the war might spread to neighboring countries; certainly there would be destabilizing refugee flows into Macedonia and Albania. So the cost of not intervening was likely to be relatively high.

The cost of intervening was expected to be slight (to all parties) – NATO expected the bombing to last only three nights or so. NATO expected Milošević to become willing to sign the Ramboulliet agreement after a short period of bombing.[119] If that did not happen, some preliminary plans were in place for a phased bombing campaign, but after a short period of time, NATO ran out of approved targets, and the war had to be conducted on an ad hoc basis. "NATO member nations began the conflict with no shared political or military plan of how to fight; they lacked a strategy on the use of ground forces and had no agreement on targeting policies."[120] Given the absence of a well-thought out "plan b," it does not appear that NATO thoroughly engaged in exploring possible scenarios and trajectories in the event that Milošević did not capitulate as expected. If NATO did engage in such an exploration, it must have underestimated the ferocity with which the Serbian regime might carry out ethnic cleansing. If it did explore that possibility, and the forced deportation of 800,000 refugees was foreseen, it is hard to say how NATO would have been able to say that the Kosovo bombings would have done less harm than good. Because the type of force applied, airpower over Kosovo, was not likely to be tactically effective at stopping the ethnic cleansing, it was likely to cause physical destruction and human casualties without remedying the just cause. This cannot be called proportionate.

General Clark argued during the campaign that the most effective way to end the conflict would be to strike at the heart of the Serb command and control in Belgrade. Implementing this strategy might have achieved NATO's objectives more quickly, allowing an earlier end to the war, fewer casualties, and less physical destruction. Striking targets in Kosovo was relatively ineffective, and because it continued for so long the bombing was extremely destructive. As a result, postwar reconstruction was more difficult than it otherwise might have been. NATO member countries could not agree to strike the targets in downtown Belgrade proposed by Clark, citing concerns about civilian suffering. It is true that if the motive for striking targets in downtown Belgrade was to cause civilian suffering and use that suffering as a lever to force Milošević's hand, this would be impermissible under the laws of war. Decision-makers are never to use the suffering of civilians to achieve a political end. This raises a question that is impossible, unfortunately, for me to answer here – whether it is sometimes okay to kill some smaller number of non-combatants to prevent some larger number from being killed. This utilitarian argument is the subject of much philosophical debate. In the Kosovo case, however, Clark's argument called for striking command and control targets, causing disruption to the regime and the military. The disruption and suffering caused to non-combatants, and even civilian casualties, would have been a foreseeable but unintentional side effect of the attacks; however, civilian suffering would not have been intended as part of a strategy to force Milošević's hand.[121] In the end, it was this strategy that won the war, and if it had been adopted earlier, the war could have been prosecuted in a way that it might have been expected to do more good than harm.

Regarding *in bello* proportionality it must be said that NATO did analyze each target in terms of the numbers of civilian casualties that were likely, and planners tried to minimize civilian casualties. General Clark gives an account of planners carefully estimating collateral damage and unintended civilian casualties, using mathematical formulas that accounted for blast and fragmentation effects for different types of weapons and data specific to the target sets. NATO also used formulas to estimate building occupancy at different times of the day to make their calculations of damage likely to be done by the bombing as accurate as possible.[122]

The NATO intervention failed to stop the ethnic cleansing in Kosovo, in fact, it may have created conditions under which 90 percent of the Kosovo Albanian population was expelled by the Serb military, or fled in fear of both the Serbs and the bombing. However, there were some successes: the conflict did not spread to neighboring Macedonia until 2001, and then it was limited. Perhaps because international forces were on the ground in neighboring areas, a much wider war did not break out in 1999. The Serb forces were eventually forced out of Kosovo, and about 800,000 refugees returned home in one of the largest refugee repatriations in history.

Conclusion

The theory Walzer constructs in *Just and Unjust Wars* allows humanitarian intervention in the case of genocide, ethnic cleansing, enslavement, and widespread massacres. Once massacres were clearly underway or ethnic cleansing had commenced, Walzer's theory finds that the just cause criterion was satisfied. In the case of Kosovo, Walzer has said that the intervention was "completely justified and perhaps obligatory."[123] Whether the massacres were provoked by the KLA is not germane to Walzer's theory; the crucial element is that the state, for whatever reason, has committed massacres of civilians. Before the massacres commenced, Walzer's theory would not have found there to be a just cause for outside intervention in the conflict between the KLA and the Yugoslav government. Nor would Walzer's theory have found just cause for an intervention to assist the Kosovo Albanian people to liberate themselves from an apartheid-like regime. Walzer's view finds that whoever can intervene in the face of massacres, should intervene. Walzer does not put much emphasis on the other categories of restraint (see Chapter 4).

My view differs from Walzer's in two major aspects. First, my view would have found a just cause for influence, interference, and intervention earlier than Walzer's view. My threshold for just cause is lower than Walzer's. As explained in Chapter 3, atrocity crimes including persecution constitute just cause in my formulation. There is little doubt that atrocity crimes were being committed against ethnic Albanians from the mid-1990s onward.[124] Both Albanians and Serbs have been victims of atrocity crimes, however. During the period 1974–1989, it is even possible that there was just cause for outside influence, interference, or even intervention to assist the ethnic Serbs if they were intentionally and severely[125] denied fundamental rights on ethnic grounds. After 1990, if there was persecution against ethnic Albanians that constituted crimes against humanity, there would have been a just cause for intervention in my view.

My view also differs from Walzer's in that the analysis is structured differently. My view interprets the other *jus ad bellum* categories of restraint differently from Walzer's view, as I explained in Chapter 4. In my view, these categories of restraint must also be satisfied in advance of a decision to resort to war, if that war is to be called completely justified. I agree with Walzer that there was a just cause. However, because we cannot say last resort, proportionality, and likelihood of success were fully satisfied, my view cannot find that NATO's intervention was clearly a justified resort to force.

Conclusions

Revision of Walzer's emphasis on aggression/defense

I tried to show that Walzer's emphasis on aggression and defense (as he defines these) leads to an insufficient and even potentially misleading framework for analysis of the justice of particular wars. One weakness of Walzer's approach is that it assumes the aggressor in a war can be easily identified, as can the party acting in justified self-defense. In practice, however, sometimes it is difficult to make a determination of which party was responsible for starting the fight. There is often some measure of aggressive behavior on all sides of a conflict. Very often there is a downward spiral of escalating tension before violent conflict breaks out, and in such cases the unjust aggressor and the just defender are not always readily identifiable.

A second problem with Walzer's formulation is that it de-emphasizes the other categories of restraint. Once a just cause is perceived, the resort to war is generally held to be permissible. Walzer does not address the *jus ad bellum* questions of proportionality, likelihood of success, right intention, or legitimate authority in great detail; once one state has attacked another with force (thus generating the just cause for defensive war), a military response is almost always justified (except in the cases of a genocidal state defending genocide or a slave state defending its practice of slavery). Walzer does discuss the category of last resort, but once a just cause is apparent, last resort is of little practical value as a restraint against war. The narrow understanding of just cause means that acceptable just causes are of such an overwhelming nature that the other categories of restraint are almost always satisfied. When the category of just cause is expanded, a more comprehensive elaboration of the meaning and significance of all the categories of restraint is useful. When all things are considered, there may be many just causes but few justifiable resorts to force. In some cases, such as Kosovo, Walzer's focus on just cause leads to a different analysis and judgment about the justice of war.

I have tried to show that the purposes of just war theory are served best by the comprehensive *jus ad bellum* framework set forth in the historical and canonical treatment of just war theory combined with the Atrocity Standard for just cause. The purposes of just war theory are to help guide decision-making before the resort to war and to help guide public discussion, debate, and judgment before, during, and after a war. The comprehensive framework is slightly less handy and immediately gratifying, I suppose, because it rarely will allow us to judge particular wars as clearly and completely just or unjust. However, it provides a richer set of principles and lenses for decision-makers and citizens to utilize in organizing their debate about whether a particular resort to force is just or unjust, and in precisely which ways. For example, perhaps in a particular case everyone agrees that there is a just cause, but it is less clear whether proportionality or likelihood of success is satisfied. The point of the comprehensive framework is to recapture the language of *the rest of* just war theory and increase the breadth and depth of the tools available (and in some sense required) for responsible public argument about complex situations.

The emphasis on "threats" and "self-defense" has been paramount in some public discussions about the resort to war in Iraq, for example. This emphasis has tended to focus the debate mainly on the question of whether a just cause was present. This fixation obscures or minimizes the other relevant questions about the justice of this conflict, and it reduces the specificity and complexity of public debate. Emphasizing the importance of all the categories of restraint, and clarifying the meaning of the categories, will help to disentangle complex situations for public debate. The move I propose away from Walzer's framework and toward the comprehensive framework should provide a complex but clear (and broad enough) means of organizing public inquiry, conversations, and judgments. Walzer's framework is attractive because it is simple and clear; but it is too compact a theory to adequately serve the analytical and discursive purposes that just war theory is meant to serve, or to deal with the complexity of contemporary international relations.

A new threshold for non-intervention

Another central argument of this book has been that the non-intervention norm as defended by Walzer rests on unstable grounds, and a more stable grounding is to be found in the idea of sovereignty as responsibility. Walzer makes an essentially realist defense of non-intervention in almost any case where the state can control its territory. For Walzer, a legitimate state is one that can fight its own internal wars,[1] and foreigners are bound to stay out of such a state's internal affairs. I aimed to show, in contrast to Walzer, that only capable and responsible states are owed the duty of non-intervention. Walzer finds intervention to have been permissible in cases where there is no functioning state apparatus that can meet the needs of its people. The examples to which he refers are Sierra Leone and Liberia; he argues intervention was permissible in these cases because these states were not "decent and effective." I endorsed Walzer's findings and further concluded that non-intervention is not owed to other states that are neither decent nor effective, like Burma and Zimbabwe. Walzer's permissiveness for intervention in a failed state but prohibition of intervention to counter "the ordinary brutality of authoritarian regimes" relies on an unsustainable moral distinction

160 *Conclusions*

between a state that does not serve its people because it does not possess sufficient capacity and an authoritarian state that uses its capacity for objectionable ends. Sometimes it will likely be difficult for outsiders to distinguish merely weak regimes from wicked ones, as Walzer would likely agree. However, outsiders can recognize the misery of the inhabitants of these states, and it is difficult to see how intervention could be sanctioned in a weak state but not a wicked one, as Walzer argues.

Anti-paternalism refuted

I tried to show why the argument from anti-paternalism, in favor of non-intervention in all but the most extreme cases, is not convincing. The anti-paternalist critic says, roughly, "a people governed in accordance with their own traditions should not have to comply with the human rights preferences of the liberal west." I aimed to establish that this position is flawed by showing that respect for human rights is not a distinctively liberal or western preference. I presented evidence of the broad international consensus on minimal human rights, which has been signed onto by every member state of the United Nations. The protestations of some who attempt to justify the denial of fundamental rights to some members of their societies on grounds of custom or tradition represent an unreasonable position, albeit one sometimes expressed loudly and with spectacular violence. Outsiders are not bound to respect the wishes that some people have to deny the fundamental rights of some other people. However, it may be the case that the advocates of the traditionalist position are not a small minority, and opposing them by means of armed force may do more harm than good; but outsiders can nevertheless justifiably take a view, and if there is a severe and intentional denial of fundamental rights on a widespread or systematic basis, there is just cause for AHI. The reason a war for human rights ought not to be fought in a case like this would likely be a prudential reason, or perhaps such a war should not be fought because less destructive means might remedy the situation. The test for whether a state has a claim to non-intervention should not be whether a people is governed in accordance with its own customs, as Walzer argued. The test should be whether human security is provided for by the state.

A new threshold for just cause

I agree with Walzer's view that the threshold for just cause for intervention ought to be at "crimes that shock the conscience of mankind" but I disagree with Walzer's specification of what constitutes such crimes. For Walzer, this is a narrow set of crimes, which he calls "massive human rights abuses." Walzer argues that there is a "radical break – a chasm" between these crimes (genocide, ethnic cleansing, enslavement, and widespread massacres) and "the common brutalities" of authoritarian regimes.[2] I argued that this wide gulf does not exist. Genocide, ethnic cleansing, widespread massacre, and enslavement are only a few of the crimes against humanity that shock the conscience of mankind, as enumerated in the Rome statute. I set the threshold for just cause at atrocity crimes as defined in Articles 6, 7, and 8 of the Rome Statute of the International Criminal Court. The negotiated character of the Rome Statute and the broad international agreement as expressed in the Statute's Preamble that all the enumerated crimes "shock the conscience of mankind" demonstrates that the Atrocity Standard threshold is not distinctively liberal or western, nor does it overreach international consensus.

One implication of this expansion of just cause is that some crimes on the "ordinary brutality" side of Walzer's wide gulf constitute just cause under the Atrocity Standard. Widespread or systematic official disappearance of persons, forced sterilization, and harmful traditional practices that rise to the level of persecution, which is a crime against humanity, are some of the additional crimes that the Atrocity Standard finds to be just cause for AHI.[3] It might be impossible to create respect for human rights or stop harmful traditional practices by force of arms, but this is not a barrier to a finding of just cause. Rather, it means that the likelihood of success criterion is not met. Perhaps it is also true that interference short of armed force might be effective, in which case the last resort criterion would not be met. The barrier to AHI in such cases is not the absence of a just cause.

In Chapter 4, I tried to show that expansion of the just cause criteria to the Atrocity Standard does not yield an excessively permissive just war theory, or even an overly permissive standard for just cause. The wider scope of just cause articulated in the Atrocity Standard does not include trivial complaints. The threshold is at those crimes against humanity acknowledged in the Preamble of the Rome Statute to "shock the conscience of mankind." Furthermore, just cause is only one element of the *jus ad bellum*. Just cause alone is never a sufficient criterion to justify the resort to war in the comprehensive framework. Instead, the comprehensive framework insists on a thorough analysis of circumstances through the lenses of the other categories of restraint as well, even in the case of self-defense.

In Chapters 5 and 6, I argued that the permissiveness of Walzer's version of just war theory can at times be more worrisome than the permissiveness of the Atrocity Standard combined with the comprehensive framework, even though Walzer's scope for just cause is narrower. The permissiveness to worry about in Walzer's position is that once armed aggression is imminent or underway and the aggressor and defender are clearly identified, the other *jus ad bellum* restraints appear to become largely moot. These differences between the two frameworks were set out in Chapter 5 and further illustrated in Chapter 6 by the divergence in the two frameworks' analyses of the Kosovo conflict.

Noted further implications of taking last resort, proportionality, and likelihood of success seriously. Taking these restraints seriously means that preventive action is required where possible; preventive action does not necessarily mean military action.

I extended Walzer's maxim that "a war fought before its time is not a just war"[4] to also say that "a war that might have been prevented by earlier action is not a just war." The significance of this change is that it becomes impermissible to ignore an intensifying conflict, and when war becomes necessary, to claim it is the last resort. The requirements of proportionality, last resort, and likelihood of success all entail that decision-makers evaluate and respond to early warning signals, when this is possible, in order to prevent war from becoming necessary and to solve conflicts in the least costly way. Prevention is always less costly than fighting. Because the just cause criteria have been expanded in the Atrocity Standard, outsiders have a right of interference in matters that under the old paradigm were considered to be matters of internal concern. The practical significance of this change is that outsiders are permitted to interfere earlier. Earlier translates to more proportionately, especially if armed conflict can be avoided all together by preventive diplomatic, economic, social, or military means.

If war becomes necessary in spite of reasonable efforts at early action and prevention, decision-makers may claim that war is the last resort. If war becomes necessary but reasonable preventive efforts were not made, decision-makers can claim that a war is necessary, but they cannot claim the justice of last resort.

Problematized the argument from moral hazard

One argument against humanitarian intervention is the moral hazard argument. It asserts that a norm permitting international intervention to stop massacres or genocide will act as an incentive for a persecuted (or perhaps just disgruntled) minority to provoke the government of its state into perpetrating massacres. I aimed to show that it is untenable to suggest that because of the moral hazard danger, outsiders should be barred from rescuing victims of massacres. Instead of the threshold being too low, as the moral hazard argument suggests, I aimed to demonstrate that the threshold is too high. If outsiders could influence, interfere, and if necessary, intervene, when persecution is taking place, there would be no incentive for the minority to provoke massacres; however, they might still provoke "lesser" atrocities to try and bring intervention to bear in their case. The moral hazard problem illuminates one important reason why, instead of waiting outside the borders for massive human rights abuses like massacres and genocide to occur, international actors should become engaged earlier. Bringing mediation to bear early in a conflict is better, even if the international community is manipulated into providing mediation, than waiting outside the border while the conflict escalates, and possibly being manipulated into AHI later.

Significance

Further refinement of the categories and further explanation and discussion of their implications in restraining the "dogs of war" (and particularly the importance generated by just war principles of the obligation to try to prevent armed conflict) will be a benefit to democratic citizens. Just war scholarship should provide, as Walzer notes so beautifully in the Preface to the first edition of *Just and Unjust Wars*, a framework for democratic citizens to argue among themselves and with their leaders.

If the comprehensive framework becomes the dominant paradigm and is adopted by a large portion of democratic citizens and academics, leaders will have to answer more questions about all the categories of restraint instead of referring only to the justice of a cause. The obligations of academics in a democratic society include insisting on deep and honest inquiry into questions with public consequences. The comprehensive framework expands the scope of the inquiry about the justice of resorting to war. The discussion is enlarged beyond questions of threat and self-defense to include questions of cost, complexity, the status of preventive efforts, legitimacy, intention, and likely outcomes, among others. If public discussion is framed in the more comprehensive way, leaders will likely have to answer additional types of questions to justify any resort to war [consider omitting: The practical effect may be little; but it will take more effort for a dishonest leader to "weave a fair pretense" of wool to pull over the eyes of a democratic people]. I am convinced that expressions of just-war thinking that hold a just cause to be a sufficient condition for the resort to war lead too easily to the use of force. It is too easy to misunderstand or even to misrepresent potential threats as imminent and grave enough to constitute a "just cause" for war. Furthermore, if the Atrocity Standard is adopted for just cause, the number of cases where many people are willing to argue that just cause is present will multiply. In cases where just cause is present but the prospective resort to war could not satisfy the other restraints, the comprehensive framework might constitute a brake on the rush to war. Whether widespread popular use of the comprehensive framework for analysis would actually result in a greater or lesser number of military conflicts is an empirical, not an ethical question, and I cannot answer it in this book. I hope that it would lead at least to deliberation rather than a rush to judgment and action based on emotional or unreflective reactions to perceived threats.

If the Atrocity Standard is widely accepted as a threshold for just cause, as I hope the reader will be convinced it should be, then it would become inconsistent for perpetrators of ongoing crimes against humanity to claim protection behind the mantle of state sovereignty while they are actively perpetrating atrocities. The atrocity threshold clarification is necessary to bring just war theory in line with not only the emerging norms of sovereignty as responsibility and the responsibility to protect, but also in line with the evolution of international legal thought and institutions. It would be inconsistent to maintain that atrocity crimes are crimes against humanity for which perpetrators should be prosecuted by international tribunals if domestic legal institutions abrogate their responsibility to do so, while at the same time accepting that state sovereignty or a right of national self-determination could be invoked to shield the perpetrators from intervention to stop the atrocities.

Just war theory is a toolkit of language about principles by which concerned citizens, including academics and decision-makers, can organize their inquiry and their debate. The just war language and principles will be most useful if they include all of the *jus ad bellum* categories. In this way, we can argue about whether a particular resort to force is just or unjust on particular counts. The comprehensive view builds on Walzer's work by re-articulating the importance for public discourse of all the other categories of restraint. The comprehensive view is more complex, and we need all the tools it provides to conduct a more adequate discussion of the justice or injustice of resorting to war.

Intractable questions and suggestions for further research

One vexing question that I have not been able to fully answer in this book is the question of where exactly is the bright shining line that says this is persecution, and this is not. I have tried to be clear that severe, intentional deprivations of fundamental rights do not include trivial instances of discrimination. Crimes against humanity can be recognized as such because they are systematic or widespread, severe and intentional, and they result in widespread or systematic lessening of life chances. This is still perhaps too vague. I have decided, of necessity, to follow the lead of international jurisprudence and leave it a bit open-ended, to be determined on a case by case basis. This is not ideal, but there is a level of uncertainty here that seems to be irresolvable.

The comprehensive framework as I have set it out is in need of further elaboration and refinement. Some areas that need more work are: a new definition of the crime of aggression, which will accommodate the understanding of states' primary purpose as providing for human security; more case studies; and *jus post bellum* planning as a part of *jus ad bellum*.

Aggression

International law prohibits offensive war, even justifiable humanitarian intervention, without the sanction of the UN Security Council. However, if it is true that offensive war is sometimes just, perhaps the legal definition of aggression will evolve to encompass that principle. Broad international acceptance of the Atrocity Standard can be reasonably hoped for, as it is consistent with the broad consensus, international cooperation, and fruitful negotiations that created the Rome Statute. If the Atrocity Standard is convincing, a new definition of aggression should reflect this new understanding of just cause. The definition of the crime of aggression under the Rome Statute is still not settled, and this is an area that needs more work.

More case studies

The Kosovo case study highlights the divergence between the judgments arrived at through Walzer's framework and the comprehensive framework. Walzer found the war to be a justified humanitarian intervention, based on his judgment that ethnic cleansing was underway when the decision for NATO to drop its first bombs was made. However, the comprehensive framework yielded a more complicated picture: just cause and legitimate authority were met, but likelihood of success, last resort, and proportionality were not fully satisfied. A rich history of the justice and injustice of particular conflicts through the lenses of the comprehensive framework would be a welcome contribution to substantive knowledge about particular wars, and such an effort would also yield a clearer understanding of the significance of the categories of restraint.

Jus post bellum planning as part of *jus ad bellum* calculations

More work should be done on *jus post bellum* obligations. Once the just cause is remedied, what constitutes a just peace? A determination of whether *jus post bellum* obligations can be met should be made prior to the resort to force. It is a substantial enough question that I think it might warrant the addition of a separate category of *jus ad bellum*. Otherwise, *jus post bellum* planning should be included as a very substantial part of the right intention, likelihood of success, and proportionality criteria. This would call for additional work on the meaning and implications of those criteria. In this case, we must be careful to always insist that remediating the just cause is only the first part of securing a just peace.

Given that the majority of conflicts that threaten human security are now intra-state instead of inter-state conflicts, just war theory is often called on to make judgments about wars of intervention. Walzer's framework, although it works well for cases where there is a clear aggressor and defender, is not sufficient to deal with the complexities of the new wars of the twenty-first century. We can update just war theory by revising the non-intervention norm in such a way as to be consistent with the emerging norms of sovereignty as responsibility and responsibility to protect.

It is also important to acknowledge that Walzer's framework does not work well when it is difficult to identify the aggressor and the defender. Re-stating the historical categories of *jus ad bellum* and using all the lenses the categories provide helps to provide citizens with guidelines for making principled decisions about whether war is, all things considered, a good idea. Insistence on using all the categories of restraint can put the brakes on the rush to judgment and to war.

Notes

Introduction

1 Thomas George Weiss, *Humanitarian Intervention: Ideas in Action* (Cambridge: MA.: Polity Press, 2007), 66.
2 Weiss quoting Kalevi Holsti, ibid., 66, n. 20.
3 Ibid. 61, n. 7. See also Peter J. Hoffman and Thomas George Weiss, *Sword and Salve: Confronting New Wars and Humanitarian Crises* (Lanham, MD: Rowman & Littlefield, 2006), 60, n. 16, quoting Peter Wallensteen and Margareta Sollenberg, "Armed Conflict, 1989–2000," *Journal of Peace Research* 38, no. 5, 632.
4 Michael Walzer, *Just and Unjust Wars: A Moral Argument with Historical Illustrations*, 3rd edn. (New York: Basic Books, 2000), xii.
5 Ibid., xv.
6 International Commission on Intervention and State Sovereignty and others, *The Responsibility to Protect* (Ottawa: International Development Research Centre, 2001), 91.
7 Michael Walzer, *Just and Unjust Wars: A Moral Argument with Historical Illustrations*, 2nd edn. (New York: Basic Books, 1992), xiii.
8 Ibid., xvi.
9 Ibid., xvi.
10 Michael Walzer, "The Moral Standing of States: A Response to Four Critics," *Philosophy and Public Affairs* 9, no. 3 (1980), 209–229.
11 Walzer, *Just and Unjust Wars: A Moral Argument with Historical Illustrations*, 2nd edn., xvi–xvii.

1 Walzer's formulation of just cause

1 Michael Walzer, "Response to Lackey," *Ethics* 92, no. 3, Special Issue: Symposium on Moral Development (1982), 547–548.
2 Michael Walzer, *Just and Unjust Wars: A Moral Argument with Historical Illustrations*, 3rd edn. (New York: Basic Books, 2000), 59. The medieval theologian referred to in this paragraph is Francisco de Vitoria. See Francisco de Vitoria, Anthony Pagden, and Jeremy Lawrance, *Political Writings* (Cambridgeand New York: Cambridge University Press, 1991), 177.
3 Walzer, *Just and Unjust Wars*, 62. (Walzer makes four exceptions to this rule, and I will introduce those exceptions below.)
4 Ibid., 51.
5 Michael Walzer, "The Moral Standing of States: A Response to Four Critics," *Philosophy and Public Affairs* 9, no. 3 (Spring 1980), 211.
6 Walzer, *Just and Unjust Wars*, 62.
7 Ibid., 54.

8 Ibid., 59.
9 Ibid., 60.
10 Ibid., 62.
11 Ibid., 59.
12 Ibid., 61–63.
13 Ibid., 74, 80–85. Walzer contrasts his view with the less restrictive formulation of Vattel, for whom preventive war might be justifiable where a regime has shown previous signs of rapacity or ambition, refused to give future securities, or in the case of augmentation of power in a traditional enemy. For a useful graphic representation depicting early conceptions of just cause where preventive war was permissible, see LeRoy Brandt Walters, *Five Classic Just-War Theories: A Study in the Thought of Thomas Aquinas, Vitoria, Suarez, Gentili, and Grotius* (New Haven, CT: S.L., 1971), 350–351.
14 Walzer's discussion of the Six-Day War is summarized in this paragraph from pp. 82–85 of *Just and Unjust Wars*. The quoted sentences in this paragraph are taken from that summary.
15 Michael Walzer, "No Strikes," *New Republic* (September 30, 2002), 20.
16 Walzer, *Just and Unjust Wars*, 62.
17 The first three points indented here are directly quoted from ibid., 90.
18 Ibid., 90.
19 Michael Walzer, "War Fair," *The New Republic* (July 31, 2006), 15.
20 Walzer, *Just and Unjust Wars*, 87–88.
21 Ibid., 96.
22 Ibid., 88, 93.
23 Ibid., 98–99.
24 Ibid., 101.
25 Ibid., 93. Of course, most of the time states do claim that secession will have these bad effects.
26 Michael Walzer, "Words of War," *Harvard International Review* 26, no. 1 (2004), 36.
27 Walzer, *Just and Unjust Wars*, 96.
28 Ibid., 88.
29 Ibid., 99.
30 Ibid., 97.
31 Ibid., 100.
32 Walzer, "The Moral Standing of States" 218.
33 Michael Walzer, "The Politics of Rescue," *Arguing About War* (New Haven, CT: Yale University Press, 2004), 70.
34 This is Walzer's phrasing, which he has used throughout his works and career (especially in speeches and interviews) to refer to the work of earlier legal scholars and just war theorists.
35 Walzer, *Just and Unjust Wars*, xii.
36 Michael Walzer, "The Argument About Humanitarian Intervention," in Michael Walzer and David Miller, *Thinking Politically: Essays in Political Theory* (New Haven, CT: Yale University Press, 2007), 240.
37 Michael Walzer, "The Politics of Rescue," *Dissent* (Winter 1995), 41.
38 Georg Meggle, *Ethics of Humanitarian Interventions*, Vol. Bd. 7 (Frankfurt: Ontos Verlag, 2004), 24.
39 Walzer, "Words of War," 36.
40 For arguments that the duty to intervene is a perfect duty, see Carla Bagnoli and Kok-Chor Tan in Meggle, *Ethics of Humanitarian Interventions* (Frankfurt: Ontos Verlag, 2004).
41 Walzer, *Just and Unjust Wars*, 237.
42 Walzer, *Arguing About War*, 208.

43 Walzer, "Arguing for Humanitarian Intervention," in Nicolaus Mills and Kira Brunner, *The New Killing Fields: Massacre and the Politics of Intervention* (New York: Basic Books, 2002); see also Walzer, "The Argument about Humanitarian Intervention."
44 Ibid.
45 Walzer, "Words of War," 36–38.
46 Michael Walzer, "How Aggressive Should Israel Be? War Fair," *The New Republic* (July 31, 2006).
47 Michael Walzer, "Just War and Terrorism," *Philosophia* 34, no. 1 (2006), 11.
48 Walzer, *Arguing About War*, 68.
49 Michael Walzer, "The Argument about Humanitarian Intervention," in Georg Meggle, ed., *Ethics of Humanitarian Interventions* (Piscataway, NJ: Transaction Books, 2004).
50 Walzer writes: "Only domestic tyrants are safe, for it is not our purpose in international society (nor, Mill thinks, is it possible) to establish liberal or democratic communities, only independent ones," *Just and Unjust Wars*, 94.
51 Michael Walzer, "The Politics of Rescue," *Dissent* (Winter 2002), 29–37.

2 Walzer's innovations

1 LeRoy Brandt Walters, *Five Classic Just-War Theories: A Study in the Thought of Thomas Aquinas, Vitoria, Suarez, Gentili, and Grotius* (New Haven, CT: S.L., 1971), 340–341.
2 Valerie Morkevicius argues interestingly that international law was not actually secularized in her paper, "Tangled Roots: International Law and the Secularization of Just War Theory," presented at the International Studies Association, 48th Annual Convention, February, 2007.
3 James Turner Johnson, *Ideology, Reason, and the Limitation of War: Religious and Secular Concepts, 1200–1740* (Princeton, NJ: Princeton University Press, 1975), 29.
4 Walters, *Five Classic Just-War Theories*, 311.
5 Terry Nardin, "The Moral Basis of Humanitarian Intervention," Symposium on the Norms and Ethics of Humanitarian Intervention, Center for Global Peace and Conflict Studies, University of California, Irvine, May 26, 2000.
6 Johnson, *Ideology, Reason, and the Limitation of War*, 38.
7 Thomas Aquinas, *Summa Theologiae, II*, Question 40 "On War," reprinted in Chris Brown, Terry Nardin, and N.J. Rengger, *International Relations in Political Thought: Texts from the Ancient Greeks to the First World War* (Cambridge and New York: Cambridge University Press, 2002), 214.
8 Psalm 82: 2–4.
9 Aquinas, *Summa Theologiae, II*, 214.
10 See Walters, *Five Classic Just-War Theories*.
11 A.J. Coates, *The Ethics of War* (Manchester and New York: Manchester University Press, 1997), 158.
12 Paul Ramsey, *War and the Christian Conscience: How Shall Modern War be Conducted Justly?* (Durham, NC: Published for the Lilly Endowment Research Program in Christianity and Politics by Duke University Press, 1961), 82–89, quoted passage appears on p. 87.
13 Coates, *The Ethics of War*, 161.
14 C.A.J. Coady, "The Ethics of Armed Humanitarian Intervention," USIP Peaceworks no. 22, August 2002.
15 James Turner Johnson, *Can Modern War be Just?* (New Haven, CT: Yale University Press, 1984), 22.
16 G.E.M. Anscombe, "War and Murder," in Richard A. Wasserstrom, *War and Morality* (Belmont, CA: Wadsworth, 1970), 136.
17 Ramsey, *War and the Christian Conscience*, xvii.

18 Alberico Gentili and others, *De Iure Belli Libri Tres*, Vol. [no. 16] (Oxford; London: The Clarendon Press; H. Milford, 1933). Book I, Chapter 13.
19 Ibid., Book I, Chapter 15, p. 61.
20 Hugo Grotius, *The Rights of War and Peace: Including the Law of Nature and of Nations*, translated by A.C. Campbell (New York: M.W. Dunne, 1901), 77.
21 Here Grotius is quoting Cicero, discussing the same topic. Ibid., 77.
22 Ibid.
23 Ibid., 78.
24 Walzer, *Just and Unjust Wars*, 81.
25 When genocide, massacre, or mass deportation is "imminently apprehended," pre-emptive force is justified for ICISS. International Commission on Intervention and State Sovereignty and others, *The Responsibility to Protect* (Ottawa: International Development Research Centre, 2001), 33.
26 Emerich de Vattel, Joseph Chitty, and Edward Duncan Ingraham, *The Law of Nations* (Philadelphia, PA: T. & J.W. Johnson & Co., 1863), Book II, Chapter 4, section 56.
27 Walters, *Five Classic Just-War Theories*, 182; see also Gesina Hermina Johanna van der Molen, *Alberico Gentili and the Development of International Law. His Life, Work and Times*, 2nd rev. edn. (Leyden: A.W. Sijthoff, 1968).
28 Michael Walzer, "The Moral Standing of States: A Response to Four Critics," *Philosophy and Public Affairs* 9, no. 3 (1980), 220–221.
29 Francisco de Vitoria, Anthony Pagden, and Jeremy Lawrance, *Political Writings* (Cambridge: Cambridge University Press, 2001), 278, 288.
30 Ibid., 288.
31 Ibid., 280–288.
32 Walzer, *Just and Unjust Wars*, xi.
33 G. Scott Davis, "Conscience and Conquest: Francisco de Vitoria on Justice in the New World," *Modern Theology* 13, no. 4 (1984), 475.
34 William V. O'Brien, "Just and Unjust Wars (Book Review)," *Political Science Quarterly* 94, no. 1 (1979), 22.
35 Grotius, *The Rights of War and Peace*, 2. See Grotius' discussion of Phalaris, Diomede, and Busiris, 288.
36 Ibid., 504–506.
37 Ibid., Book 2, Chapter 25, paragraph vii.
38 Ibid.
39 Emerich de Vattel, *The Law of Nations*, section 18, on the equality of states.
40 Ibid., 155.
41 In the section on right intention, I will argue that mixed-motives are permissible, even desirable, as long as the intervener's intention is limited to rectifying the just cause.
42 Grotius, *The Rights of War and Peace*, 289.
43 Samuel Pufendorf, *On the Duty of Man and Citizen*, James Tully, ed., (Cambridge: Cambridge University Press, 1991), 170.
44 Charles R. Beitz, "Bounded Morality: Justice and the State in World Politics," *International Organization* 33, no. 3 (1979), 406.
45 Walzer, "The Moral Standing of States," 228.
46 Also see "The Communitarian Critique of Liberalism," in Michael Walzer and David Miller, *Thinking Politically: Essays in Political Theory* (New Haven, CT: Yale University Press, 2007).
47 Walzer, "The Moral Standing of States," 211.
48 Ibid., 212.
49 Gerald Doppelt, "Walzer's Theory of Morality in International Relations," *Philosophy and Public Affairs* 8, no. 1 (1978), 3–26; Ernest van den Haag, "Yoo-Hoo! Yooganda?," *National Review* 30, no. 15, 475.

50 Doppelt, "Walzer's Theory of Morality in International Relations," 6; Darrel Moellendorf, "Marxism, Internationalism, and the Justice of War," *Science and Society* 58, no. 3 (1994), 264.
51 Doppelt, "Walzer's Theory of Morality in International Relations," 6.
52 Ibid., 8.
53 Ibid., 10–11.
54 Walzer, *Just and Unjust Wars*, 97.
55 Doppelt, "Walzer's Theory of Morality in International Relations," 13.
56 Charles R. Beitz, *Political Theory and International Relations* (Princeton, NJ: Princeton University Press, 1999), 69.
57 Ibid.
58 Walzer, *Just and Unjust Wars*, 87.
59 Charles R. Beitz "Bounded Morality: Justice and the State in World Politics," *International Organization* 33, no. 3 (1979), 415.
60 Beitz, *Political Theory and International Relations*, 87.
61 David Luban, "Just War and Human Rights," *Philosophy and Public Affairs* 9, no. 2 (1980), 168.
62 Ibid., 166.
63 Ibid., 169.
64 Ibid., 179–180.
65 Ibid., 180.
66 Ibid.,
67 Ibid., 165.
68 Richard Wasserstrom, "Just and Unjust Wars (Book Review)," *Harvard Law Review* 92, no. 2 (1978), 542.
69 Ibid., 542.
70 Ibid.
71 Ibid.
72 Doppelt, "Walzer's Theory of Morality in International Relations," 7.
73 Walzer, *The Moral Standing of States*, 210.
74 Ibid.
75 Ibid., 215.
76 Ibid., 216.
77 Walzer, *Just and Unjust Wars*, 101; and affirmed in Walzer, *The Moral Standing of States*, 215: "A state that is stable, that manages to control its own people, is therefore legitimate."
78 Wasserstrom, "Just and Unjust Wars (Book Review)," 542.
79 Walzer, *The Moral Standing of States*, 215.
80 Ibid., 212.
81 Ibid., 216.
82 Ibid., 225.
83 Ibid., 222.
84 Luban, *Just War and Human Rights*, 180.
85 Gerald Doppelt, "Statism without Foundations," *Philosophy and Public Affairs* 9, no. 4 (1980), 399–400.
86 Ibid., 403.
87 Charles R. Beitz, "Nonintervention and Communal Integrity," *Philosophy and Public Affairs* 9, no. 4 (1980), 386.
88 David Luban, "The Romance of the Nation-State," *Philosophy and Public Affairs* 9, no. 4 (1980), 395–396.
89 Ibid., 393.
90 Ibid., 394.
91 Walzer, *The Moral Standing of States*, 221.
92 Walzer, *Just and Unjust Wars*, 96.

93 Walzer, *The Moral Standing of States*, 214.
94 Walzer, *Just and Unjust Wars*, 101.
95 Ibid., 86.
96 Ibid., 135.

> The ban on rape and murder is a matter of right. The law recognizes this right, specifies, limits, and sometimes distorts it, but it doesn't establish it. And we can recognize it ourselves, and sometimes do, even in the absence of legal recognition.

97 In his essay, "The Argument about Humanitarian Intervention," Walzer affirms a similar analogy, "a brutal husband and a scream in the night," referring to cases of genocide. However, he would reject my argument, I think, that the analogy extends to cases less grievous than genocide. In such cases Walzer uses the analogy of the individual rather than the household. The individual represents, I suppose, communal integrity – the community as one body.
98 Walzer, *Just and Unjust Wars*, 93, 101.
99 Fernando R. Teson, "The Liberal Case for Humanitarian Intervention," (November 2001). FSU College of Law, Public Law Research Paper No. 39.
100 Walzer, *Just and Unjust Wars*, 90.
101 John Stuart Mill, "A Few Words on Non-intervention," *Collected Works of John Stuart Mill*, Vol. xxi: *Essays on Equality, Law and Education* (Toronto: Toronto University Press, 1984).
102 I will discuss each of these reasons further in Chapters 4 and 5.
103 Martha Craven Nussbaum, *Women and Human Development: The Capabilities Approach* (Cambridge and New York: Cambridge University Press, 2000), 34.
104 Valerie Morkevicius, "Tangled Roots: International Law and the Secularization of Just War Theory," Paper presented at the annual meeting of the International Studies Association 48th Annual Convention, Hilton Chicago, Chicago, Illinois, February 28, 2007.
105 Elizabeth Anscombe uses similar words to explain why the aggressor/defender paradigm is not sufficient for a theory of justice about war, and David Luban uses the same phrase as well.

3 A reformulation of the non-intervention norm and a revised conception of just cause

1 For a discussion of this type of tension regarding widow immolation in India, see Anne Hardgrove, "Sati Worship and Marwari Public Identity in India" *The Journal of Asian Studies* 58, no. 3. (1999), 723–752.
2 David Scheffer has suggested using the term "atrocity crimes" to capture the meaning of the entire list in his essay "Why International Law Matters in God's World," in Jonathan Rothchild, Matthew Myer Boulton, and Kevin Jung, *Doing Justice to Mercy: Religion, Law, and Criminal Justice* (Charlottesville, VA: University of Virginia Press, 2007).
3 The expression "organizing the debate," captures just what I think just war theory is useful for. The expression is used by David Little in his unpublished lecture on "The Role of the Academic in a Time of War."
4 Michael Walzer, *Just and Unjust Wars: A Moral Argument with Historical Illustrations*, 3rd edn. (New York: Basic Books, 2000), 90.
5 International Commission on Intervention and State Sovereignty, *The Responsibility to Protect* (Ottowa: International Development Research Centre, 2001), 91; Jerome Slater and Terry Nardin, "Nonintervention and Human Rights," *The Journal of Politics* 48, no. 1 (1986), 86–96.
6 David Scheffer suggests the shorthand use of the term "atrocity crimes" in his essay, "Why International Law Matters in God's World."

7 Michael Walzer, "The Argument About Humanitarian Intervention," in Georg Meggle, ed., *Ethics of Humanitarian Interventions* (Frankfurt: Ontos Verlag, 2004), 22–23.
8 Walzer, *Just and Unjust Wars*, 101.
9 International Commission on Intervention and State Sovereignty, *The Responsibility to Protect*, 13.
10 United Nations, High-Level Panel on Threats, Challenges, and Change and United Nations, *A More Secure World: Our Shared Responsibility: Report of the High-Level Panel on Threats, Challenges, and Change* (New York: United Nations, 2004), 15–16.
11 Ibid., 2.
12 Ibid.
13 Ibid., 129.
14 Ibid., 27, 30, 47.
15 United Nations Charter, Chapter XV, Article 99.
16 Stephen Stedman, personal conversation, Spring 2005.
17 Simon Chesterman has recorded the practical expansion in the use of the term "threat to international peace and security" by the United Nations Security Council in Simon Chesterman, *Just War Or Just Peace? Humanitarian Intervention and International Law* (Oxford and New York: Oxford University Press, 2002). See also Elizabeth Reid, "A Future, if One is Still Alive: The Challenge of the HIV Epidemic," in Johnathan Moore, ed. *Hard Choices: Moral Dilemmas in Humanitarian Intervention* (Lanham, MD: Rowman & Littlefield, 1998), 269–286.
18 International Commission on Intervention and State Sovereignty, *The Responsibility to Protect*, 7.
19 Capacities are universal raw material, prospective capabilities. Capabilities refer to what you could actually do and be if you choose to do so (taking into account your resources and political situation), and functioning refers to what you are and do (achievements). Also see Martha Craven Nussbaum, "In Defense of Universal Values," *Women and Human Development: The Capabilities Approach* (New York: Cambridge University Press, 2000); Amartya Sen, "Functionings and Capability," *Equality Reexamined* (Cambridge, MA: Harvard University Press, 1992), 39–54.
20 Martha Craven Nussbaum, *Women and Human Development*, 238.
21 Ibid.
22 See Michael Walzer, "The Politics of Rescue," *Arguing About War* (New Haven, CT: Yale University Press, 2004), 75; also Walzer "The Argument About Humanitarian Intervention" and Michael Walzer, "Arguing for Humanitarian Intervention," in Kira Bruner and Nicolaus Mills, eds., *The New Killing Fields: Massacre and the Politics of Intervention* (Cambridge, MA: Basic Books, 2002). Also see Walzer's preface to the third edition of *Just and Unjust Wars*, xiii.
23 Carla Bagnoli, "Humanitarian Intervention as a Perfect Duty. A Kantian Argument," *Nomos* 47 (2004); Kok-Chor Tan, "The Duty to Protect," *Nomos* 47, (2004).
24 Allen E. Buchanan, *Justice, Legitimacy, and Self-Determination: Moral Foundations for International Law* (Oxford and New York: Oxford University Press, 2004). See also Allen Buchanan and Robert O. Keohane, "The Legitimacy of Global Governance Institutions," *Ethics and International Affairs* 20, no. 4 (2006), 405–437.
25 Terry Nardin, "International Political Theory and the Question of Justice," *International Affairs* 82, no. 3 (2006). Also see Thomas Pogge, ed. *Freedom from Poverty as a Human Right: Who Owes What to the Very Poor?* (Oxford: Oxford University Press, 2007).
26 Walzer, *Just and Unjust Wars*, 51.
27 Ibid., 86.
28 See David Scheffer, "Why International Law Matters in God's World."
29 For a discussion of the state as the means by which goods and services are delivered,

Notes 173

see United Nations, High-level Panel on Threats, Challenges, and Change and United Nations, *A More Secure World: Our Shared Responsibility: Report of the High-Level Panel on Threats, Challenges, and Change.*

30 Ibid., 129.
31 When I use the term right, I mean an "all-things-considered" right as opposed to a *prima facie* right.

4 Just cause

1 Michael Walzer, *Just and Unjust Wars: A Moral Argument with Historical Illustrations*, 3rd edn. (New York: Basic Books, 2000), xiv.
2 Michael Walzer, "The Argument About Humanitarian Intervention," in Georg Meggle, *Ethics of Humanitarian Interventions* (Frankfurt: Ontos Verlag, 2004), 22.
3 Ibid.
4 International Commission on Intervention and State Sovereignty and others, *The Responsibility to Protect*, 16.
5 Ibid., 33.
6 David Little, in conversation with John P. Reeder and in unpublished work, has suggested that Articles 6, 7, and 8 of the Rome Statute might be a reasonable threshold for AHI. I do not suggest that Little endorses my argument or my interpretation of the Atrocity Standard, however.
7 See especially Simon Chesterman, *Just War Or just Peace? Humanitarian Intervention and International Law* (Oxford: Oxford University Press, 2001).
8 See the Rome Statute of the International Criminal Court.
9 *Prosecutor* v. *Kupreskic et al.*, Trial Judgment, International Criminal Tribunal for the Former Yugoslavia (ICTY), January 14, 2000, paragraph 595.
10 Ibid., paragraph 623.
11 Ibid., paragraph 595.
12 Ibid., paragraphs 598, 599.
13 Ibid., paragraph 627.
14 United Nations, High-level Panel on Threats, Challenges, and Change and United Nations, *A More Secure World: Our Shared Responsibility: Report of the High-Level Panel on Threats, Challenges, and Change* (New York: United Nations, 2004), 129.
15 Some just war theorists do fold in proportionality to just cause, but I reject this approach because it has the effect of reducing complexity and specificity in our arguments. I will say more about this in the section on proportionality in Chapter 5.
16 McMahan, "Just Cause for War," *Ethics and International Affairs* 19, no. 3 (Fall 2005).
17 David Little, unpublished work.
18 Rome Statute of the International Criminal Court, Article 7.
19 Michael Walzer, "Words of War," *Harvard International Review* 26, no. 1 (2004) 32–34.
20 Ibid.
21 United Nations. High-level Panel on Threats, Challenges, and Change and United Nations, *A More Secure World:* 129.
22 Jeff McMahan, "Just Cause for War," *Ethics and International Affairs* 19, no. 3 (2005), 1–21.
23 Francisco de Vitoria, Anthony Pagden and Jeremy Lawrance, *Political Writings* (Cambridge: Cambridge University Press, 2001), 267; Anthony Coates, *The Ethics of War* (Manchester: Manchester University Press, 1997), 148.
24 James Turner Johnson, *Ideology, Reason, and the Limitation of War* (Princeton, NJ: Princeton University Press, 1975), 188–195.
25 John Rawls, *The Law of Peoples: With, the Idea of Public Reason Revisited* (Cambridge, MA: Harvard University Press, 1999), 78–79.

26 Fernando R. Teson, "Ending Tyranny in Iraq," *Ethics and International Affairs* 19, no. 2 (2005), 1–20.
27 Rawls, *The Law of Peoples*, 95, n. 8.
28 Ibid., 81.
29 Ibid., 79.
30 Ibid., 93–94, n. 6.
31 Fernando R. Teson, "Of Tyrants and Empires," *Ethics and International Affairs* 19, no. 2, 27–30.
32 Rawls, *The Law of Peoples*, 94, n. 6.
33 Human Rights Watch, *World Report 2000: The Events of 1999* (United States: Human Rights Watch, 1999), 167.
34 Human Rights Watch Reports, *Afghanistan: Humanity Denied: Systematic Violations of Women's Rights in Afghanistan* 13, no. 5 (C) (October 2001), 11.
35 Allen E. Buchanan, *Justice, Legitimacy, and Self-Determination: Moral Foundations for International Law* (Oxford: Oxford University Press, 2007), 287.
36 Rawls, *The Law of Peoples*, 75–78.
37 Ibid., 80, n. 23.
38 Ibid., 71.
39 David Little, "Belief, Ethnicity and Nationalism," *Nationalism and Ethnic Politics* 1, no. 2 (1995). Little notes,

> Article 2 of the *Universal Declaration* and the *Covenant on Civil and Political Rights* are the general provisions against discrimination, and Article 7 of the *Universal Declaration* and Article 26 of the *Covenant on Civil and Political Rights* guarantee equal protection of the law. (There are similar articles in all other major international human rights instruments).

40 Little, "Belief, Ethnicity, and Nationalism" (note 2) quoting Craig Calhoun, "Nationalism and Civil Society: Democracy, Diversity and Self-Determination," *International Sociology* 8, no. 4 (1993), 405.
41 Kevin Boyle and Juliet Sheen, *Freedom of Religion and Belief: A World Report* (London: Routledge 1997), 1. Boyle and Sheen cite the complaint of the Special Rapporteur on Religious Intolerance to the Human Rights Commission, December 15, 1995. E/CN1996/96, cited by David Little, "Rethinking Human Rights: A Review Essay on Religion, Relativism, and Other Matters," *Journal of Religious Ethics* 27, no. 1 (1999).
42 Allen Buchanan, "Taking the Human out of Human Rights," in Rex Martin and David A. Reidy, *Rawls' Law of Peoples: A Realistic Utopia?* (Oxford: Blackwell Publishers, 2006), 151; citing Rawls, *The Law of Peoples*, 65.
43 Rawls, *The Law of Peoples*, 10.
44 Kok-Chor Tan has noted this as well in "The Problem of Decent Peoples," in Martin and Reidy, *Rawls' Law of Peoples*, 85.
45 Rawls, *The Law of Peoples*, 75, n. 15.
46 Ibid. 10.
47 I am not sure about this point as a just cause point, only as a prudential point. David Mellow argues that intervention need not be welcomed by the victims of oppression. He asks us to imagine that

> you and your armed hunting buddies came upon a scene where people were being murdered, and you pointed your weapons but the victims urged you not to shoot because they were pacifists and would rather die than have you kill in their defense.

Mellow argues you would not be bound by their wishes not to stop the murders and extrapolates this to just war thinking. See David Mellow, "Iraq: A Morally Justified Resort to War," *Journal of Applied Philosophy* 23, no. 3, 293–310, (example given on page 297).

48 Nussbaum, *Women and Human Development*, 111.
49 Kok-Chor Tan, "The Problem of Decent Peoples," 86.
50 Martha Craven Nussbaum, *Sex and Social Justice* (New York and Oxford: Oxford University Press, 1999), 95. Also see Kok-Chor Tan, "The Problem of Decent Peoples," 85: he argues that "the structures for expressing dissent are constrained by the hierarchical values of the society that are themselves the very source of contention."
51 Nussbaum, *Sex and Social Justice*, 151.
52 Amartya Sen, "Gender Inequality and Theories of Justice," in Martha Craven Nussbaum, Jonathan Glover, and World Institute for Development Economics Research, *Women, Culture, and Development: A Study of Human Capabilities* (Oxford and New York: Clarendon Press; Oxford University Press, 1995), 260.
53 S. Sudha and S. Irudaya Rajan "Female Demographic Disadvantage in India 1981–1991," in Shara Razavi, ed., *Gendered Poverty and Well-Being* (Blackwell, 2000).
54 It should be noted that Teson rejects the justifications the Bush administration actually gave about weapons of mass destruction and a connection between Iraq and Al-Qaeda, but he thinks the war was justified anyway as a humanitarian intervention, even though it was not explicitly argued for in those terms by the Bush administration. This quotation is from a public event of the Carnegie Council, "Ending Tyranny in Iraq: A Debate" with Kenneth Roth, Fernando R. Teson, and Paige Arthur. A transcript is available at www.cceia.org/resources/transcripts/5268.html.
55 Alan J. Kuperman, "Reducing the Moral Hazard of Humanitarian Intervention: Lessons from Economics," American Political Science Association Annual Meeting, 2004, Chicago, IL; also Testimony in the ICTY seems to bear this out (cited in Chapter 5), as well as comments made by members of the KLA. I will say much more about the details of this case in Chapter 5.
56 Alan J. Kuperman "Suicidal Rebellions and the Moral Hazard of Humanitarian Intervention," in Timothy W. Crawford and Alan J. Kuperman, *Gambling on Humanitarian Intervention: Moral Hazard, Rebellion and Civil War* (New York: Routledge, 2006), 100.
57 Jack Straw Memo – March 25, 2002, memo from Jack Straw (UK Foreign Secretary) to Tony Blair in preparation for Blair's visit to Bush's Crawford ranch, covering Iraq–Al-Qaeda linkage, legality of invasion, weapons inspectors, and post-war considerations.
58 John Stuart Mill, "A few words on non-intervention," in Brown, Nardin and Rengger, *International Relations in Political Thought*, 122.
59 www.downingstreetmemo.com/strawtext.html accessed September 14, 2008.
60 Michael Walzer, "The Argument About Humanitarian Intervention," *Dissent* 49, no. 1 (2002), 29.
61 Mervyn Frost raised this objection to me in response to my paper on "Pre-emption and Prevention" at the ISA convention in 2006, and this objection is also mentioned by David Rodin in his chapter "The Problem with Prevention," in Henry Shue and David Rodin, eds., *Preventive War: Military Action and Moral Analysis* (Oxford: Oxford University Press, 2007), 165.
62 For an interesting exploration of this issue, see Ryan Goodman, "Humanitarian Intervention and Pretexts for War," *The American Journal of International Law* 100, no. 1 (January 2006), 107–141.
63 Hugo Grotius, *The Rights of War and Peace: Including the Law of Nature and of Nations,* translated by A.C. Campbell (New York: M.W. Dunne, 1901), 289.
64 An interesting question for future research is whether a United Nations all-volunteer multinational force or paid private armies operating on behalf of legitimate public authorities might be effective and morally appealing.
65 William F. Schulz was Executive Director of Amnesty International USA from 1994 to 2005.

66 Michael S. Lund, *Preventing Violent Conflicts: A Strategy for Preventive Diplomacy* (Washington, DC: United States Institute of Peace Press, 1996), 22, 23.
67 See Chesterman, *Just War Or just Peace?*
68 Charter of the United Nations, Article 1(2).
69 Secretary-General Kofi Annan, Ditchley Lecture 2 (June 26, 1998) quoted by David Little in "Humanitarian Intervention: A Theoretical Approach," in Joseph I. Coffey, Charles T. Mathewes, and Tanenbaum Center for Interreligious Understanding, *Religion, Law, and the Role of Force: A Study of their Influence on Conflict and on Conflict Resolution* (Ardsley, NY: Transnational Publishers, 2002), 123.
70 This paragraph draws from Martha Nussbaum's ideas published in several articles and books including "In Defense of Universal Values" and *Women and Human Development* and on John Rawls' idea of "political liberalism" as opposed to "comprehensive" or "ethical" liberalism, from his book *Political Liberalism*.
71 Sumner B. Twiss, "Comparative Ethics and Intercultural Human Rights Dialogues," in Lisa Sowle and James F. Childress, *Christian Ethics: Problems and Prospects* (Cleveland, OH: Pilgrim Press, 1996), 363.
72 David Little, "Rethinking Human Rights: A Review Essay on Religion, Relativism, and Other Matters," *Journal of Religious Ethics*, 1996.
73 My view is on non-intervention as owed to capable and responsible states is similar to the concept of sovereignty as responsibility, but because I am only talking about one attribute of sovereignty, the right to non-intervention, I have decided to use the term non-intervention and not to use the term, sovereignty. I do not wish to say states are no longer sovereign if they violate human rights systematically; remediation of the just cause is the limit of permissible intervention.
74 Nussbaum gives an account of how capabilities are related to human rights in several texts. For one very clear discussion, see Martha Craven Nussbaum, "In Defense of Universal Values," *Women and Human Development: The Capabilities Approach* (Cambridge: Cambridge University Press, 2000).
75 Ibid., 56.
76 See Nussbaum, Glover, and World Institute for Development Economics Research, *Women, Culture, and Development*, 95.
77 Sumner B. Twiss, "Comparative Ethics and Intercultural Human-Rights Dialogues: A Programmatic Inquiry," in Sowle and Childress, *Christian Ethics: Problems and Prospects.*
78 Amartya Kumar Sen, *Development as Freedom*, 1st edn. (New York: Knopf, 1999), 5.
79 Amartya Sen's definition.
80 Martha Craven Nussbaum, *Frontiers of Justice: Disability, Nationality, Species Membership* (Cambridge, MA: Harvard University Press, 2006), 76–78.
81 Ibid., 79.
82 Nussbaum, "Religion and Women's Human Rights," in Paul Weithman, ed., *Religion and Contemporary Liberalism* (Notre Dame: University of Notre Dame Press, 1997), 112–113.
83 Nussbaum, *Frontiers of Justice*, 79.
84 Ibid.
85 Ibid.
86 Interestingly, Eric Hobsbawm and Terence Ranger argue that traditions (and nations) only *seem* old because traditionalists (and nationalists) rewrite their history. See Eric Hobsbawm and Terence Ranger, *The Invention of Tradition* (Cambridge: Cambridge University Press, 1982).

5 Other *jus ad bellum* categories

1 Hugo Grotius, *The Rights of War and Peace*, vol. 2, edited and with an Introduction by Richard Tuck, from the edition by Jean Barbeyrac (Indianapolis: Liberty Fund, 2005), 1311.
2 Michael Walzer, *Just and Unjust Wars: A Moral Argument with Historical Illustrations* (New York: Basic Books, 2000), 361; Michael Walzer, "The Moral Standing of States: A Response to Four Critics," *Philosophy and Public Affairs* 9, no. 3 (1980), 209–229, http://links.jstor.org/sici?sici=0048-3915%28198021%299%3A3%3C209%3ATMSOSA%3E2.0.CO%3B2-G.
3 Paul Roe, "The Intrastate Security Dilemma: Ethnic Conflict as a 'Tragedy?'" *Journal of Peace Research* 6, no. 2 (1999), 183.
4 Susan L. Woodward and Brookings Institution, *Balkan Tragedy: Chaos and Dissolution After the Cold War* (Washington, DC: Brookings Institution, 1995), 94, 220.
5 Also see David Rodin, *War and Self-Defense* (Oxford and New York: Clarendon Press; Oxford University Press, 2002), 40–42.
6 Walzer, *Just and Unjust Wars*, 59, 68, 72.
7 Ibid., 72.
8 Ibid., 84.
9 Michael Walzer, *Arguing About War* (New Haven, CT: Yale University Press, 2004), 88.
10 Ibid. Michael Walzer, "The Argument about Humanitarian Intervention," in Georg Meggle, ed., *Ethics of Humanitarian Interventions* (Piscataway, NJ: Transaction Books, 2004), 28.
11 Walzer, *Just and Unjust Wars*, preface to the 2nd edition (Basic Books, 1992), xiv.
12 Walzer, *Just and Unjust Wars*, 218.
13 Ibid., 21.
14 Michael Walzer, "Excusing Terror," *The American Propsect* 12, 18 (October 21, 2001), 17; in very slightly different language, Walzer made exactly the same point in "Terrorism and Its Excuses" in 1988, reprinted in *Arguing About War*.
15 Ibid., 75.
16 Ibid., 84.
17 Ibid., 218.
18 *Dissent*, March 2003, Reprinted in *Arguing About War*.
19 *DJB* I, 13, 60; I, 14, esp. 65, quoted in LeRoy Brandt Walters, *Five Classic Just-War Theories: A Study in the Thought of Thomas Aquinas, Vitoria, Suarez, Gentili, and Grotius* (New Haven, CT: S.L., 1971), 318.
20 Alberico Gentili, *Three Books on the Law of War*, Book I, Chapter 15.
21 Grotius, *The Rights of War and Peace*, Book II, Chapter 23, sections vii and viii.
22 Ibid., section viii.1.
23 Hugo Grotius, *The Rights of War and Peace: Including the Law of Nature and of Nations,* translated by A.C. Campbell (New York: M.W. Dunne, 1901), 74–75.
24 Ibid., Book II.1.2.1, 50.
25 Here Grotius is quoting Cicero, discussing the same topic.
26 Ibid., 77.
27 Ibid., 78.
28 Ibid., 76.
29 Walzer, 2003.
30 David A. Welch, *Justice and the Genesis of War*, vol. 29 (Cambridge and New York: Cambridge University Press, 1993), 335; John Langan, "Just and Unjust Wars (Book Review)," *Theological Studies* 40, no. 3 (1979).
31 C.S. Lewis, *Mere Christianity* (San Francisco, CA.: Harper Collins, 2001), 119. The full quotation reads

> War is a dreadful thing, and I can respect an honest pacifist, although I think he is entirely mistaken. What I do not understand is this sort of semi-pacifism you get nowadays which gives people the idea that though you have to fight, you ought to do it with a long face and as though you were ashamed of it.

32. Michael S. Lund, *Preventing Violent Conflicts: A Strategy for Preventive Diplomacy* (Washington, DC: United States Institute of Peace Press, 1996), 220.
33. Alexander George and Jane Hall, "The Warning-Response Problem," in Bruce W. Jentleson and Carnegie Commission on Preventing Deadly Conflict, ed., *Opportunities Missed, Opportunities Seized: Preventive Diplomacy in the Post-Cold War World* (Lanham, MD: Rowman & Littlefield, 2000).
34. Allen Buchanan and Robert O. Keohane, "The Preventive Use of Force: A Cosmopolitan Institutional Proposal," *Ethics and International Affairs* 18 (2004), 1–22.
35. International Commission on Intervention and State Sovereignty and others, *The Responsibility to Protect*, xii, 32, 74.
36. Personal conversation with Ramesh Thakur, member of the International Commission on Intervention and State Sovereignty.
37. This objection was raised by Mervyn Frost in response to my paper presentation at 2006 ISA convention, San Diego, California.
38. Gregory H. Stanton, "The Eight Stages of Genocide," Working Group Paper, Yale Program in Genocide Studies, 1996.
39. Ted Robert Gurr, *Peoples Versus States: Minorities at Risk in the New Century* (Washington, DC: United States Institute of Peace Press, 2000), 399; also see Stanton, noted above.
40. Ted Robert Gurr, *Minorities at Risk: A Global View of Ethnopolitical Conflicts* (Washington, DC: United States Institute of Peace Press, 1993).
41. Wibke Kristin Timmerman, "The Relationship between hate propaganda and Incitement to Genocide: A New Trend in International Law Towards Criminalization of Hate Propaganda?" *Leiden Journal of International Law* 18 (2005), 263–264.
42. Michael N. Barnett, *Eyewitness to a Genocide: The United Nations and Rwanda* (Ithaca, NY: Cornell University Press, 2002), 77–79.
43. Anthony Coates, *The Ethics of War* (Manchester: Manchester University Press, 1997) 190.
44. Henry Allen Stephenson, "The Justice of Preventive War," Master's Thesis, Naval Postgraduate School, Monterey, CA., 2004.
45. See the 2002 National Security Strategy of the United States.
46. Jeff McMahan, "Preventive War and the Killing of the Innocent," in Richard Sorabji and David Rodin, *The Ethics of War: Shared Problems in Different Traditions* (Aldershot and Burlington, VT: Ashgate, 2006), 174.
47. Peter S. Temes, *The Just War: An American Reflection on the Morality of War in our Time* (Chicago, IL: Ivan R. Dee, 2003), 168.
48. Thomas B. Biersteker, Sue E. Eckert, and Peter Romaniuk, *Targeted Financial Sanctions: A Manual for Design and Implementation (Contributions from the Interlaken Process)* (Providence, RI: Watson Institute for International Studies, 2001). For a list of publications on sanctions reform, see the *Targeted Sanctions Bibliography* maintained by the Targeted Sanctions Project of the Watson Institute for International Studies at Brown University and available online at www.watsoninstitute.org/pub/Targeted_Sanctions_Bibliography.pdf.
49. Neta Crawford and Audie Klotz, *How Sanctions Work: Lessons from South Africa* (New York: St. Martin's Press, 1999).
50. Walzer, *Just and Unjust Wars*, 51.
51. Walters, *Five Classic Just-War Theories*, 320.
52. Grotius, *The Rights of War and Peace* (1901), 281.
53. Hugo Grotius, *Commentary on the Law of Prize and Booty*, ed. and with an Intro-

duction by Martine Julia van Ittersum (Indianapolis: Liberty Fund, 2006). Chapter III: *Question I* Accessed from http://oll.libertyfund.org/title/1718/77222/1870685 on 2008-09-28.
54 Francisco de Vitoria, "On the American Indians," in *Political Writings*, (Cambridge: Cambridge University Press, 2003), 286.
55 Walters, *Five Classic Just-War Theories*.
56 Paul Ramsey quoting Father Ford on the idea of using nuclear weapons against military targets, in: Paul Ramsey, *War and the Christian Conscience: How Shall Modern War be Conducted Justly?* (Durham, NC: Published for the Lilly Endowment Research Program in Christianity and Politics by Duke University Press, 1961), 82.
57 Taylor B. Seybolt and Stockholm International Peace Research Institute, *Humanitarian Military Intervention: The Conditions for Success and Failure* (Oxford and New York: Oxford University Press, 2007); Matthew Krain, "International Intervention and the Severity of Genocides and Politicides," *International Studies Quarterly* 49, no. 3 (2005), 363–387.
58 Francisco de Vitoria, "On the American Indians," *Political Writings* (Cambridge: Cambridge University Press, 2003), 286.
59 Lund, *Preventing Violent Conflicts*, 1; also see Jerome Slater and Terry Nardin, "Nonintervention and Human Rights," *The Journal of Politics* 48, no. 1 (1986), 86–96.
60 Seybolt and Stockholm International Peace Research Institute, *Humanitarian Military Intervention*, 294; see also Matthew Krain, "International Intervention and the Severity of Genocides and Politicides," *International Studies Quarterly*, 49, no. 3: 363–387.
61 Michael Walzer, "The Politics of Rescue," *Dissent* 142, no. 4 (1995), 39.
62 Placeholder endnote please delete.
63 Walzer, *Just and Unjust Wars*, 94–95.
64 Walzer, *Arguing About War*, 76.
65 Walzer, *Just and Unjust Wars*, 192.
66 Ibid., 120.
67 Ibid., 192.
68 Paul E. Sigmund, ed., *St Thomas Aquinas on Politics and Ethics* (New York: Norton, 1988), 65.
69 Walters, *Five Classic Just-War Theories*, 318.
70 Grotius, *The Rights of War and Peace* (1901), 280.
71 Walters, *Five Classic Just-War Theories*.
72 International Commission on Intervention and State Sovereignty and others, *The Responsibility to Protect*; Lund, *Preventing Violent Conflicts*.
73 International Commission on Intervention and State Sovereignty, *The Responsibility to Protect*, 20.
74 The cost to interveners, not to the parties in conflict was calculated. "Comparing Costs of Prevention and Conflict" in Michael E. Brown and Richard N. Rosecrance, *The Costs of Conflict: Prevention and Cure in the Global Arena* (Lanham, MD: Rowman & Littlefield Publishers, 1999).
75 Thomas Hurka, "Proportionality and the Morality of War," *Philosophy and Public Affairs* 33, no. 1 (2005), 34–66.
76 See also David Mellow, "Counterfactuals and the Proportionality Criterion," *Ethics and International Affairs* 20, no. 4 (2006), 454.
77 Jefferson McMahan, "Just Cause for War," *Ethics and International Affairs* 19, no. 3 (2005), 5.
78 Lund, *Preventing Violent Conflicts*, 220; James Turner Johnson, *Ideology, Reason, and the Limitation of War: Religious and Secular Concepts, 1200–1740* (Princeton, NJ: Princeton University Press, 1975), 291.
79 I owe this point to P. Terrence Hopmann.

80. Gregory Kavka, "Was the Gulf War a Just War?" *Journal of Social Philosophy* 22, no. 1 (1991), 24.
81. Tetlock and Belkin write, "The ferocity of the critics is a bit unnerving. Moreover, they are right that counterfactual inference is dauntingly difficult. But they are wrong that we can avoid counterfactual reasoning at acceptable cost." Philip Tetlock and Aaron Belkin, *Counterfactual Thought Experiments in World Politics: Logical, Methodological, and Psychological Perspectives* (Princeton, NJ: Princeton University Press, 1996), 1.
82. For 25 methods of approaching this type of thought experiment, see Jerome C. Glenn, *Futures Research Methodology v2.0* (Washington, DC: American Council for the United Nations University, 2003).
83. Jeff McMahan and Robert McKim, "The Just War and the Gulf War," *The Canadian Journal of Philosophy* 23, no. 4 (1993), 509.
84. Mellow, "Counterfactuals and the Proportionality Criterion," 446–447.
85. See also Thomas Hurka, "Proportionality in the Morality of War," *Philosophy and Public Affairs* 33, no. 1 (2005), 34–66.
86. Fernando Teson has referred to interventions commenced dishonestly behind a false claim of humanitarian intentions as "mendacious interventions."
87. See David Little, "Response to Scheffer," in Jonathan Rothchild, Matthew Myer Boulton, and Kevin Jung, *Doing Justice to Mercy: Religion, Law, and Criminal Justice* (Charlottesville, VA: University of Virginia Press, 2007).
88. Paul Ramsey, *The Just War: Force and Political Responsibility* (Lanham, MD: University Press of America, 1983), 259.
89. Daniel M. Bell, Jr., "Just War Engaged: Review Essay of Walzer and O'Donovon," *Modern Theology* 22, no. 2 (2006), 295.
90. Walzer, *Just and Unjust Wars*, 102, 107.
91. Ibid., xxi.
92. See Johnson, *Ideology, Reason, and the Limitation of War*; Sumner B. Twiss, "History, Human Rights, and Globalization," *Journal of Religious Ethics* 32, no. 1 (2004).
93. Walters, *Five Classic Just-War Theories*, 351–355.
94. Ibid., 353.
95. Samuel Pufendorf, *On the Duty of Man and Citizen*, ed. Tully (Cambridge: Cambridge University Press, 1991), 170.
96. See John Stuart Mill, *The Collected Works of John Stuart Mill*, Vol. X, *Essays on Ethics, Religion, and Society*, ed. John M. Robson, Introduction by F.E.L. Priestley (Toronto and London: University of Toronto Press, Routledge and Kegan Paul, 1985), Chapter 2.
97. See also Fernando R. Teson, "Ending Tyranny in Iraq," *Ethics and International Affairs* 19, no. 2 (2005), for an application of the distinction between motive and intention to the 2003 Iraq War.
98. See Taylor Seybolt, "What Makes Humanitarian Intervention Effective," *SIPRI*, 2001.
99. See John Stuart Mill, *The Collected Works of John Stuart Mill*, Chapter 2, paragraph 3289.
100. Taylor Seybolt, *Effective Humanitarian Interventions: The Conditions for Success and Failure* (Oxford: Oxford University Press, 2007), 20.
101. Ibid.
102. Oliver Ramsbotham and Tom Woodhouse, *Humanitarian Intervention in Contemporary Conflict: A Reconceptualization* (Oxford: Polity, 1996), 73.
103. Quoted in Seybolt and Stockholm International Peace Research Institute, *Humanitarian Military Intervention*, 12.
104. Immanuel Kant, *Perpetual Peace*, Sixth Preliminary Article.
105. Walzer, *Arguing About War*, 80.
106. Walzer, *Just and Unjust Wars*, 105.

107 Walzer, *Arguing About War*, 78.
108 Walzer, *Just and Unjust Wars*, preface to the 3rd edition, xiv
109 Thomas Aquinas, *Summa Theologiae II*, Question 40, objection 4.
110 John Kelsay, "Just War Tradition, *Ahkam al-jihad*, and Political Decision-Making," Delivered at the Omani Training Institute for Diplomats, Muscat, Oman, February 8, 2006. Used by permission of the author.
111 Martha Finnemore, *The Purpose of Intervention: Changing Beliefs about the use of Force* (Ithaca, NY: Cornell University Press, 2003), 173.
112 This insight is from Ruggie's introductory chapter John Gerard Ruggie, *Multilateralism Matters: The Theory and Praxis of an Institutional Form* (New York: Columbia University Press, 1993).
113 Walzer, *Just and Unjust Wars*, 107.
114 David Little, "Humanitarian Intervention: A Theoretical Approach," in Joseph I. Coffey, Charles T. Mathewes, and Tanenbaum Center for Interreligious Understanding, eds., *Religion, Law, and the Role of Force: A Study of their Influence on Conflict and on Conflict Resolution* (Ardsley, NY: Transnational Publishers, 2002), 124.
115 Ibid.
116 Robert G. Kennedy "Is the Doctrine of Pre-emption a Legitimate Element of the Just War Tradition?" presented to the Joint Services Conference on Professional Ethics, Washington, DC, January 2005.
117 Wesley K. Clark, *Waging Modern War: Bosnia, Kosovo, and the Future of Combat*, 1st edn. (New York: Public Affairs, 2001).
118 Radio Mille Collines broadcast hate propaganda, including detailed instructions on whom the Interhamwe were to kill and where the targeted victims could be found.
119 www.pbs.org/wgbh/pages/frontline/shows/ghosts/interviews/moose.html (accessed March 8, 2007).
120 Buchanan and Keohane, "The Preventive Use of Force: A Cosmopolitan Institutional Proposal," 1–22; Allen Buchanan and Robert O. Keohane, "Justifying Preventive Force," *Ethics and International Affairs* 19, no. 2 (2005), 109–111. Similar arguments are made by Carla Bagnoli and Kok-Chor Tan in Georg Meggle, *Ethics of Humanitarian Interventions* (Frankfurt: Ontos/Verlag, 2004).
121 See also Brian Orend, "Michael Walzer on Resorting to Force," *Canadian Journal of Political Science/Revue Canadienne De Science Politique* 33, no. 3 (2000), 113.
122 For a description of the threats under which conscripts fight, see *International Law Reports*, edited by Elihu Lauterpacht and C.J. Greenwood, (Cambridge: Cambridge University Press, 1992), 10.

6 Intervention in Kosovo

1 Julie Mertus, *Kosovo: How Myths and Truths Started a War* (Berkeley, CA: University of California Press, 1999), xviii.
2 Stephen T. Hosmer, *The Conflict Over Kosovo: Why Milosevic Decided to Settle When He Did* (Santa Monica, CA: Rand, 2001), 9, n. 5.
3 Tim Judah, *Kosovo: War and Revenge* (New Haven, CT: Yale University Press, 2000), 313.
4 Noel Malcolm, *Kosovo: A Short History* (New York: New York University Press, 1998), 332–333.
5 Malcolm, *Kosovo*, 333.
6 Mertus, *Kosovo*, 110.
7 United States Holocaust Memorial Museum. Online exhibit: Jasenovac. www.ushmm.org/museum/exhibit/online/jasenovac.
8 Mertus, *Kosovo*, 110.
9 Malcolm, *Kosovo*, 253; Alex J. Bellamy, *Kosovo and International Society* (Houndsmill and New York: Palgrave, 2002), 3.

10 Malcolm, *Kosovo*, 254.
11 This historical section is informed by Alex J. Bellamy, *Kosovo and International Society* (Houndsmill and New York: Palgrave, 2002); Judah, *Kosovo*; Susan L. Woodward, *Balkan Tragedy: Chaos and Dissolution after the Cold War* (Washington, DC: Brookings Institution, 1995); Malcolm, *Kosovo*.
12 Mertus, *Kosovo*, 287–288.
13 Ibid., 287.
14 Woodward, *Balkan Tragedy*, 62.
15 Judah, *Kosovo*, 38.
16 Malcolm, *Kosovo*, 327.
17 Woodward, *Balkan Tragedy*, 65.
18 Bellamy, *Kosovo and International Society*, 94.
19 Woodward, *Balkan Tragedy*, 78.
20 Judah, *Kosovo*, 52.
21 Bob Allen, *Why Kosovo? Anatomy of a Needless War* (Ottawa: Canadian Center for Policy Alternatives, 1999), 10.
22 Woodward, *Balkan Tragedy*, 78.
23 Allen, *Why Kosovo?*. Allen quotes the *New York Times* November 1, 1987, as circulated by Fairness and Accuracy in Reporting.
24 Judah, *Kosovo*, 52.
25 Ibid.
26 Mertus, *Kosovo*, 143.
27 Woodward, *Balkan Tragedy*, 15.
28 Mertus, *Kosovo*, 155.
29 Malcolm, *Kosovo*, 342.
30 Woodward, *Balkan Tragedy*, 382.
31 Malcolm, *Kosovo*, 346.
32 Independent International Commission on Kosovo, *The Kosovo Report: Conflict, International Response, Lessons Learned* (Oxford and New York: Oxford University Press, 2000), 44.
33 Ibid., 1; Bellamy, *Kosovo and International Society*, 11.
34 Independent International Commission on Kosovo, *The Kosovo Report*, 40.
35 Independent International Commission on Kosovo, *The Kosovo Report*, 42.
36 Ibid.
37 Ibid.
38 Malcolm, *Kosovo*, 60.
39 Independent International Commission on Kosovo, *The Kosovo Report*, 343, n. 18.
40 Hugh Miall, Oliver Ramsbotham, and Tom Woodhouse, *Contemporary Conflict Resolution: The Prevention, Management and Transformation of Deadly Conflicts* (Cambridge: Polity Press, 1999), 121.
41 Ibrahim Rugova quoted in Judah, *Kosovo*, 61.
42 Independent International Commission on Kosovo, *The Kosovo Report*, 43–45.
43 Judah, *Kosovo*, 78.
44 Dominic McGoldrick, "The Tale of Yugoslavia: Lessons for Accommodating National Identity in National and International Law," in Stephen Tierney, ed., *Accommodating National Identity: New Approaches in International and Domestic Law* (The Hague: Martinus Nijhoff Publishers, 2000), 27.
45 Bellamy, *Kosovo and International Society*, 41–43.
46 Judah, *Kosovo*, 75–77.
47 Ibid., 78–79.
48 Allen, *Why Kosovo?*; see also Judah, *Kosovo*, 77; see also Miranda Vickers, *Between Serb and Albanian: A History of Kosovo* (New York: Columbia University Press, 1998), 268.
49 Mertus, *Kosovo*, 305.

50 Independent International Commission on Kosovo, *The Kosovo Report*, 372.
51 Judah, *Kosovo*, 126.
52 Vickers, *Between Serb and Albanian*, 243.
53 For one example, see Bruce W. Jentleson, "Preventive Diplomacy and Ethnic Conflict: Possible, Difficult, Necessary," Institute on Global Conflict and Cooperation (June 1, 1996), IGCC Policy Papers, Paper PP27. http://repositories.cdlib.org/igcc/PP/PP27, 11.
54 Stacy Sullivan, *Be Not Afraid, for You have Sons in America: How a Brooklyn Roofer Helped Lure the U.S. into the Kosovo War*, 1st edn. (New York: St. Martin's Press, 2004), 144–149.
55 Judah, *Kosovo*, 129.
56 Sullivan, *Be Not Afraid, for You have Sons in America*, 150–151.
57 Alan Kuperman, "Transnational Causes of Genocide," in Raju G.C. Thomas, *Yugoslavia Unraveled: Sovereignty, Self-Determination, Intervention* (Lanham, MD: Lexington Books, 2003), 16–18, 70.
58 International Criminal Tribunal for the Former Yugoslavia, p. 32911 transcripts of testimony October 12, 2004; Hutsch's level of objectivity is unknown.
59 Page 32942 transcript of ICTY testimony quotation reads:

> The clear objective was to tie down Serb forces, to provoke the Serb forces, and to accompany the Rambouillet negotiations with the images which became very well known. In other words, images where Serb forces were shooting at Kosovo Albanian villages.

60 Kuperman, "Transnational Causes of Genocide," 60.
61 Amnesty International, "A Human Rights Crisis in Kosovo Province, Document Series A, no. 2: *Violence in Drenica*, February–April 1998." (AI Index: EUR 70/33/98).
62 Sullivan, *Be Not Afraid, for You have Sons in America*, 161, 163.
63 Independent International Commission on Kosovo, *The Kosovo Report*, 55.
64 OSCE Report: *Kosovo/Kosova, As Seen, As Told: The human rights findings of the OSCE Kosovo Verification Mission*, 10.
65 Ibid., 14.
66 P. Terrence Hopmann, "Failure in Kosovo," *Brown Alumni Magazine*, 1999.
67 OSCE, *Kosovo/Kosova*, 62.
68 Madeleine Korbel Albright and William Woodward, *The Mighty and the Almighty: Reflections on Power, God, and World Affairs* (London: Macmillan, 2006), 62.
69 Bellamy, *Kosovo and International Society*.
70 Transcript of Peter Boyer's interview with Amb. Richard Holbrooke, *Frontline 1812*, "War in Europe," Part 1.
71 Hosmer, *The Conflict Over Kosovo*, 12.
72 www.state.gov/www/regions/eur/ksvo_rambouillet_text.html/
73 Jasna Dragovic Soso, "Western Policies and the Milošević Regime," in Peter Siani-Davies (ed.), *International Intervention in the Balkans since 1995*, (London: Routledge 2003) 128.
74 Richard Holbrooke, quoted in David J. Rothkopf, *Running the World: The Inside Story of the National Security Council and the Architects of America's Power* (New York: Public Affairs Press, 2006), 378.
75 Hosmer, *The Conflict Over Kosovo*, 25.
76 Ibid., 30–31.
77 Bellamy, *Kosovo and International Society*, 151.
78 Independent International Commission on Kosovo, *The Kosovo Report: Conflict, International Response, Lessons Learned*, 88.
79 Ibid., 3.
80 Hosmer, *The Conflict Over Kosovo*, 20.

81 Wesley K. Clark, *Waging Modern War: Bosnia, Kosovo, and the Future of Combat*, 1st edn. (New York: Public Affairs, 2001), 224, 227.
82 Bellamy, *Kosovo and International Society*, 147–152; also Clark, *Waging Modern War: Bosnia, Kosovo, and the Future of Combat*, 206.
83 *Political Killings In Kosova/Kosovo: March–June 1999: A Cooperative Report* (American Bar Association Central and East European Law Initiative, 2000) and Independent International Commission on Kosovo, *The Kosovo Report: Conflict, International Response, Lessons Learned*, 3.
84 *Political Killings In Kosova/Kosovo*, 25; also see *Policy or Panic? The Flight of Ethnic Albanians from Kosovo, March–May 1999* (American Association for the Advancement of Science: Science and Human Rights Program, 2000).
85 Michael Walzer, "Kosovo" in Michael Walzer, *Arguing About War* (New Haven, CT: Yale University Press, 2004), 99.
86 Michael Walzer, *Just and Unjust Wars: A Moral Argument with Historical Illustrations* (New York: Basic Books, 2000), 59.
87 Independent International Commission on Kosovo, *The Kosovo Report*, 1.
88 For a discussion of persecution against ethnic Albanians and against Serbs before March 1999, see OSCE, *Kosovo/Kosova*, Part 3.
89 Amb. William Walker, interviewed by Peter Boyer, *Frontline 1812*, "War in Europe," Part 1.
90 OSCE, *Kosovo/Kosova*.
91 Lund, *Preventing Violent Conflicts*, x.
92 It is unclear exactly when this decision was made; Bellamy quotes an anonymous army ranger who speculates that NATO did rely on the KLA to call in air strikes until Serb forces obtained a radio from a captured KLA fighter and used its codes to order the strike that killed a convoy of more than 80 refugees at Korishe/Korisa.
93 Clark, *Waging Modern War*, 183.
94 Matthew Krain, "International Intervention and the Severity of Genocides and Politicides."
95 Ivo H. Daalder and Michael E. O'Hanlon, *Winning Ugly: NATO's War to Save Kosovo* (Washington, DC: Brookings Institution Press, 2000), 160.
96 Ibid., 160, (citing Hersh and others, "NATO's Game of Chicken").
97 Independent International Commission on Kosovo, *The Kosovo Report*, 94, also see Daalder and O'Hanlon, *Winning Ugly*, 240–242 for a list of "collateral damage" incidents.
98 www.cnn.com/WORLD/europe/9904/12/nato.attack.07 (according to Daalder, the death toll was "about twenty people.".
99 Bellamy, *Kosovo and International Society*.
100 Clark, *Waging Modern War*, 241.
101 Paul Mojzes, "Religion and AHI in the Former Yugoslavia," in Joseph I. Coffey, Charles T. Mathewes and Tanenbaum Center for Interreligious Understanding, *Religion, Law, and the Role of Force: A Study of their Influence on Conflict and on Conflict Resolution* (Ardsley, NY: Transnational Publishers, 2002), 142.
102 General James P. McCarthy, "Ethical Implications of Kosovo Operations," in John D. Carlson and Erik C. Owens, *The Sacred and the Sovereign: Religion and International Politics* (Washington, DC: Georgetown University Press, 2003), 71.
103 James Satterwhite, "Forestalling War in Kosovo: Opportunities Missed," *Peace and Change* 27 (2002), 600–611.
104 Lund, *Preventing Violent Conflicts*.
105 Satterwhite, *Forestalling War in Kosovo*, 600–611.
106 Judah, *Kosovo*, 92.
107 Bellamy, *Kosovo and International Society*, 26.
108 Ted Robert Gurr, *Minorities at Risk: A Global View of Ethnopolitical Conflicts* (Washington, DC: United States Institute of Peace Press, 1993).

109 Bellamy, *Kosovo and International Society*, 41.
110 Miall, Ramsbotham and Woodhouse, *Contemporary Conflict Resolution*, 126.
111 Independent International Commission on Kosovo, *The Kosovo Report*, 49.
112 Ibid., 51.
113 I owe this point to P. Terrence Hopmann.
114 Miall, Ramsbotham, and Woodhouse, *Contemporary Conflict Resolution*.
115 Independent International Commission on Kosovo, *The Kosovo Report*.
116 Miall, Ramsbotham, and Woodhouse, *Contemporary Conflict Resolution*, 126.
117 Judah, *Kosovo*, 125.
118 Richard Ned Lebow, *Between Peace and War: The Nature of International Crisis* (Baltimore, MD.: Johns Hopkins University Press, 1981), 24–36.
119 Independent International Commission on Kosovo, *The Kosovo Report*, 86.
120 General James P. McCarthy, "Ethical Implications of Kosovo Operations," in John D. Carlson and Erik C. Owens, eds, *The Sacred and the Sovereign: Religion and International Politics*, (Washington, DC: Georgetown University Press, 2003), 70.
121 The doctrine of double effect, which excuses this strategy, is not accepted by all just war theorists. I have accepted it here, following Walzer.
122 Clark, *Waging Modern War*, 179.
123 Michael Walzer, "Kosovo," in *Arguing About War*, (New Haven, CT: Yale University Press, 2004), 99. Walzer's essay, "Kosovo," also appears in the very broad and diverse collection of short essays edited by William J. Buckley, *Kosovo: Contending Voices on Balkan Interventions* (Grand Rapids, MI and Cambridge: Eerdmans, 2000).
124 See OSCE's report *Kosovo/Kosova: As Seen, As Told*, especially Part III, and also see *The Kosovo Report* for a description of discriminatory measures taken against the Albanian inhabitants of Kosovo during the 1990s.
125 As noted in Chapter 4, "severe" means, in my understanding of the term, "leading to large scale or systematic death or lessening of life chances."

Conclusions

1 Michael Walzer, *Just and Unjust Wars: A Moral Argument with Historical Illustrations* (New York: Basic Books, 2000), 101.
2 Michael Walzer, "The Argument about Humanitarian Intervention," in Georg Meggle, ed., *Ethics of Humanitarian Interventions* (Piscataway, NJ: Transaction Books, 2004), 22.
3 The Atrocity Standard is explained in detail in Chapter 4.
4 Walzer, "Five on Iraq" in *Arguing About War* (New Haven, CT: Yale University Press, 2004) 161, 163.

Index

"A Few Words on Non-intervention" (Mill) 4, 13
A More Secure World: Our Shared Responsibility (UN) 47
actions 115–17
Afghanistan 16–17, 64–6, 70, 84
aggression 164; crime of 2, 8, 29; overt 90–1; victims of 10
aggressor–defender paradigm 8, 20–1, 89, 123–4; revision of 158–9
Ahtisaari, Martti 148
Al-Qaeda 16–17, 64–5, 78
Albania 128, 129, 136
Albanians in Kosovo 126–37, 139–43, 145–9, 152–4, 156–7
Albright, Madeleine 140, 141
Algeria 28, 35–6, 37
Annan, Kofi 82
Anscombe, G.E.M. 21
anti-paternalism 82–4, 160
apartheid 55, 56–7, 132
Aquinas, St. Thomas 20, 63, 107, 114, 118, 119–20
arbitration 93
Arguing About War (Walzer) 118
armed humanitarian intervention (AHI) 2, 43, 45, 161; Atrocity Standard and 67–8, 74–5; human rights and 77–9; and just cause 53, 55–6, 60–1; proportionality and 111–12; thresholds for 63–6; *see also* humanitarian intervention
atrocity crimes 43, 45, 61, 63, 65, 111, 157, 161; past atrocities 64, 74, 80
Atrocity Standard 5, 54, 55–61, 161, 163, 164; objection of strength 66–73; objection of weakness 73–4; threshold for AHI 63, 64, 65–6
Augustine 20, 21, 22, 114
Aztecs 64

Bagnoli, Carla 49
Barisha, Sali 136
Beitz, Charles 27, 30–1, 37
Belgrade 122, 127, 129, 131–2, 147, 148, 155–6
Belkin, A. 110
Bell, Daniel 113
Bellamy, Alex 134, 152
Berger, Samuel "Sandy" 140, 141
Berisha, President 153
Blair, Tony 78
Bosnia 129, 136, 154
Buchanan, Allen 49, 66, 70, 97, 123
bureaucracy 122
Burma 41, 45, 159
Bush, George H.W. 132, 135
Bush, George W. 78

cannibalism 25
capabilities 172; humans' 48–9, 51, 84–8; state 49–50, 51
"capable and responsible" state 43, 45–6, 48, 50–2, 71
capacity 172; humans' 48–9, 84–8; state 45, 46, 49–50, 51
Carnegie Commission on Preventing Violent Conflict 108
Carnegie Endowment commission 128
Carrington, Lord 152
cease-fire: at Kosovo 138–9
Chernomyrdin, Viktor 148
Childress, James 95
Christmas Ultimatum 132, 135, 137
civic virtue 40, 41
civil war 2, 19, 23–4; and just cause 53, 60, 61–6
"Civilization" (Mill) 40–1
Clark, General Wesley K. 122, 149–50, 155–6
Clinton, Bill 132, 140, 142, 150

Coady, C.A.J. 21
Coates, A.J. 21
collective self-defense 9–10, 21–2, 45
"communal integrity thesis" 30, 37
communitarianism 28, 83
competence de guerre 62
conflict resolution 96–7
conscience of mankind: outrage of 5, 15, 54, 160–1
conscripts 123
constructivism 1
costs: conflicts 108–10; of non-intervention 81, 110, 155
counter-factual analysis 109, 110–11
counter-intervention 13–14, 30
crimes against humanity 45, 55, 61, 164; *see also* atrocity crimes
critics: Walzer's innovations 29–38
Croatia 129, 135

Dallaire, General Romeo 98
Dayton Accords 135, 136, 137, 138, 153, 154
defense of a neighbor 21–2, 54
defensive interventions 99
defensive wars: likelihood of success in 102, 103–4; Walzer's view on 4, 8, 20–1, 89, 101–2, 158; *see also* aggressor–defender paradigm
dehumanizing propaganda 98, 105
democracy 66–7, 73–4, 77–8, 162–3
demographics: in Kosovo 127
descriptive realism 80
deterrent effect 99, 111–12
diplomacy 91, 92–3; backed by threat 99–100; preventive 99, 104–5, 146–7, 151–2
discrimination 52, 56–7, 58–9; Atrocity Standard and 67–71, 72–3; ethnic 132; threshold for AHI and 64–6; *see also* gender discrimination; religious discrimination
dissent 71, 72–3
doctrine of double effect 101
domestic analogy 30, 31, 39
Doppelt, Gerald 29–30, 34, 36–7

early warning indicators 97, 99–100, 112, 162
economic sanctions 53
elections 67, 78, 105
enforced disappearance 55–6
"equal in status" 13
equality in dignity and rights 71

ethnic cleansing 2, 14, 16, 33, 45, 98; in the Atrocity Standard 55, 56; in Kosovo 105, 122, 128, 139–45, 147–8, 155–6; *see also* forced resettlement/migration; refugees
ethnic discrimination 132

failed states 43; intervention in 11, 15, 16–17, 40–1; and just cause 61
Federal Republic of Yugoslavia 126, 129–34, 138, 139, 141, 145, 154
female genital mutilation 88
female infanticide 73
force: of arms 77–9; liberalism imposed by 105–6; resort to 54, 93, 95, 97, 144; threat of 99–100
forced resettlement/migration 17, 33, 75, 128, 155; *see also* refugees
forecasting 110
formal multilateralism 121, 150
free assembly 57
free speech: restriction on 87; right to 57
Frontiers of Justice: Disability, Nationality, and Species Membership (Nussbaum) 86
functioning 49, 85, 86, 87, 172
fundamental rights 56–8, 65, 66–8; moral hazard and 75

gender discrimination 65, 70, 72–3, 84–5, 88, 104
genocidal violence 75, 79–80, 98
genocide 2, 9, 14, 15–16, 33, 45, 54; actual or apprehended 97; in the Atrocity Standard 55, 56; *see also* Rwanda
Gentili, Alberico 22–3, 93, 117
Grotius 23, 24, 25–6, 27, 72, 80, 93–4, 102, 107–8, 114, 118, 124
guerrillas 62

Haradinaj, Ramush 137
health care 47, 70, 81
hierarchical societies: decent 67–9, 71–2
Hitler, Adolf 80
HIV/AIDS 47, 81
Holbrooke, Ambassador Richard 138, 140, 141, 142, 154
Holsti, Kalevi 1
honor killings 73, 88
Hosmer, Stephen 141
Hoxha, Fadil 130
human rights 8–9, 11, 28–9, 32–4, 37; and force of arms 77–9; fundamental 56–8, 65, 66–8, 75; international agreements

human rights *continued*
    41; non-intervention and 50, 52; norms 69; overlapping consensus on 83, 84–8; thresholds for AHI and 63–4
human rights abuses/violations 5, 8, 14–15, 17, 44, 160; Atrocity Standard and 56–9; *see also* genocide; massacres; persecution; slavery
Human Rights Watch 65, 74, 149
human sacrifice 25
human security 22, 44, 45, 46, 47, 51, 73; threats to 59; UN document on 84
humanitarian imperialism 64
humanitarian intervention 14–16, 33; and moral hazard 162; permissibility of 49; and political will 116–17; pre-emptive 23–7, 54, 79–80; *see also* armed humanitarian intervention (AHI)
humanitarian outcome 117
Hurka, Thomas 109
Hutsch, Franz Josef 137

In Our Own Best Interests (Schulz) 81
incapable state 45, 47
India 87, 88
individual rights *see* human rights
individuals: *versus* the state 39
Inequality Re-examined (Sen) 86
influence 53, 60
information: sources of 109, 110, 112–13
intentional and severe deprivation 56, 58
intentions 115–17
interference 53, 60
international aid organizations 132
International Commission on Intervention and State Sovereignty 23, 44, 48, 54; "the responsibility to prevent" 97
International Commission on Kosovo 142, 153
International Criminal Tribunal for Yugoslavia 56–7, 58–9, 137
international human rights agreements 41
international law: just cause and 82
international peace and security 47, 48, 51, 59, 73
interventions 11–17; continuum of 53–4, 60; counter-intervention 13–14, 30; in failed states 11, 15, 16–17, 40–1; norm of 75; secessions 12–13, 61–6, 74–5; self-interested 111, 112; *see also* armed humanitarian intervention (AHI); humanitarian intervention; just cause; Kosovo; last resort
Iraq 77, 78

Iraq war 74, 93, 100, 116, 159
irresponsible state 45, 47
Israel: Six-Day War 10–11, 92

Jasenovic concentration camps 127–8
Jashari family 138
Jewish people 58–9
Johnson, James Turner 21, 62–3, 95, 114
jus ad bellum 1, 3, 6, 19, 65, 158–9, 161, 165; in Kosovo 144; non-intervention and 43–52; other categories 89–125; Walzer's formulation of 31, 32; *see also* just cause; last resort; likelihood of success; proportionality; right intention
jus in bello 8, 19, 60, 62, 90; and last resort 100–1, 124; and legitimate authority 123; and likelihood of success 102; and proportionality 107, 113, 156; and right intention 118, 148–9
jus post bellum 79, 106, 111, 165
Just and Unjust Wars (Walzer) 1, 2, 162–3; on just cause 53, 61, 62; on Kosovo 138, 143, 156; other *jus ad bellum* categories 90, 91, 101–2, 118, 119; on W's formulation of just cause 10, 11, 12, 13, 14, 15; on W's formulations 25, 27, 28, 32, 33–4, 36
just cause 4–5, 53–88; aggressor–defender paradigm 8, 20–1; Atrocity Standard and 54, 55–61; author's comments on critics debate 38–42; civil war and secession 53, 60, 61–6; collective self-defense 9–10, 21–2, 45; critics of Walzer's innovations 29–38; failed states and 61; innovations in 19–20; interventions 11–17; and Kosovo 145–6; likely objections to author's view 66–88; national self-defense 8–9, 45; a new threshold for 160–2; pre-emption 10–11, 22–7, 45, 54; reasons for innovations 27–9; *see also* interventions; *jus ad bellum*; non-intervention rule
just peace 103, 106, 114–15, 117, 149, 165
just war doctrine/theory 1, 3, 54, 71, 100, 158, 163, 165
"justice as fairness" 28

Kant, Immanuel 49, 118
Kazanistan 52, 67, 69, 71
Kelsay, John 120
Kennedy, Robert 122
Keohane, R.O. 97
kleptocratic state 49
Kosovo 6; cease-fire 138–9; historical

background 126–38; "Operation Allied Force" 105, 143–56; Prekaz and 138; Racak 139–43; *see also* NATO
Kosovo Liberation Army 75, 136–9, 140, 142, 145–6, 147, 153, 157
Kosovo Verification Mission 138–9, 141
Kuperman, Alan 75, 137
Kupreskic decision 57–8

Las Casas, Bartholome 25
last resort 9, 42, 44, 54, 76; author's view on 94–8, 124; diplomacy backed by threat 99–100; historical views on 93–4; *jus in bello* implications of 100–1, 124; and Kosovo 151–4; post-9/11 arguments 100; Walzer's views on 91–3, 94, 97
lastness 91
law enforcement: wars of 9–10
Law of Peoples (Rawls) 5, 64–5, 67, 69, 70–1, 123
League for a Democratic Kosovo 133–4, 135, 153
legitimate authority 9, 42, 44, 54; comprehensive view on 120–3, 125; historical view on 119–20; *jus in bello* considerations 123; and Kosovo 150–1; Walzer's view on 118–19
legitimate government 13, 33, 34–6, 38–40; *see also* "capable and responsible" state
liberalism 1, 66, 71, 160; by force 105–6
Liberia 159
liberty 29–30, 49, 50, 63, 77–8
life chances 52, 56, 59, 65, 70, 73
likelihood of success 4, 9, 42, 44, 54, 73, 79; comprehensive view on 103–5, 124; historical views on 101–2; and Kosovo 146–8; and proportionality 103, 108; strong states imposing liberalism 105–6; Walzer's view 101–2
Little, David 5, 54, 69, 83, 121
Livy 23, 94
London conference 134, 135, 136, 152
love: *versus* self-interest 21–2
Luban, David 31–2, 36, 37
Lund, Michael 81, 105, 151

McCarthy, General James P. 151
Macedonia 129, 156
McKim, Robert 110–11
McMahon, Jefferson 60, 100, 109–10, 110–11
mass deportation *see* forced resettlement/migration; refugees

massacres 2, 14, 15–16, 33, 75–6, 79, 162; in Kosovo 128, 135, 137, 139–40, 156–7
Mellow, David 111, 174
Melos 103
Mexico 25
might and right 40, 51, 82
military intervention 53, 54; legality of 55; in secession 61–2; *see also* armed humanitarian intervention (AHI); interventions
Mill, John Stuart 4, 13, 31, 32, 38–9, 40–1, 77–8, 115
Milošević, Slobodan 130–8, 140–2, 147–8, 152–6
"Mission of Long Duration" 132, 133–4, 152
Mojzes, Paul 150
Montenegro 129, 153
Moose, George 122–3
moral hazard objection 74–7, 162
"Moral Standing of States: A Response to Four Critics, The" (Walzer) 33–6
motives 115–18
multilateralism 119, 121–3, 125, 150–1
Muslims 67, 72, 127, 128

naming and shaming 53
Nardin, Terry 49, 64
Nasser, Gamal Abdel, President 10
National Security Strategy of the United States 2002 100
national self-defense 8–9, 45, 102, 103
nationalism: Serbian 131
NATO: in Kosovo 122, 126, 136, 138, 140–1, 142–3; "Operation Allied Force" 105, 143–56
Nazis 58–9
necessary war 95–6
neighbors: defense of 21–2, 54
neutrality 13–14; rights to 16, 22, 38
"no losses" strategy 147–8
nominal rights 84–5
non-combatants: deaths of 149; immunity 101; in Kosovo 126, 127, 137, 138
non-derogable rights *see* fundamental rights
non-governmental organizations 81, 88, 104
non-intervention: costs of 81, 110, 155; a new threshold for 159–60
non-intervention rule 4, 43–52, 108; *see also* just cause
North American Indians 25

nuclear weapons 21
Nussbaum, M.C. 84–5, 86, 87

offensive wars: likelihood of success in 102; Luban's view on 32; Walzer's view on 4, 8, 20–1
"Operation Allied Force" 105, 143–56
"Operation Horseshoe" 142, 146
"ordinary brutality" 17, 27, 45, 64, 144
Organization for Security and Cooperation in Europe (OSCE) 132, 133–4, 138–40, 141, 146, 152
Ottomans 126–7, 131
overlapping consensus 41, 70, 71, 83, 84–8
overt aggression 90–1

Panić, Milan 133–4, 152
past atrocities 64, 74, 80
past conflicts 109
patriarchal societies 72
"peace with rights" 50
"peoples" 70–1
permissiveness 5, 143, 161
persecution 55, 56–60, 164; freedom from 51; and religion 69; threshold for AHI and 64–6
poisoning 132
political agency 61
political will 116–17
pre-emption 10–11, 22–7, 45, 54, 79–80; last resort and 91, 92, 94, 97
Prekaz 138, 145
prescriptive realism 80–1
presumption against war 95
prevention: diplomacy 99, 104–5, 146–7, 151–2; last resort and 92, 93, 94, 95–7, 100; proportionality and 108–9; Walzer's innovations on 22–7
propaganda: dehumanizing 98, 105
proportionality 2, 9, 42, 44, 54, 60, 73, 76; comprehensive view on 108–13, 124; and force of arms 78; historical view on 107–8; *jus in bello* concerns in 107, 113, 156; and Kosovo 154–6; and likelihood of success 103, 108; Walzer's view 106–7, 108, 113
public authority 120
Pufendorf, Samuel 27, 115
punishment 79

Racak 139–43, 145
Rambouillet Accords 136, 137, 140–1, 146, 154, 155
Ramsbotham, O. 117

Ramsey, Paul 21, 22, 112
Rawls, John 5, 28, 52, 86, 87, 123; and the Atrocity Standard 67–71; threshold for AHI 63–5
Raymond of Penafort 114
realism 1, 44, 80–1
rebel groups 13–14, 74–5, 76; Walzer's views on 38
refugees 47, 62, 143, 149, 155, 156; *see also* forced resettlement/migration
religious discrimination 65, 67, 68–9, 70, 72
remediation 78, 88, 147, 148
Report of the International Commission on Intervention and State Sovereignty 49
repression: government 98
reprisals 92, 99
resort to force 54, 93, 95, 97, 144
"responsibility to prevent" 1, 84, 96, 97
"responsibility to protect", the 1, 2, 4, 24, 96
revolution: right to 34, 35, 38
right intention 8, 9, 42, 44, 54, 80; comprehensive view on 115–18, 124–5; historical view on 114–15; *jus in bello* implications of 118, 148–9; and Kosovo 148–50; Walzer's view on 113–14
"rights worth dying for" 8–9
rights: political 28–9; state 10, 31–3; *see also* human rights; nominal rights
"Romance of the Nation-State, The" (Luban) 37
Rome Statute of the International Criminal Court 5, 43, 45, 54, 55–6, 57, 61, 63, 161
Roth, Ken 74
Rubin, Jamie 141
Rugova, Ibrahim 132–3, 134, 135, 136, 152, 153
rules of disregard 11–17; counter-intervention 13–14, 30; in failed states 11, 15, 16–17, 40–1; humanitarian intervention 14–16, 23–7, 33; limits of 17–18; secessions 12–13, 61–6
Rwanda 15, 97, 98, 106–7, 108, 122–3

sanctions 101
Sandinistas 36
Sarin 132
Saudi Arabia 73
Schulz, William F. 81
secessions 12–13, 61–6, 74–5
second original position 70
self-defense 54; collective 9–10, 21–2, 45;

national 8–9, 45, 102, 103; pre-emption 10–11, 22–7, 45, 54, 79–80; suicidal 103
self-determination 12, 14, 19, 27–9, 30, 35, 38; non-intervention and 46
self-help test 12–13, 14, 15, 60, 61
self-interest 19, 21–2; interventions 111, 112
Sen, Amartya 73, 86
Serbia 128, 129–31, 145
Serbians 126–37, 138–43, 145–50, 152–3, 155, 157
Sierra Leone 45, 61, 159
Six-Day War 10–11, 92
slavery 2, 9, 14, 15, 33, 64, 88; in the Atrocity Standard 55
Somalia 15, 41
South Africa 101, 132
sovereignty: "capable and responsible" state 43, 45–6, 48; concept of 34; as control 45–6; as responsibility 1, 2, 4, 24, 26, 45–6; rights of 31–2
Spaniards: as conquerors 24–5
stability: states-system 22
Stambolic, Ivan 130–1
"standing occupations" 106
state: *versus* the individual 39
"Statism Without Foundations" (Doppelt) 36–7
Stephenson, Henry Alan 100
Straw, Jack 77, 78
strong states: and liberalism by force 105–6
Suarez, Francisco 25, 102
substantive multilateralism 121, 150
success *see* likelihood of success
Sudetenland 80
sufficient importance 107
sufficient threat 10
suicidal self-defense 103
Sullivan, Stacey 138
supreme emergency exemption 113
Swedish magic water 35–6, 37

Taliban 64–6, 70
Tan, Kok-Chor 49, 72
targeted killings 16
Temes, Peter S. 100–1
terrorism 92
Teson, Fernando 5, 40, 175; and the Atrocity Standard 73–4; on past atrocities 80; threshold for AHI 63, 64, 65, 66
Tetlock, P. 110

threats: diplomacy backed by 99–100; to human security 59; to international security 47; sufficient 10
Tito, Marshal 129, 131
traditional practices: harmful 43, 87, 88, 161
Trotsky, Leon 128
trust 120
tuberculosis 47, 81
"turning savagely on the people" 25
Twiss, Sumner B. 83
tyrannical regimes 29, 32, 38; legitimacy of 34–6, 39–40

UN: Charter 82; *Declaration on the Elimination of All Forms of Intolerance and Discrimination Based on Religion or Belief* 69; *Outcome Document of the High-level Plenary Meeting 2005* 83–4, 96–7; Secretary-General's High-level Panel on Threats, Challenges and Change 47, 49, 59; Security Council 55, 150, 164; security failures 122
unequal access 72–3
unilateralism 118–19, 122, 125
United States: Al-Qaeda killings 16–17, 64–5; and Kosovo 132, 136–7, 138–9, 140–1, 148; post-9/11 arguments 100; and prescriptive realism 81; Vietnam War 27–8, 107
Universal Declaration of Human Rights 50, 52, 56, 57, 58, 67–8

Vattel, Emerich de 23–4, 26, 115, 167
Vickers, Miranda 135
Vietnam War 27–8, 107
Vitoria, Francisco de 24–5, 27, 62, 102, 104, 120
Vojvodina 128, 129–30, 131, 134

Walker, Ambassador William 140, 146
Walzer–Mill doctrine 31, 32, 38–9, 40–1, 78
Walzer, Michael: author's comments on critics debate 38–42; critics of 29–38; on defensive wars 4, 8, 20–1, 89, 101–2, 158; on failed states 61; on force of arms 78; formulation of just cause 4, 8–18; innovations in theory 4, 19–42; on interventions 53–4; on last resort 91–3, 94, 97, 99; on legitimate authority 118–19; on likelihood of success 101–2; on non-intervention 159–60; and the non-intervention norm 44–5, 49; on

Walzer, Michael *continued*
  "Operation Allied Force" 143–56; other *jus ad bellum* categories 89, 90–1; on proportionality 106–7, 108, 113; reasons for innovations 27–9; revision of emphasis on aggression defense 158–9; on right intention 113–14; on secession 61–2; threshold for AHI 55–6, 60, 63–4; threshold for just cause 160–1; *see also Just and Unjust Wars* (Walzer)
war crimes 45, 60
wars of law enforcement 9–10
wars of secession 62
Wasserstrom, Richard 33, 34, 35

weapons of mass destruction 100
Weiss, Thomas G. 1
Welch, David 94
widow immolation 73, 87
Woodhouse, T. 117
Woodward, Susan 90, 130, 131

Yemeni desert 16–17
Yugoslav Constitution 1974 129–30, 131, 134
Yugoslavia *see* Federal Republic of Yugoslavia

Zimbabwe 41, 45, 61, 159

eBooks – at www.eBookstore.tandf.co.uk

A library at your fingertips!

eBooks are electronic versions of printed books. You can store them on your PC/laptop or browse them online.

They have advantages for anyone needing rapid access to a wide variety of published, copyright information.

eBooks can help your research by enabling you to bookmark chapters, annotate text and use instant searches to find specific words or phrases. Several eBook files would fit on even a small laptop or PDA.

NEW: Save money by eSubscribing: cheap, online access to any eBook for as long as you need it.

Annual subscription packages

We now offer special low-cost bulk subscriptions to packages of eBooks in certain subject areas. These are available to libraries or to individuals.

For more information please contact webmaster.ebooks@tandf.co.uk

We're continually developing the eBook concept, so keep up to date by visiting the website.

www.eBookstore.tandf.co.uk

For Product Safety Concerns and Information please contact our EU representative GPSR@taylorandfrancis.com
Taylor & Francis Verlag GmbH, Kaufingerstraße 24, 80331 München, Germany

www.ingramcontent.com/pod-product-compliance
Lightning Source LLC
Chambersburg PA
CBHW061830300426
44115CB00013B/2322